Praise for *The Art of Business*

"It is with humility that I commend Dr. Raymond Yeh, and thank him, for writing this most important book, the Art of Business. As an engineer and past corporate executive, I am well grounded in Western thought and practice (science or high-tech), yet my life's path has led me into the realms of Eastern philosophies and indigenous spiritual practices (cultural wisdom or high-touch). Perhaps the most important lesson of all is one that my life in Hawaii continues to teach me. That is the importance of balance in life—of honoring wholeness, mind-body-spirit-nature-community in harmony, whether it is in an individual or an organization. Of tempering the brilliance of looking into the future that science and research promises us, with an open heart that listens to the subtle whisperings of Ancient wisdom passed on by our ancestors. In Hawaii, this balance and harmony of life is known as *lokahi*. In Dr. Yeh's book, every example, every story speaks of *lokahi*."
—Earl E. Bakken, Co-founder, Medtronic

"Raymond Yeh has done it again. If you thought *Zero Time* was good, *The Art of Business* is great!"
—Jim Botkin, Ph.D., Chairman, InnerCALL

"*The Art of Business* is a major contribution to understanding the world of business. It brings together lessons related to vision, timing and the future, continuous learning, the importance of the customer, and leadership. It is a great effort by the authors to weave, under one theoretical umbrella, important lessons from outstanding leaders of the world."
—John Sibley Butler, Professor, McCombs Graduate School of Business and Director, IC2 Institute, the University of Texas at Austin

"Reading *The Art of Business* allowed me, for the first time, to understand the wisdom behind Sun Tzu's 'Five fundamental arts of strategy'. The story format utilized by the author greatly simplifies the task of interpretation for these complex principles. I strongly recommend this book as a required reading for CEOs, managers and entrepreneurs."
—Augustine Y. Cheung, Ph.D., CEO and Founder, Celsion Corporation

"Dr. Raymond Yeh writes clearly, joyfully and brilliantly about the 'soul' of organizations and the vision of their leaders. While providing us with a practical guide to nurturing a successful business, he shares with us true stories that read like novels with larger-than-life heroes, and offers us the freedom to become heroes ourselves."

—Margo Dover, President, Business Connection Catalyst

"Today's business practitioner and student focuses on the 'how' of business, not the 'why.' That's why people from the best business schools create monsters like Enron. In this brilliant book, Raymond Yeh talks about what really matters—the soul and spirit of business. It's about time!"

—Gary E. Hoover, Founder, Hoover's, Inc., and author, *Hoover's Vision*

"The concepts presented in *The Art of Business* as with *The Art of War* help format the foundation and basic principles necessary to build any significant, successful organization."

—Stephen H. Hochschuler, MD, Chairman, Texas Back Institute

"As one of the many successful American entrepreneurs in the footsteps of giants—from laundry to banking—I find Dr. Yeh's *The Art of Business* most fascinating and most enlightening. It's a must read for those interested in improving or expanding their businesses or to become a giant."

—Henry Hwang, Chairman, Rock- Asia and Founder, Far East National Bank

"Using a fascinating blend of studies of important businesses, and incorporating timeless insights from their leaders as well as Oriental sages, Raymond Yeh provides us a wealth of wisdom and guidance for successfully conducting business in the 21st century.

These insights will enable us to more successfully interrelate with and manage relationships among employees, shareholders, customers and the many other constituencies of business in a fair and appropriate manner, leading to the competitive advantage in an environment of accelerating change and increasing expectations.

More importantly, the lessons embodied in *The Art of Business* even more broadly apply directly to the 'The Art of Life.' This book is full of knowledge and experiences presented in a thoughtful and intriguing way."

—Cordell W. Hull, Former CFO and Director (retired), Bechtel Group

"*The Art of Business* is aptly titled. Ray and Stephanie Yeh combine their wise heads, warm hearts, and surpassing understanding to reveal that success in business and life is an 'art', not solely the product of a mechanistic, statistically quantifiable application of science. Their profound insight into the ways, not just the means, of successful undertakings is holistic in nature and exalts the importance of the mental and spiritual over that of the purely material. In my opinion, their book is an inspirational revelation and a seminal contribution."

—Herb Kelleher, Chairman, Southwest Airlines

"In a global marketplace where international competition and domestic culture blur to create dynamic, kaleidoscopic environments, *The Art of Business* provides new tools and unique insights for both strategic positioning and operational decision making. By linking theory and practice, applying classic truths of human behavior to modern examples of real-world companies, and drawing on his remarkable cross-cultural experiences, Dr. Raymond Yeh enables managers to learn and apply key principles of success. This book is a great read."

—Robert Lawrence Kuhn, Ph.D., Managing Director, Smith Barney/ Citigroup, Former President, The Geneva Companies

"In my experience of working in many different countries, including Germany, England, Libya, Korea, and the U.S., I have found that there are no major differences among different business environments if we know how to deal with the people. Dr. Yeh's previous book *Zero Time* focused on management skills. *The Art of Business* tells us what to aim for in doing business. The great people in business share the common trait of being able to read and move people correctly."

—Sung Lee, former President, Samsung Austin Semiconductor

"The founders of GSD&M have long embraced *The Art of War*, compiled well over two thousand years ago by a mysterious Chinese warrior-philosopher, as a powerful philosophy of business. Raymond Yeh's *The Art of Business* confirms our belief that business is a war for consumers' minds and hearts. I suspect it is no coincidence that the cover of Ray's book depicts the ancient symbol for Tao, *the way*. I've nicknamed this profound book *Ray's Way*, as he is most certainly on the right path."

—Tim McClure, Co-founder, GSD&M and President, Omnicom Group

"My first read of this book had such a positive impact that I went back to page one for my exciting re-read. This book is positive and timeless."
—Red McCombs, Chairman, McCombs Enterprises

The Art of Business rises far above the typical business book through its use of rich historical anecdotes and literary references. Although it is deeply instructive, this book is a joy to read.
—Michele Moore, former Vice President of Corporate Communications, Dell Inc.

"*The Art of Business* is a pragmatic yet spiritual volume providing deep and sustainable values. At a moment when management books are appearing everyday, yet our problems grow more intense, out of a desultory pack has risen this elegant and insightful masterpiece. For all those interested in aesthetic or organizational success, these lessons regarding possibilities, timing, leverage, and mastery will remain at the core of any reader's professional and personal values."
—Barry Munitz, President and CEO, J. Paul Getty Foundation

"Ray Yeh is truly one of this country's wise business leaders. The stories in *The Art of Business* from other wise business leaders not only will delight and amaze you, but will also enable you to think strategically!"
—Craig and Patricia Neal, Co-founders, Heartland Institute

"Raymond Yeh has given us a great gift in making the ancient teachings of Sun Tzu relevant to the practice of building successful social organizations. This is not a how-to manual but the sharing of stories of those who are engaged in creating meaning in life through collective action. Read the stories in this book as koans. They inspire deep regard for the joy of life and the knowing that we all can contribute to the building of a better future."
—Jim Pelky, Former Chairman, Santa Fe Institute

"The next frontier in competitiveness is corporate culture. In a world where everybody and her brother are organizational development consultants, why do we have so many dysfunctional enterprises? The answer is that firms will succeed only by embracing the multi-dimensional blend of strategies Dr. Yeh proposes.

The Art of Business is a fascinating book, with engaging life stories of 'giants' who exemplify the Tao of organization, and with their principles for success expertly abstracted. (The figures in Chapter Four alone are worth many times the price of the book.)

You too can follow this Tao, whether you are an entrepreneur or part of a large organization. Start now, persevere with good spirit, and always refer to *The Art of Business.*"

—Fred Phillips, Research Professor, Oregon Health & Science University and author, *The Conscious Manager: Zen for Decision Makers*

"Raymond Yeh has taken the teachings of Sun Tzu to a new level of thoughtfulness and completeness. His analysis brings new meaning—in a relevant and timely fashion—to established wisdom. Any and all of us in the crazy world we live in today—should take the time and opportunity to re-focus our business and personal lives through Raymond's fresh perspective. I commend him for his perspicacity, vision and courage and urge you to read this very fine work. The experience will make a difference in the quality of your life!"

—Pike Powers, Managing Partner, Fulbright & Jaworski L.L.P., Austin, Texas

"In an age of Enron and Global Crossing, my academic colleagues, given a choice, would rather focus on the bad versus the good in organizations. Truth also be told, I'd like to tell them to 'Get a life.' But I'll settle for a more genteel response, something along the lines of: 'My dear colleagues, you've missed the point. Two points actually.' First, someone has to focus on the 'good' in organizations since it tends to be so systematically ignored. We need to know what to preserve, what to foster, where to center our aspirations and values. Dr. Yeh excels in this quest, on a par with the Peters & Waterman classic *In Search of Excellence.* But he goes beyond their treatment, which gets me to my second point. Ray Yeh isn't trying to be 'scientific' or systematic in the Western sense. What he's achieved is a new prism forged by merging Eastern and Western concepts of business and life. He's used that prism to shed light on great organizational achievements. And that's no small achievement. The result is so, so refreshing and so 'good.'"

—Robert Ronstadt, DBA, Vice President of Technology Commercialization, Boston University

"This book is a must read for anyone interested in a unique look at success factors for business growth, with historical accounts of business across diverse areas. While Dr. Yeh provides factual data to support his very interesting theory, his accounts of real business support for this theory makes this book extremely readable. Rarely will you find an informative business book so enjoyable to read."

—Stephen A. Szygenda, Ph.D., P.E., Dean, School of Engineering, SMU

"In *The Art of Business*, Raymond Yeh brings us the eternal wisdom of Sun Tzu, using stories that not only bring to life the five fundamental arts which comprise the lessons of the book, but reveal the powerful contemporary wisdom of Ray Yeh as well. To characterize this book as a 'business book' is to do it a great injustice. It is a guide for life and for leaders in any endeavor. As a graduate of the U. S. Military Academy at West Point, and a retired Army General with a second career in industry, I can confidently say that military leaders can benefit as much as those in the world of business from this outstanding and highly readable treatise."

—Alan B. Salisbury, Ph.D., Major General, USA (Ret), Chairman, Avilar Technologies

"Yeh writes a terrific book! Practical yet poetic, it inspires while it informs. Read it to become a better leader. Use it to build a better company."

—Ray Smilor, PhD, President, Beyster Institute/Foundation for Enterprise Development

"*The Art of Business* takes the reader on an unexpected spiritual journey into the world of management and successful leadership. Building on the foundation of Sun Tzu's five fundamental arts, author Raymond Yeh tells the stories of several highly successful corporations. In each story, the keys to designing and implementing a successful corporate strategy are revealed, and in each case the role of principled, value-driven leadership is highlighted. Anyone who thought that humility, patience, and peace of mind were absent from the board rooms of today's successful companies had better read Yeh's important and uplifting book."

—Steadman Upham, President, Claremont Graduate University

"Managers and executives seeking to improve their leadership skills can either study the principles of leadership or explore the characteristics of successful leaders. In *The Art of Business*, Raymond and Stephanie Yeh integrate both approaches, together with a leavening measure of oriental wisdom. The book utilizes five 'Arts' to provide a structure for achieving

leadership mastery. Moreover, the practical application of these Arts is effectively demonstrated by examining the characters and actions of proven leaders in a wide range of fields, including business, government, and sports. One cannot read this book without finding concepts and principles that will enhance his or her leadership potential."
—John Vanston, Chairman, Technology Futures

"*The Art of Business* is Insightful, analytical, inspirational, and creative—illustrated by compelling cases. This book will be required reading in my management courses."
—Ken Walters, Professor, Bothell Business Program, University of Washington

"Awesome and inspiring! *The Art of Business is* an enlightening, must-read for thoughtful leaders of business and government. Raymond Yeh brilliantly uses the framework of Sun Tzu's principles to reflect his insights on the nature of man and business. The stories he tells of successful companies are fascinating and demonstrate his deep understanding and clarity of thinking. He writes with passion and purpose, engaging his readers. This book is an important and valuable contribution to contemporary management theory."
—Po Chi Wu, Ph.D., General Partner, Position Smith(TM) and CEO, Story Manager, Inc.

"Great work! Useful anecdotes for aspiring and established business leaders."
—Philip Yeo, Chairman, Economic Development Board and A*Star, Singapore

The Art of Business
In the Footsteps of Giants

Raymond T. Yeh, Ph.D
with Stephanie H. Yeh

Zero Time
Publishing

The Art of Business

Copyright© 2004 by Raymond Yeh

Requests for permission should be addressed to
  Zero Time Publishing
  1145 Church Avenue
  Olathe, CO 81425
  info@zerotimepublishing.com

ISBN: 0-9754277-0-9

Printed in Taiwan

To the memory of
George Kozmetsky and K.T. Li
and their vision of
Service, Compassion and Global Prosperity

Acknowledgments

We are greatly indebted to the many individuals who helped make this book a reality. We first thank all the people who graciously allocated time out of their busy schedules to be interviewed: Herb Kelleher, Colleen Barrett, Jim Wimberly, and Ron Ricks of Southwest Airlines; Earl Bakken and Art Collins of Medtronic; Gordon Moore and Albert Yu of Intel; Adam Kahane of the Center for Generative Leadership; Michael Dell, Michele Moore, Tom Meredith, Scott Eckert, and Keith Maxwell of Dell, Inc.; George Kozmetsky, formerly of the University of Texas at Austin; John Wooden of UCLA; Neal Kocurek of St. David's Healthcare Systems; Red McCombs of McCombs Enterprises; Sung Lee of Samsung Austin Semiconductor; Jim March of Stanford University; Tim McClure of GSD&M; Bob Inman of the University of Texas; Dick Lampson, Barbara Waugh, and Andrew Liu of Hewlett-Packard; Henry Hwang of Rock Asia; Carl Rosendorf of Smartbargains.com; Michael Blasgen of Sony America. K. T. Li, Y. C. Wang of Formosa Plastic, Stan Shih of Acer, and C. L. Wang in Taiwan; Kanji Kobayashi, formerly of NEC, and T. Kobayashi, formerly of Fujitsu, in Japan; Philip Yeo and Carmee Lim in Singapore; Ney Araujo, formerly of Agroceres and Atilano Sobrinho of Inepar, in Brazil, we thank you. We have learned so much through our interviews with you, interviews that made this book possible. Thank you!

We received invaluable advice from the many people who read drafts of the chapters and gave us ideas to make this a better book. Specifically, we are most grateful for Herb Kelleher who, in spite of his extremely busy schedule, read the entire manuscript, providing detailed notes and thoughtful comments. We benefited from C.V. Ramamoorthy and Jim March's wisdom, H. T. Yeh's constant encouragement and careful reading of many drafts, Jim Pelky's urgings to do better, and Syed Shariq's insightful questions. Michele Moore has been most gracious in going over the details of several drafts. Barbara Waugh, Nancy Lee Hutchins, Tim McClure, Ann Daly, and Kate O'Keefe all provided valuable suggestions. Hiroshi Yamaguchi of NEC was so gracious in helping with NEC's history and story. Flory Chowe not only designed a brilliant cover, but her Chinese calligraphy graces pages throughout the book. Debbie Buxton did a stellar job editing and proofing the draft. We thank all of you.

Last but not least, we want to thank Priscilla, wife to Ray and mother to Stephanie, who provided the constant support and love that made everything we undertook a success. Thanks also to Alan Joel for his support and counsel throughout the writing process. We love you both!

We are proud of this book and the ideas in it. Thanks to all of you who made this possible.

Preface

The Art of Business is a meditation on leadership that has emerged from Ray Yeh's personal communion with those among us who lead with heart. It illuminates and enlightens the wisdom of compassionate engagements that are capable of transforming the spirits of the organizations. Ray synthesizes the wisdom of the East and the knowledge of the West to articulate insights that show the way for experiencing wholeness and for nurturing the gift of the leadership in our daily engagements, wherever we are.

The Art of Business shows the path to compassionate leadership, not often seen or traveled by many. This path requires engagement with the courage of one's conviction, and unfolds the promise of soaring to the call of service, with compassion, to those with whom we share our lives everyday. Art Collins, CEO of Medtronic, expresses the essence of his journey on this path when he talked with Ray about what he would say if his grandchildren asked him, "Grandpa, what did you do in your life that was really important?" He said he would reply:

> *"I don't tell them I delivered an extra penny per share, not that that isn't important. But I tell them about all the good Medtronic did for millions of people around the world, and the small, but hopefully important, part I played in that effort."*

The Art of Business challenges us all to create a 'sacred space' of engagements with others, at home and at work. It is a call to embrace the spirit of the Dutch to reclaim the sacred space (over 60% of the Dutch population live on land that they have reclaimed from the ocean) for compassionate acts of leaders within the organizational culture that motivates engagements, more often than not, with the logic of consequences. Ray's message is an inspiration for renewed exploration and action, for reclaiming the sacred within any organization in order to create a truly compassionate and trusting culture.

Dr. Syed Shariq, Co-Chair, Kozmetsky Global Col-laboratory,
Stanford University

Contents

Prologue

This book is a result of more than twenty years of curiosity beginning in the late 1970s, when I was a research fellow at Fujitsu, the giant Japanese computer and systems company. I noticed that many top Japanese executives read and extensively utillized two strategic books: *The Art of War* by Sun Tzu and *The Book of Five Rings* by Miyamoto Musashi, the famed samurai of ancient Japanese history and Sun Tzu's disciple. As I began to read these two oriental classics, I found them difficult to understand, especially Musashi's book. Years later, when I was running my own companies, I felt frustrated by many of the gung-ho, systematic approaches advocated in popular management books. Peter Senge's book, *The Fifth Discipline*, proved helpful because he treated the organization as a living system rather than a machine. His ideas jarred my memory and reminded me of Sun Tzu and Musashi. Sun Tzu, as I understand him from his book, always views any organization—even an army—as an organic whole.

It is interesting to note that the word *business* in Chinese consists of two characters: *Sheng* (生), which is life, and *Yi* (意), which is meaning. So the word *business* in Chinese translates into "the meaning of life." In other words, the ancient Chinese thought of organizations as living, organic systems long before the arrival of the Newtonian model. Since I believe that wisdom transcends time and culture, I began a research project to determine whether the best modern companies currently practice Sun Tzu's wisdom. This book is the result of my private research project that delved into the business practices of more than 30 leading companies and their leaders.

My research revealed that a great organization must first of all have a soul, which creates meaning for the people who work there. Such an organization knows where it is going and somehow always seems to *flow* with the changing world, arriving at its destiny in perfect synchrony. A great organization cleverly *leverages* everything in its environment, including competitors, to effectively and efficiently utilize its resources. It is also the *master* of its trade, constantly treading on the leading edge while maintaining effective balance. Finally, a great organization is made of *leaders* who help to actualize the organization's vision by aligning their own dreams to it.

Although many books attempt to translate Sun Tzu's wisdom into systematic guidelines for business, the wisdom of this ancient teacher actually needs to be experienced rather than simply analyzed. To offer you, the reader, that experience, I have chosen to present Sun Tzu's teachings in story format. These stories describe how the best companies in the world have put Sun Tzu's strategies to work, allowing you to follow in the footsteps of giants—the business leaders who have walked before us. The story format frees you to select and read any story that interests you, even before you read the introduction to each chapter. The wisdom is in the stories themselves, in the actual experiences of these leaders and their organizations. The introduction in each chapter captures the essential wisdom of these companies and their leaders, providing a framework for insight. There is no specific sequence for reading or using this book. If you have a specific problem, pick a story and dive in. I also included Southwest Airlines in every chapter to give you a deeper look at a company that uses all the strategic arts introduced in this book.

The power of Sun Tzu's teachings lies in the five fundamental arts of strategy that he used, in various combinations, to influence his environment to his advantage. These five arts, outlined at the beginning of *The Art of War*, are Tao, Tien, Dee, Jiang, and Fa. According to Sun Tzu:

> *"War is a matter of vital importance to the State; the province of life or death; the road to survival or ruin. It is mandatory that it be thoroughly studied. Therefore, appraise it in terms of the five fundamental elements... The first of these elements is Tao; the second, Tien; the third, Dee; the fourth, Jiang; and the fifth, Fa."*

Table i expresses the meaning of the Chinese characters and the essence of Sun Tzu's wisdom as I interpret it. The specific arts listed in italics in the essence column are the titles of the five chapters in this book.

The great organizations included in this book are from around the world, and include for-profit and non-profit companies as well as both young and mature organizations. The practice of these strategic arts empowers an organization to hold a steady course in the quest for its vision, resisting the temptations and pressures in its environment. This steady aim is crucial because of our society's focus on the short term bottom-line, which often causes a company to lose its *soul*. Enron, WorldCom, and Arthur Andersen so ably demonstrate the dire consequences of the loss of corporate soul. Finally, this book assists leaders at any level with insights from great leaders on the application of these arts for guiding their organizations in this ever changing and unpredictable world.

Enjoy!

Chinese Character	Translation	Essence
Tao 道	Vision/Truth/Path	Pure Potentiality *The Art of Possibility*
Tien 天	Weather	Synchronize with Destiny *The Art of Timing*
Dee 地	Terrain	Utilize What You Have *The Art of Leverage*
Fa 法	Discipline/Process	Balance on the Edge *The Art of Mastery*
Jiang 將	Commander	Service *The Art of Leadership*

Table i. The Essence of Sun Tzu's wisdom.

I

The Art of Possibility

"The Tao that can be told is not the eternal Tao.
The name that can be named is not the eternal name.
The nameless is the beginning of heaven and earth.
The named is the mother of ten thousand things.
Ever desireless, one can see the mystery.
Ever desiring, one can see the manifestations.
These two spring from the same source but differ in name;
This appears as void.
Void within void…
The gate to all possibility."
–Lao Tzu–

A young disciple serves his Zen master while listening to two older disciples, A and B, arguing just outside the door. After a few moments, disciple A enters the room and relates the argument to the master as well as his own point of view. The master smiles at disciple A and says, "You are right." As soon as disciple A happily leaves the room, disciple B walks in. Disciple B proceeds to elaborate his side of the argument to the master. The master smiles at disciple B and says, "You are right," and disciple B also happily departs. By this time, the young disciple, who is still in the room, is thoroughly confused and says to the master, "It seems that disciples A and B cannot both be right." The master smiles at the young disciple and says, "You are also right."

In classical Chinese literature, Tao is like a multi-faceted crystal, encompassing multiple different meanings that are difficult to behold all at once. Tao is the way or ultimate destination. Tao is also moral purpose, enlightenment, and truth. At the same time, Lao Tzu tells us, "The Tao that can be told is not the eternal Tao." In other words, no written definition or intellectual understanding ever captures the true essence of the eternal Tao. Tao cannot be grasped with the intellect, only glimpsed with the eyes of the spirit through experience.

Figure 1.1 The Yin/Yang Symbol.

Classical Chinese authors often use the Yin/Yang symbol (see Figure 1.1) to capture the multiple expressions of Tao. For instance, Tao is:

- **Holistic:** While we cannot predict the amount of Yin or Yang at any given moment, we know the whole is always there.
- **Dynamic:** The Yin and Yang are fluid, and they tug and pull each other—the makeup is constantly changing.
- **Inclusive:** There is always Yin within Yang (the dark spot within the white space) and Yang within Yin (the white spot within the dark space).
- **Harmonious:** The ebb and flow of nature automatically balances itself.

Tao is the dynamic flowing force that constantly seeks to create in the world. As such, Tao can be thought of as the pure potentiality or pure consciousness of which everything is a manifestation. In Tao, mind and body are no longer separable, but are the complementary aspects of life co-evolving together as the Yin and Yang.

The Tao Experience

A common experience of Tao for many people is that of being "in the zone." When athletes are in the zone, they describe feeling light and effortless as their bodies automatically and instinctively reach peak performance. Legendary coach and track star John Smith recalls being in the zone the day he set the world record in the 440 meter race: "It feels as if gravity is pulling the body along rather than impeding it." Whether in sports, music, business, or art, we've all tasted Tao. Tao could be a runner's high, a musician's groove, or a feeling of being "on." Tao is the life force that constantly seeks to manifest through each of us in different aspects of our lives.

Perhaps the easiest way to begin experiencing Tao on a personal level, to get in touch with one's soul as it were, is to answer three basic life questions:

- What is my dream?
- How do I realize my dream?
- Who am I or what do I stand for?

When we begin to answer these questions, we have begun our quest for the soul. Indeed, the answers to these questions are the end game for many people on the spiritual path and the tools of many masters past and present. While the Tao cannot be grasped, these questions can be answered. They are doorways into the possibilities of the soul.

Just as it is the omnipresent fabric woven into every aspect of the living world, Tao is also a part of the man-made systems of business and commerce. If Tao is pure consciousness, the essence of the creative processes of life, then any organization that wishes to evolve and grow as a living system must have Tao. While many of the artificially created systems of man are mechanical, there are organizations that are true living systems, true expressions of Tao. These are organizations with soul.

I have developed a keen awareness of the difference between organizations that are living systems and those that are simply mechanical expressions of man-made goals over the years. Those organizations that were living, growing, and dynamic systems seemed to be informed by some intelligent presence influenced by a higher purpose. In every aspect of those companies I saw that same soul, that same drive to create something beyond individual selfish desires. What I saw were living expressions of Tao in a business setting; a situation in which we have come to expect automation and lifelessness.

After many years of walking in and out of companies that were both living and mechanical, I realized that only those companies possessed of a soul had any hope of longevity in the constantly changing business climate. Only those companies with Tao could evolve at the pace of life, matching the dynamic creative processes of life itself. For years I was unsure of how to describe and explore the presence of something which, by its very nature, cannot be named. While there are libraries of books devoted to the personal exploration of the soul, I found a scarcity of books that focused on the exploration and development of an organization's soul. Yet, we devote years of our lives to the growth and creation of business and commerce. How, then, can we knowingly and deliberately nurture the development of an organizational soul?

The answer lies in the same three questions that we must ask ourselves when we seek our own souls. In organizations, the answers to these questions have long been expressed as the Vision, Purpose, and Values (VPVs):

- *Vision:* What is our dream?
- *Purpose:* How do we fulfill our shared vision?
- *Values:* What do we stand for and how do we behave ethically?

In a marketplace that thrives on the Darwinian principle of "survival of the fittest," strong VPVs are the guiding forces that help living organizations keep their aim and stay the road despite dramatic changes in the business climate. If the vision defines the ultimate destination of the path, then the purpose and core values form the path itself. While there are numerous ways of traveling from a starting point to a destination, the purpose and core values help leaders choose the way and stay on track despite obstacles and trials. In other words, the quest for vision must be *value-centered* and *purpose-driven* as illustrated in Figure 1.2.

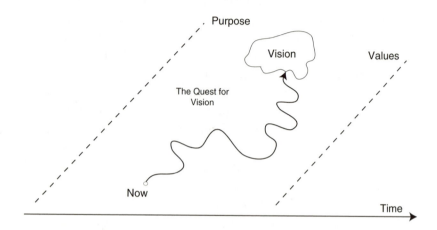

Figure 1.2 Vision, purpose, and values.

Most organizations, living or mechanical, have a set of VPVs. However, not all VPVs are equal. In ordinary organizations that are not inspired from within by a compelling vision, the VPVs may be duly written and recorded in the dusty back issues of annual reports or even posted on the walls. Yet, as a guiding force they lack power and do little to influence the employees and officers—the very people for whom they were intended. The VPVs exist, but fail to guide the daily decisions of the organization. In these companies, the people may be active and busy, but they often fail to create lasting results.

In a dynamic organization with soul, however, the VPVs are expressed in every moment and every interaction. VPVs can be heard in casual conversations between co-workers, in speeches and press releases to sources in and out of the company, in celebrations, and in what is celebrated. The VPVs consistently inform and influence decisions both trivial and major, and guide the steady and deliberate evolution of the organization.

The Yin/Yang Formula

In a marketplace based on survival of the fittest, competition is the beginning and end of the story. Within any industry, companies struggle and fight with each other to be the top dog, to have the next great breakthrough that will send profit margins soaring through the proverbial roofs. Within any company, corporate directors nurture the killer instinct by enticing employees with stock options and raises at one end while lashing them with the threat of layoffs and downsizing at the other. Few can see beyond the next quarterly report and most live or die by market analyst reports. The same game of competition is played as avidly among employees as among companies.

But to the giants of business, who represent only a small percentage of players in the market, the dog eat dog world is not only the lowest form of evolution but also a poor form of strategy. These players are true strategists who understand that corporate longevity and success come from working for a higher purpose, or working in Tao.

In companies with Tao, there is the urge to create something real and beneficial in the world, not just achieve top dog position. Indeed, rather than always looking outwardly at the competition, these companies are inwardly focused on their higher purpose while having a high degree of awareness of all things around them.

Lifting one's gaze from mere survival to living in Tao is no simple task when competition is all around. Competition seems real and self-evident, easy to grasp, while Tao is often only an ephemeral concept or a fleeting glimpse of what might be possible. One formula that helps us get a better grasp of Tao is the Yin/Yang formula. Tao is difficult to grapple with because it is pure potentiality, a single presence that is in all things, the one force behind all creation. While Tao is one, everything that manifests as an expression of Tao is a duality; hence, the Yin/Yang symbol is the perfect expression of Tao.

The Yin/Yang symbol beautifully expresses the duality of all manifestations. For instance, light and dark are dual manifestations of the same thing. Without dark there cannot be light, and vice versa. The same is true of good and evil. Or, in the case of the elemental particle theory, the building block of the universe exists as both wave and particle at the same time.[1] In these dualities, you cannot have one without the other. The dark enhances and emphasizes the light while the light provides contrast for the dark.

To see the Tao of an organization and begin to develop a living Tao in your own organization, apply the Yin/Yang formula. For instance, in a mechanical organization the basis for guidance and management is control, which is the Yang. As a result, employees often lack initiative and investment in the organization and live only to serve their own selfish desires—this is the Yin. By contrast, in organizations with Tao, the Yang is freedom and empowerment. Employees are given the freedom to handle situations in their own way. The flip side of the coin is accountability and discipline—this is the Yin. With freedom must come accountability and responsibility lest individual decisions run riot or contrary to the Tao. Control necessarily breeds self-serving (which leads to the need for even greater control) while freedom and empowerment leads to accountability and investment in the organization. The Yin/Yang formula always describes a cycle that feeds itself continuously.

Fueling the Winning Formula

The Yin/Yang formula is akin to any mathematical formula in that the results differ depending on the initial values that are fed into the formula. For the formula to produce freedom and accountability, one must create trust as the fuel. In this fuel there must be something that invites each person in the organization to step beyond the natural human instinct to ask, "What's in it for me?" The human DNA, programmed through millennia of evolution for survival and indoctrinated by the marketplace in competition, naturally reverts to selfish and self-serving behaviors before all else.

Trust is the bridge that allows each person in the organization to step beyond his or her selfish instincts to take part in something much greater. To really exist, trust must be a two-way bridge. For instance, when employees trust the organization, they are saying, "I trust that you have chosen a strong and worthy set of VPVs. I trust that you will empower me to help achieve the VPVs. I trust that you will take care of me." This allows employees to focus on creating real meaning in their work rather than constantly worrying about job security. For instance, Southwest Airlines pilots and flight attendants willingly work more hours than employees at any other U.S. airline. Why? Because they trust that the company will take care of them through job security, profit sharing, and employee benefits.

At the same time, an organization must trust its employees. When an organization trusts its employees, it is saying, "I have faith in the VPVs. I trust that you see they are worthy and will do your part to achieve them. I will help you." Inepar, an energy and telecommunications company with headquarters in Curitiba, Brazil, demonstrates this high level of trust. The company's symbol is a Brazilian bird called Quero Quero, meaning in Portuguese, "I want, I want." The first "I want" symbolizes the wants of employees, including a better quality of life, a higher salary, opportunities for professional growth, and more training. The second "I want" symbolizes the needs of the company, including total quality, higher productivity, the expansion of business, the incorporation of new technologies, and environmental preservation. Together, the stakeholders find the common "I want" and work toward achieving these common goals.

Atilano Sobrinho, Inepar's co-founder and President, told me: "I learned from the poor people that they don't have a problem with being poor, but having no prospects in life is a big problem." To expand the life possibilities for employees and their families, the company pays the educational expenses of every employee's dependent children. In response to this level of corporate trust, Inepar's productivity and quality have increased steadily.

Finally, employees must trust each other. When they do, they are saying, "I trust that we are all on the same path, seeking to achieve the same goal." Organizations must provide conditions in which team members are encouraged to trust each other rather than compete with one another. At Intel, for instance, the sharing of technical knowledge is an essential part of the culture, and is acknowledged as being the key to gaining speed and competitive advantage. These three forms of trust are all invitations for every member of the organization to step beyond the self-serving, competitive goals that are the norm in companies without Tao. Trust invites people to expand their horizons and take part in living a dream.

As a result of taking the time to cultivate trust, soulful organizations reap all the benefits sought by "dog eat dog" organizations, including profitability, longevity, adaptability, and innovation. Indeed, these are all the indicators of conscious, living evolution. In contrast, "dog eat dog" organizations fuel their Yin/Yang formulas with fear—the fear of being fired, the fear of financial loss and the fear of non-survival. The result is a constant state of reaction, lack of unity, and the failure to evolve purposefully.

Companies fueled by trust and living in Tao access the wisdom and ingenuity of every single employee by offering them freedom in exchange for accountability and discipline. In addition, employees are inspired by the pride of creating something of real benefit in the world, which leads to continuous innovation and almost no resistance. While the journey to living in Tao cannot be defined in concrete detail, the major pieces of the puzzle are clearly in evidence: a compelling vision, freedom, accountability, and trust.

One More Piece of the Puzzle

A final maverick piece of the puzzle must be mentioned before we start you on the journey of exploring the Tao. In every soulful organization we have explored, we find that the Tao has always begun with the dreamers. There are always one or two dreamers, usually the founders of the organization but not always, who spark the Tao into life. These dreamers then feed and nourish the dream, which is often considered to be an impossible dream, with raw inspiration, sheer determination, and contagious enthusiasm. They often create the VPVs as a way to communicate that dream to others and ground the dream into reality.

Consider the founding of the United States. On the night of July 2, 1776, word reached the delegates attending the Second Continental Congress in Philadelphia that hundreds of British warships and troop transports were arriving New York. As the delegates cast their initial votes, the British Empire struck, intending to annihilate the budding democracy of its rebel colony. By August there were 32,000 British troops in New York, ready to march on Philadelphia, a city with a population of only 30,000. George Washington's pickup army of 7,000 untrained, ill-equipped farmers stood as the only line of resistance.

Each of the delegates who signed the Declaration of Independence was fully aware of the death sentence that awaited them if their bid for freedom failed. As Benjamin Franklin said so well, "We must all hang together, or most assuredly, we will hang separately." The dream of freedom, the declaration that "All men are created equal; that they are endowed by their Creator with certain inalienable rights," meant more to these men than life itself. The fight for this dream has been renewed time and again by the great leaders of American history: by Abraham Lincoln during the Civil War, by Martin Luther King, Jr. in the civil rights movement, and by Lyndon Baines Johnson with his vision of a Great Society. Though every fight was different, each of these leaders was guided by the dream of freedom, of creating a society in which, "all men are created equal."

At heart, all of these dreamers have an irrepressible urge to create a freer, more beautiful and more dignified world than the one that exists today. Being with these dreamers can light up your life, and many people join great organization simply to be part of the dream. In the three stories that follow, we offer you a heavenly taste of those dreams and the dreamers. These three organizations each live in Tao in their own unique way: Medtronic, the leading medical technology company in the world, restores people to full life; Grameen Bank, the bank in Bangladesh that started micro-lending for the poor, uplifts the poorest of the poor to dignity and pride; and Southwest Airlines, the best airline in the U. S., brings democracy to the skies. Let the journey in the footsteps of giants begin!

Medtronic[2]
Restoring People to Full Life

During a visit to the Medtronic headquarters, where I gave a lecture, in Minneapolis, MN in December 2000, I was utterly surprised to discover that the company had created a corporate meditation room, a tranquil spot where any employee could get a few moments of quiet during an otherwise busy daily routine. I was also awed by the company's symbol of a rising man, created by artist Alan O. Hage, with the company's motto of "Towards Full Life." Both the symbol and motto serve as a constant inspirational reminder to each of Medtronic's 30,000 employees of the purpose they serve. When I saw the symbol, I knew then and there that the story of this marvelous company had to be told. I was truly delighted when I met Earl Bakken, the creator of the wonderful Medtronic story over the past 50 years and the company's co-founder, in November 2001 at a symposium in Hawaii.

The dream began in a tiny, un-insulated garage in the heart of the freezing Minnesota winter. It was 1949, and Earl Bakken, an earnest and unknown engineer, and his brother-in-law Palmer Hermundslie were cooking up red-hot ideas that would eventually change the face of medical technology. Bakken dreamt of a time when doctors would actually implant tiny electronic devices on or in the human body to reduce the debilitating effects of major diseases. As a child Bakken was fascinated with using electricity to heal the human body, a practice that dates back to the Roman Empire. With a directness known only to the young and the great, the two decided to form a company to produce electrical devices for healing the human body, promptly naming their venture Medtronic, a cross between the words "medicine" and "electronic." Thus began a tiny company with a huge dream, a company that today ranks in the Fortune 500, is considered one of the top 100 companies to work for, employs approximately 30,000 people worldwide, reported more than $7.7 billion in revenue for FY03 and was ranked #11 by *Money* magazine[3] on return to shareholders with 19.46% annual return over 30 years. Medtronic is also the leader in most of its markets. In

1949, however, this great company earned exactly $8 in revenue during its first month of operation.

First Success

Like most startups, Medtronic was fed on raw inspiration and meager dollars. Bakken and Hermundslie scrounged what work they could by repairing electronic medical devices for local hospitals and representing several medical equipment companies. Their first breakthrough product was the world's first external wearable, battery-powered pacemaker, which they created for Dr. C. Walton Lillehei at the University of Minnesota. Bakken describes the inspiration for this device:

> *"Dr. Lillehei had these babies he was doing open heart surgery on and he lost one during a power failure. He was upset about that. We had an AC pacemaker, a big AC pacemaker that was keeping this child's heart going during the surgery and it was working fine. During a power failure, they lost the child. I envisioned the whole story there and then."*

It turns out that "the whole story" is told not in words, but in pictures. Bakken developed a two dimensional graph (see Figure 1.3), in which he captured every type of medical device he could imagine in terms of function (prosthetic, therapeutic, monitorial, and analytic) and placement on the body (no contact, external contact, temporary entrance into the body, and permanent implant). He then drew a diagonal slash across the entire graph and proclaimed that Medtronic would create products only for those areas below the slash. Why? Because he held true to his original vision of inventing devices that would be used on or in the body itself.

In his early vision Bakken saw devices that could be implanted into the body, devices that had to be of the highest quality and reliability. He describes why Medtronic initially veered away from monitoring equipment and other products above his diagonal slash:

> *"Medtronic couldn't make monitoring equipment cheap enough. This stuff has to be built very cheaply if you're going to do business,*

and if it fails, you just get it fixed. But if a pacemaker fails you can't get it fixed. The person's gone. We only knew how to make tremendously high quality products."

With the creation of the first battery-powered pacemaker, Medtronic entered the medical community with a splash. An article about the new pacemaker appeared in the *Saturday Evening Post*. Bakken laughs about what happened next: "Our insurance agent called us up and said, 'What a marvelous thing you've done. It's great what you're doing for these kids. By the way, you're insurance is now $30,000 a year'—up from $300, which was a blow to a little company in a garage." In 1957, Dr. Lillehei successfully performed the first open-heart surgery using the new battery–powered pacemaker, and a new market was born. Today, Medtronic's pacemaker is a silver-dollar sized device that assists about 300,000 new patients every year worldwide.

	Prosthetic	Therapeutic	Monitorial	Analytic
No Contact	Cybernetics; Simulation (Nerve Cell, etc.); Breath Simulator	Cobalt; X-Ray; Laser; Hyperbaric Chambers; Ultraviolet and Infrared Lamps	Closed Circuit Television; Communication Systems; Thermography; Capacity Plethysmograph; X-Ray; Cineradiography; Computers	pH Meter; Flame Photometer; Colorimeter; Electronic Microscope; Blood Cell Counters; Radio-isotope Scanning; Osmometers; Electrophoresis Autoanalyzers
External Contact	Artificial Limbs; Artificial Larynx	Cardiac Massage; Defibrillators; Pacemakers; Respirators; Walking Aids; Electric Beds; Ultrasonics; Hypothermia; Phlebo Bynostat; Stimulators; Electric Sleep; Labor Stimulators	Electroplethysnograph; ECG; EEG; EMG; Pressures; Labor Monitoring; Telemetry	Audiometer; Breath Gas Analyzers; Pulmonary Function; Basal Metabolism; GSR; Eye Pressure; Ultrasonic Scanning
Temporary Entrance Into Body	Heart Lung; Booster Pumps; Artificial Kidney (Dialysis)	Electrophremic Respirator; Pacemakers (5800); Catheters; Coagulation Forceps; Paired Pulse; Vein Eraser; Plasma Gas Scalpel; Brain Stimulator; Cyrosurgical Pain Inhibitors	Densitometers (Dye); Radio Pills (Pressures, etc.); Blood Flow Meters; Enderadiosondes; Catheters; Transducers	Angiocardiography; Fiber Optics; Radio Pills (pH, etc.); Foreign Body Locators
Permanent Implant	Artificial Pancreas; Artificial Heart; Oral Vibrator	Implantable Hearing Aid; CSX; Implantable Pacemakers; Incontinence Stimulator; Bladder Stimulators; Drug Capsules; Bone Heaters; Transplant Aids	Potency Detector; Transponders; Expendable Monitors	

Figure 1.3 The Original Medtronic Roadmap

Desperate Days

Even with the resounding success of its first major product, Medtronic experienced the growing pains typical of any small company struggling to break into the big time. By 1960, the company had run out of money, and Bakken and Hermundslie were rapidly running out of time. Not a single banker or investor would put up the badly needed cash and the two struggling founders barely found time to woo potential investors. They juggled repair work and equipment distribution duties with the creation of custom electronic devices for physicians and the mass production of the model 5800 pacemakers. They were drowning in their own attempts to keep the company capitalized.

It gradually became clear that Medtronic had become so distracted from its original vision that bankers and investors had no idea what the company actually did. With this realization, Bakken, with the help of the company's Board of Directors, drafted the defining *Tao* for Medtronic:

The Medtronic Mission Statement

1. To contribute to human welfare by application of biomedical engineering in the research, design, manufacture, and sale of instruments or appliances that alleviate pain, restore health, and extend life.

2. To direct our growth in the areas of biomedical engineering where we display maximum strength and ability; to gather people and facilities that tend to augment theses areas; to continuously build on these areas through education and knowledge assimilation; to avoid participation in areas where we cannot make unique and worthy contributions.

3. To strive without reserve for the greatest possible reliability and quality in our products; to be the unsurpassed standard of comparison; and to be recognized as a company of dedication, honesty, integrity, and service.

4. To make a fair profit on current operations to meet our obligations, sustain our growth, and reach our goals.

5. To recognize the personal worth of employees by providing an employment framework that allows personal satisfaction in work accomplished, security, advancement opportunity, and means to share in the company's success.

6. To maintain good citizenship as a company.

Nearly half a century later, the Mission Statement continues to serve as both the ethical and practical framework for Medtronic's strategy and operations. These mission statements clearly define the company's vision (1st statement), purpose (2nd statement), and values (4th, 5th, and 6th statements). In 1962, soon after Bakken drafted the mission statement, Medtronic was able to secure long-term financing in the form of a $100,000 note from Central Northwestern Bank and a $200,000 private placement from Community Investment Enterprises, a local venture capital firm. In addition to funding, the venture capitalists also brought savvy managers to Medtronic's Board for strategic and management advice.

The founders of almost every company sit down at some point in their company's evolution to write a vision or mission statement, but history shows us that it is not the statement itself that creates success, longevity, or dominance. It is the ability to stay inspired and re-create that statement on a daily basis. Medtronic has leaned on these six statements for more than 40 years, and judging by its dominant presence—the company has been called "the best medical device company in the world" and the "Microsoft of the medical device industry"—such devotion to *Tao* is a worthwhile endeavor.

The Tao of Medtronic (extracted from its Mission Statement)

Vision: To contribute to the restoration of people toward full life.

Purpose: To direct growth in the areas of biomedical engineering where the company displays maximum strength and ability.

Values:
- The greatest possible quality and reliability.
- Being the unsurpassed standard of comparison.
- Being recognized as a company of dedication, honesty, integrity, and service.
- Making a fair profit.
- Recognizing the personal worth of employees.
- Maintaining good citizenship.

Back to the Garage

Great leaders of exceptional companies seem driven from some inner source of inspiration, and motivate others around them with their desire for greatness. But in a company of approximately 30,000 employees, how do you connect every employee, from janitors and bookkeepers to corporate officers, to the original vision that kept Bakken and Hermundslie on fire in the midst of meager circumstances? How do you bring every person in the company back into the experience of that tiny garage lab? With pomp and circumstance!

In the early 1960s, Bakken and a group of company officers created the "Mission and Medallion Ceremony," a rite of passage every new employee must experience six months or so after joining the company. This rite of passage is a journey back in time, a virtual trip back to the garage where the dream began. For a recent ceremony, Bakken, who is long retired from the company, flew from his home in Hawaii to co-host the occasion with current Chairman and CEO Art Collins. Not only did Bakken review Medtronic's mission and discuss its meaning in detail, he took the new employees on a virtual tour of the important events in the company's history. He showed slides of the company's first AC-powered pacemaker and the tiny garage that was the company's first lab. Finally, he and Collins gave each employee a bronze medallion depicting a person rising up and walking toward a full life, with the words "Toward Full Life" inscribed on the edges. On the back of the medallion is the first statement from the Medtronic Mission Statement. With each medallion, Bakken urged the new employees to remember,

"Your work here at Medtronic is not just to make money for yourself or the company, but to restore people to fuller lives."

Every December at the Medtronic annual holiday program, the company invites six patients, along with their families and physicians, to tell their personal stories, in which Medtronic products play a vital role, and to offer thanks for restoring them back to full life. At the 2001 party, more than 1,500 people attended in-person and thousands more were linked-in via videoconferencing. For Medtronic employees, it's a day of personal inspiration and connection when the true meaning of their work is literally brought to life in every patient's story.

The year-end program is also a way to reinforce the company's tradition of serving its customers well and focusing on quality. Art Collins says, "When I'm in the operating room and see the product being used on a person, that customer is no longer a statistic but an individual. It reinforces the need for quality in our business." For instance, famed comedian Jerry Lewis recently filmed a video for Medtronic in which he talked about his own story of healing. He had been in pain for 37 years, the result of performing all of his own stunts. In the early part of 2002, he could endure his pain no longer and was seriously considering taking his own life. Luckily, he found out about Medtronic's "pain pacemaker," a device that helps him to control his pain. He is now virtually pain free, can work on his book, conduct his telethon, and pick up his 10 year-old daughter. He has been restored to full life. Jerry's experience is representative of what people with chronic pain go through to find a solution that works.

Bill George, the former Chairman and CEO of Medtronic, and Art Collins proclaim the holiday program to be the most important meeting of the year, outranking even the annual shareholder meeting. They say,

"Medtronic is not in the business of maximizing shareholder value. We are in the business of maximizing value to the patients we serve."

Adds Collins: "We are so fortunate with this combination of doing a tremendous amount of good for millions of people and, in the process, having a very sound, financially successful business." Bakken concludes with this comment on Medtronic's holiday program:

> *"The presence at the holiday program of those wonderful patients, from all around the world, is not merely intended to make us feel good at Christmas time. Their bright, smiling, pain-free faces and their bold words of hope and triumph remind us why we do what we do, why we are what we are—365 days of the year."*

To the Letter

Medtronic officers are savvy enough to know that just having core values does little in terms of daily action. To give these values weight and significance, the company requires employees to sign a code of conduct statement each year that states their compliance with these core values. Immediate action is taken against violators of this code. For instance, when former CEO Bill George discovered that a newly promoted executive of Medtronic had violated the code, he asked for the man's immediate resignation. In addition, George publicized the event with full disclosure to the appropriate authorities so that "customers and employees would know with certainty what Medtronic stands for." On the acquisitions level, the company stands firm on its values and strives never to acquire another company that does not share its values.

Medtronic's success hinges on its unshakable ability to focus on its well-articulated vision "to contribute to human welfare by application of biomedical engineering in the research, design, manufacture, and sale of instruments or appliances that alleviate pain, restore health, and extend life." For over 40 years, this vision has provided meaning and motivation for Medtronic employees. This total focus on its vision is exemplified when Collins was asked how he managed the stock of the company. He answered:

> *"I don't manage the stock. We manage taking care of patients. That's our business. The stock isn't our business. There's nothing we do that's different because the stock is temporarily dropping. We're in this for the long haul."*

What Tomorrow Brings

Through all of the business fads over the last 50 years, Medtronic has never allowed itself to get bogged down in projects outside the scope of its vision. While the company has reinvented itself many times during this period, it has always stuck to Bakken's original mission statement of "restoring people to full life," a vision which continues to breathe life and motivation into the workforce even today. Bill George summarized the results of such focus:

"Over time, an innovative idea for a product or a service will be copied by your competitors. Creating an organization of highly motivated people is extremely hard to duplicate."[4]

To keep its executives focused on the company's vision and not on exotic perks, Medtronic does not maintain a corporate jet, nor provide company cars for its officers. In fact, it does not even offer reserved parking for its executives. Instead, the company traditionally spends around 10 percent of its revenue on research and development, one of the highest among major corporations. The company encourages innovation in a number of ways, including a program where employees who have good ideas are given the opportunity to try them out with $50,000 of initial funding. As a result of continued R&D spending and acquisitions, currently more than two-thirds of Medtronic's revenue comes from products introduced within the last two years.

By 1999, the company's 50th anniversary, Medtronic had enlarged its focus to include technology for treating a range of chronic diseases and conditions including heart failure, sudden cardiac arrest, coronary artery disease, spinal conditions, diabetes, back pain, chronic pain, and Parkinson's disease. Since its first month, when it earned only $8 in revenue, Medtronic has never slowed its pace. Art Collins elaborates, "Well, think about the way the body works. Not exclusively, but in large part, the body functions because of a series of chemical and electrical reactions. The brain, the spinal cord, the heart—you have nerves that run all over as well as electrical conduction pathways. For example, if you have heart block, you basically then recreate the electrical pathway with the pacemaker. Therefore, anything involved in the correction of a faulty electrical pathway is our business." Bakken jokingly said during the Induction ceremony, "At one time Medtronic only wanted your heart. Now they want every organ of your body."

As Art Collins looks into the future, he declares, "The lifeblood of our company is creating new products and ensuring that patients who have a need for our products will have appropriate access. Reducing cycle time through the patient access chain from product definition and development through product launch and availability is key to our future." What is his vision for Medtronic's future?

> "Medtronic can be characterized by the statistic that every seven seconds someone in the world is being helped by a Medtronic product. So my vision for Medtronic is we will continue to use medical technology and taking advantage of two other major, significant technological trends, which are the advances in information technology and biotechnology. We will incorporate those so that we are treating larger and larger populations of people that have a need for our products. The 7-second statistic keeps going down."

Before his retirement, Art Collins aims to reduce those seven seconds to one.

Grameen Bank
Micro Lending for the Poor

Mufia Khatoon used to be a beggar in the streets of Bangladesh. Most days, she only managed to beg a few ounces of rice, hardly enough for her and her three children. Besides having to scrape a thin living from begging, she had to deal with regular upheavals living in Bangladesh, a land of frequent natural disasters. Khatoon starved through the famine of 1974, and a storm destroyed her makeshift house in 1978. Life looked bleak. But Khatoon's life took a turn for the better when she became a member of Grameen Bank in 1979 and received a small loan of 500 taka (about $25). That tiny loan, now popularly referred to as a *micro loan*, transformed her from a poverty-stricken beggar to a proud, independent businesswoman. Khatoon is only one of the thousands of former beggars and millions of women, all considered to be unworthy of loans by conventional banks, who now live dignified lives because of micro loans from Grameen Bank.

During the famine of 1974, Muhammad Yunus, a Professor of Economics at the University of Chittgong, was shocked at the utter devastation he found in the villages situated around the University. He came to understand that the poor people in these villages were committed to a form of labor, or slavery, in which they traded their labor for a mere 22 cents per day, barely enough for survival. This cycle continues day in and day out, from one generation to the next. Yunus recalls,

> *"I never heard of anyone suffering for the lack of 22 cents. It seemed impossible to me, preposterous."*[5]

He personally lent the equivalent of $27 to 42 people, which amounted to about 62 cents per person. With this money, each person bought materials for the day's work, weaving chairs or making pots. At the end of their first day as independent business owners, each of the 42 people sold their wares and paid back the loan. Thus began the micro credit movement and the subsequent formation of Grameen Bank, which means "village." Based on this experience, Yunus, together with a group of like-minded colleagues and students, formed Grameen

Bank as a micro-lending organization dedicated to lifting the poor out of the perpetual cycle of poverty.

A Basic Human Right

More than 25 years later, Grameen Bank is 93% owned by 2.4 million borrowers. Ninety-five percent of those borrowers are women, and the bank has loaned out more than $3.5 billion dollars. More importantly, the practice of micro credit lending has spread to 43 countries, including some highly developed countries such as the United States. Furthermore, an unprecedented 98% of borrowers have paid their loans back in full.

Grameen Bank was created out of the deeply held belief that the poor are as trustworthy as the wealthy or middle class. By studying the villages around him, Yunus came to understand that the poor are poor not because they are untrained or illiterate, but because they cannot retain the returns of their labor since they have no control over capital. Once they are economically empowered, however, they "are the most determined fighters in the battle to solve the population problem, end illiteracy, and live healthier, better lives."[6]

Grameen Bank considers credit to be a basic human right, and operates on the faith that the poor will repay their debts. Unlike traditional banks, Grameen exists in a counter-culture of its own creation, focused not on making money but on helping people get out of poverty. While profit is a necessary condition of success, the officers at Grameen Bank use profit only as a measure of efficiency. If borrowers are unable to repay loans, the bankers at Grameen focus on assisting borrowers in overcoming problems, not punishing them. This unconventional approach, rare in the banking industry, springs from the belief that each person should be given the necessary tools and assistance to control his or her destiny.

Since many of the bank's borrowers are illiterate, Grameen keeps the repayment formula very simple:

- Loans last for one year.
- Loan installments are paid weekly.
- Repayment begins one week after the loan.

- Weekly loan payments are 2 percent of the loan amount each week for 50 weeks.
- Interest payments are 2 taka per week for every 1,000 taka loaned.

Micro credit lending provides small, collateral-free loans to the poor as capital for building small businesses. It is the logical extension of small business loans that provide reasonable loans to entrepreneurs unable to qualify for traditional bank loans. Micro lending has proven itself to be an effective and popular countermeasure against poverty, enabling people without access to traditional lending institutions to borrow at market rates to start small businesses. More importantly, micro loans structured by Grameen Bank force borrowers to set aside savings as guarantees for their loans, which increases the wealth and financial standing of not only the borrowers, but also the villages, towns, and the entire nation. More than eight million people currently receive micro credit and approximately half of them live in Bangladesh.

A no-handout, inexpensive program that helps the poor with a hand-up to build businesses, micro credit goes directly to the poor. In contrast to many welfare programs, micro credit actually creates long-term jobs in the villages, and helps women develop confidence and independence in a masculine-dominated culture. The economic multiplier effect of micro lending is significant because the poor reinvest the money they earn back into the local economy, buying basic goods such as food, clothing, and shelter. By limiting the size of the loans to small amount of money, micro credit institutions are able to avoid borrowers motivated by greed.

Grameen Bank pioneered the micro credit movement by becoming the first micro lending institution. Since most of its borrowers are women, who in the 1970s were considered the property of their husbands, bankers had to physically visit each village to encourage the women to step out and create independent lives with the help of micro loans. As such, Grameen Bank created a set of core values for its staff and borrowers. The VPVs of Grameen Bank are listed below:

The Tao of Grameen Bank

Vision: A poverty-free society.

Purpose: Extending credit as a human right.

Values:

- Discipline
- Unity
- Courage
- Hard work

How It Works

One of Grameen's major successes has been the discipline of its borrowers in repaying loans in spite of the regular cataclysms, natural disasters, and personal tragedies that occur. To achieve such success, Grameen has a policy of never canceling a loan because of such tragedies. Rather, bankers will restructure any loan into a very long-term loan, even if it reduces the repayment amount to half a penny each week. Such discipline helps the borrower maintain a sense of self-reliance and confidence.

The majority of Grameen borrowers are women, who have fewer opportunities for work and who are more likely to spend new earnings on their children rather than investing in their businesses. Therefore, Grameen requires that all borrowers have unity, and organize themselves into groups of five. All five are considered in default if a single borrower in the group defaults. The group meets once a week to make their loan payments and to critique one another's business plans. Grameen also requires that all borrowers deposit 5% of their loan into a group fund. Any borrower can take an interest-free loan from the group fund so long as all the other members of the group approve the amount and its usage, and the loan does not exceed half of the fund's total amount. Such loans help borrowers stave off seasonal malnutrition and pay for medical and educational needs. Groups can also request help from other groups in their "center," which is a federation of up to eight groups in a village that meets weekly with a bank worker. This kind of unity encourages members to assist each other, spot problems before they occur, and promote discipline among all members. As of 1998, the total amount of savings in all group funds exceeded $100 million.

Both bank workers and the majority of Grameen's women borrowers must overcome tremendous obstacles and demonstrate enormous courage to carry out the bank's mission. Bank workers must overcome the traditional male-dominated poverty culture of the villages, personally meeting with potential clients and encouraging them to create new lives. The women borrowers, most of whom are illiterate, must overcome their fear and uncertainty and become willing to help themselves and their children break free of the vicious cycle of hand-to-mouth poverty. They must take the first bold step of applying for a micro loan without the approval of their husbands. Both bank workers and women borrowers are often at the mercy of outraged husbands and religious conservatism.

Hard work is a natural and necessary part of working with Grameen Bank. Within the five-person groups, everyone ensures that each borrower is putting forth the necessary effort so that no one will default. The bank's staff works hard, too. Most bank workers do not have offices and must walk for miles each day to meet with potential clients. Twelve-hour days are the norm for these workers. Hand-in-hand with hard work, however, is an environment of trust. Grameen trusts each of its bank workers to analyze situations and create necessary solutions. This trust is one of the reasons that the workers are so creative. Unlike other bank workers, the workers at Grameen consider themselves to be teachers who help borrowers realize their full potential as human beings. Perhaps this is the most satisfying part of working with Grameen—the ability to be creative in helping others to create solutions. In summary, the bank's secret is that it facilitates poor people helping themselves while helping each other. People without credit are organized into borrowing support groups such that each borrower has a real financial stake in all the others in the group.

Along with Grameen's core values of discipline, unity, courage, and hard work, the majority of Grameen Bank members—mostly poor women from the different villages in Bangladesh—developed another set of core values for themselves called the Sixteen Decisions. They are:

- We shall follow and advance the four principles of the Grameen Bank—discipline, unity, courage, and hard work—in all parts of our lives.
- We shall bring prosperity to our families.
- We shall not live in dilapidated houses. We shall repair our houses and work toward constructing new houses at the earliest opportunity.
- We shall grow vegetables all year round. We shall eat plenty of them and sell the surplus.
- During the planting season, we shall plant as many seedlings as possible.
- We shall plan to keep our families small. We shall minimize our expenditures. We shall look after our health.
- We shall educate our children and ensure that they can earn enough to pay for their education.
- We shall always keep our children and the environment clean.
- We shall build and use pit latrines.
- We shall drink water from tube wells. If they are not available, we shall boil water or use alum to purify it.
- We shall not take any dowry at our sons' weddings; neither shall we give any dowry at our daughters' weddings. We shall keep the center from the curse of dowry. We shall not practice child marriage.
- We shall not commit any injustice, and we will oppose anyone who tries to do so.
- We shall collectively undertake larger investments for higher incomes.
- We shall always be ready to help each other. If anyone is in difficulty, we shall all help him or her.

31

- If we come to know of any breach of discipline in any center, we shall all go there and help restore discipline.
- We shall introduce physical exercises in all our centers. We shall take part in all social activities collectively.

One of the means for the Grameen community to sustain its culture is through celebrations. Alex Counts, President of the Grameen Foundation in Washington, D.C. related his experience when he first arrived at Bangladesh to witness the celebration that borrowers of the Bank organized in one village to commemorate the founding of their local branch office. He recalled that Yunus whispered to him towards the end of that huge celebration:

> *"These events are times when the poor can show off, be heard, be loud, make a stir. The slogans, the fanfare, it's all part of a process of overcoming the shame and isolation of poverty. Society has always told the poor, 'Stay in your crummy houses; you are neither to be seen nor heard.' Grameen invites them to come together, hold their heads up high. Be seen! Be heard."*[6]

Sending Poverty to the Museum

Given Grameen Bank's success over the last 25 years, what is its vision for the future? Professor Yunus' vision is to create a poverty-free society by 2050. In a summit for micro credit held in Feb. 1997, he said:

> *"Only one hundred years back, men were still struggling to find a way to fly. Many people seriously thought men would never fly. Those people who were committed to the idea of flying were looked at as crazy people. In 1903, the Wright brothers flew their first plane. It stayed in the air for just 12 seconds. Yes, 12 seconds. It covered 120 feet. At that moment the seed of a new world was planted. Only 65 years later, man confidently went to the moon, picked up moon rocks and returned to the world. The whole world watched every moment of it on the television.*

In the micro credit field, we are just flying our Wright brothers' plane. We are covering 120 feet here, 500 feet there. Some find our plane unsafe, some find it clumsy, and some find it not good enough for the job. We can assure you we'll soon fly our Boeings, our Concords; we'll be ready with booster rockets.

We believe that poverty does not belong to a civilized human society. It belongs to museums. This summit is about creating a process which will send poverty to the museum.... Sixty-five years after this summit, we will also go to our moon. We will create a poverty-free world."[7]

Southwest Airlines[8]
Being Whole

I was totally charmed the first time I strolled through the Southwest Airlines (SWA) headquarters on Love Field Airport, Dallas. The walls were filled with captivating photos, news clippings, articles, letters, and mementos of employees at various company events. Unlike many of the company headquarters of the Fortune 500, characterized by marble floors and works of original art, the SWA corporate headquarters felt like a big family room filled with the love and warmth emanating from the family photos.

Snowstorms are not unusual in New York; however, in December of 2001 an impossible seven feet of snow hit the Buffalo area causing air traffic to grind to a halt. A SWA plane had been trapped on the ground long enough to warrant a routine maintenance check, but maintenance crews were unable to reach the plane through the heavy snow. Because of SWA's lean scheduling system the airline had no replacement planes, and a grounded plane meant loss of revenue. Undaunted by the blizzard conditions, certified maintenance mechanic Johnny Bomaster commandeered a snowmobile to reach the plane, performed the required maintenance check, and sent the plane on its way.

Is Bomaster a hero? Perhaps, but such heroic acts happen every day at SWA. Despite being the most unionized airline in the industry, SWA also has the most dedicated workforce. SWA pilots willingly fly an average of 80 hours a month while pilots from other major airlines fly just over 50 hours each month.

In fact, this upstart Texas airline is the most profitable airline in the industry, with over 35,000 employees spanning 59 airports and 75 locations. It has the lowest unit costs and highest customer satisfaction. SWA was valued at $10.8 billion[9] in October 2002, more than all the other major U.S. airlines combined at the time. Employees own more than 10% of the airline's outstanding shares, and the company was ranked by *Money* magazine[10] as having the top return on investment over a 30 year period, bringing annual returns of 25.99% since 1972. More importantly, since its inception the airline has never laid off a single employee, and employees often stay at SWA for life. Herb Kelleher, Chairman and co-founder, describes the experience of one recently retired pilot:

> *"Nobody [else] in the airline industry has ever had total job security for 30 years—any airline, anywhere in the world. One of our pilots just left, and with his profit sharing alone he took $8 million with him. That was an extra $276,000 a year for every year that he has been here, over and above his wages and his 401(k)."*

How does SWA garner such loyal dedication from their people and create such prosperous returns for its stakeholders? By holding true to a clear and simple purpose of *total job security, profitability, and affordable fares.*

The SWA purpose flies in the face of all traditional wisdom, which insists that permanently low fares reduce revenue and profitability. The airline's stellar returns prove otherwise, due in part to the fact that SWA fares are low enough to compete not only with other airlines but also with ground transportation. When it enters a new market, SWA effectively slashes ticket prices by 65% and increases passenger volume by 30% on average.[11] This so-called *Southwest Effect* is simply another manifestation of the airline's stunningly simple yet effective purpose and efficient execution.

According to Mike Levine, former president of New York Air, "You know, it's very easy to be expensive and good, and it's very easy to be inexpensive and bad. But Southwest Airlines walks the tightest rope in our industry because it's inexpensive and good at the same time."[12] Kelleher agrees:

> *"You can provide [low fares and excellent service] together. I think frequently business people in America think it's one or the other. You know, it's either got to be very expensive and way upscale, or it has to be very inexpensive and way downscale. But we think that you can do both and I think in that sense we're very much akin to Wal-Mart."*

While this Wal-Mart of airlines is incredibly successful today, the story wasn't always so rosy. In fact, the airline had such a rocky start that it almost didn't take off at all. Baptized by fire from the very beginning, SWA developed an irrepressible spirit of warriorship that is a major part of its character even today.

The Crusaders

Although originally organized in 1967 to fill a need for intrastate airline routes between Dallas, San Antonio, and Houston, the first SWA plane did not actually take off until four years later. Competing airlines Braniff, Texas International, and Continental fought in court to keep the new carrier out of the Texas intrastate market. During those first four years, cofounder and former CEO Herb Kelleher fought as the lone-ranger lawyer against as many as 15 opposing lawyers.

While Kelleher fought in the courtroom for the airline's right to remain at Love Field, employees found ways to compete with the other airlines in the sky. The airline strongly encouraged every employee, from maintenance crewmen to ticket agents and back office personnel, to contribute fresh, innovative ideas. Today, the culture is no different. Every SWA employee is still on a crusade to empower more people to travel. In fact, Kelleher points out that he chose the Signature Line Symbol of Freedom for SWA because it communicates to employees that they are doing more than a job. It tells them that they are liberating many new passengers to travel each year. Says Kelleher, "When we go into a new city-pair market, we increase the number of passengers in that market often by a thousand percent in one year. That means an awful lot of people who wanted to fly, who wished they could fly, now can. We set them free to fly."

Kelleher resolved never to lose sight of SWA's vision of democratizing the skies, which translates into affordable air travel for the masses, profitability for the airline, and job security for every employee. More specifically, the official mission statement published in January 1988 states:

The Mission of Southwest Airlines

The mission of Southwest Airlines is dedication to the highest quality of Customer Service delivered with a sense of warmth, friendliness, individual pride, and Company Spirit.

To Our Employees

We are committed to provide our employees a stable work environment with equal opportunity for learning and personal growth. Creativity and innovation are encouraged for improving the effectiveness of Southwest Airlines. Above all, employees will be provided the same concern, respect, and caring attitude within the organization that they are expected to share externally with every Southwest Customer.

SWA employees are never under the illusion that they are just "doing their job." Rather, every employee is a crusader in the business of *freedom*, the business of empowering ordinary people with the opportunity to do things they never dreamed of because flying was expensive. Employees are charged with a sense of moral imperative and duty to fulfill their mission of bringing democracy to air travel. A clear purpose helps to foster a sense of pride and ownership. Ron Ricks, Vice President of Government Affairs, related the following example of employee ownership:

"One of the first cases I handled when I started working here involved a claim against an outside contractor, who had damaged an aircraft engine. I was interviewing the mechanic who knew the most about this whole situation because we had a court case coming up. So here's a mechanic who has got the blue overalls, the Teamsters union cap with the buttons and grease under his fingernails. After the interview he said, 'Now I want to ask you a question. You are going to get all of that money back, aren't you?' I said, 'Well, it's a tough case, it's a lawsuit, you can't predict victory and all that.' He put his hand on my shoulder and said, 'Son, I don't think you understand. That's my money you're messing around with.' It crystallized in my mind then the difference between a Southwest employee and that of other airlines. Here

was a member of the Teamster's union who understood that it was his money."

Every member of the original SWA team believed in a dream— they had to. SWA was an upstart airline with a tenuous position in the market and no track record. They were the original dream makers. They wanted to see the dream come alive. This dream creates meaning at work for every employee of SWA. The following poem, written by John Turnipseed, Director of People Services, expresses the spirit of SWA people.

Dare To Dream[13]

"Some people only look at life through eyes that seldom gleam
while others look beyond today as they're guided by a dream.
And the dreamers can't be sidetracked by dissenters who may laugh
for only they alone can know how special is their path.
But dreams aren't captured easily;
there's much work before you're through
but the time and efforts are all worthwhile
when the impossible comes true.
And dreams have strength in numbers
for when a common goal is shared
the once impossible comes true because of all who cared.
And once it's seen as reality a dream has just begun
for magically from dreams come dreams
And a walk becomes a run.
But with growth of course comes obstacles
and with obstacles come fear
but the dream that is worth dreaming
finds its way to the dear.
And the dream continues growing
Reaching heights before unseen
And it's all because of the courage of the dreamers
and their dreams."

If this poem and the corporate vision give the impression that working for SWA is a perpetual cake walk filled with dreamy moments and freedom-filled declarations, don't be fooled. While the airline has a reputation for caring and fun, it also operates like a highly calibrated precision machine, doing a daily dance of activity that belies the carefree attitude of the employees.

The Daily Dance

SWA is the only airline that has ever won the Triple Crown Award (for fewest delays, complaints, and mishandled bags) five years in a row, from 1992 to 1996.[14] Other airlines rarely win this award for more than one month at a time. This achievement is staggering for an organization that must coordinate 35,000 employees in 59 airports and operate almost 3,000 flights a day, seven days a week. SWA operates at this rate 365 days a year and never takes a holiday. Ron Ricks describes daily operations at SWA:

"The success at Southwest Airlines is 1,000 steps a day. It's not seven easy steps to anything. It's 1,000 baby steps. I tell people that I'm not surprised that a Southwest Airlines flight is late occasionally. I'm surprised that one is ever on time because of the thousands of little things that have to take place before the airplane ever takes off. If you looked at it on paper you would say, 'It's not possible. You can't do that. And yet, somehow we do it.'"

In the departure process alone, personnel from up to 11 functional areas, including pilots, flight attendants, mechanics, gate agents, ticket agents, baggage transfer agents, ramp agents, caterers, fuelers, freight agents, and operations agents must coordinate with each other and complete their tasks within the 20 minute window that the airplane is at the gate. Colleen Barrett, President and Chief Operating Officer of SWA, elaborates that on-time performance is the ultimate measure of success for any airline, and does not happen unless every employee is ready to go the moment the airplane lands. In fact, she goes on to say that every employee involved in the departure process is in such a state of readiness that they are literally "perched and ready for that door to open."

With such a complicated array of steps happening 3,000 times a day, delays are bound to occur no matter how diligent the crew and staff. In spite of these inevitable delays, though, SWA manages to deliver reliable service, even if it means being accurate in predicting the length of the delay.

During a severe ice storm in Dallas, for instance, most airlines were making vague statements to the effect of, "We're canceling a lot of flights and we're not sure if we're going to be operating," which created uncertainty and anxiety for passengers. In contrast, SWA offered the bold statement that all flights before 9 AM would be cancelled and all flights after 9 AM would operate as scheduled. Some passengers, uncertain as to whether this statement could be trusted, called a radio talk show and voiced their worries, wondering whether to go to the airport or stay home. Without missing a beat, the radio talk show host replied, "Well, let me tell you, based on my experience with Southwest, if they say they are going to operate after 9 o'clock they might not be perfect, but I think they'll do it." When a flight attendant on her way to work heard the exchange over the radio, she called the radio station from her cell phone. She said she was scheduled for a certain flight departing after 9 AM, and she personally guaranteed that she would be there. While SWA can't control the weather, employees and staff do their utmost to offer the reliable, dependable service that the public has come to trust.

Control? What Control?

With so many factors to coordinate in the daily routine of launching 3,000 flights, many assume that SWA operates on a tight leash of strict control. Nothing could be further from the truth! In fact, Kelleher jokingly recounts his reaction when asked about control:

> "When I was with the New York Society of Airline Analysts, the 'splinter group' as they call them, I was describing Southwest Airlines and one of the analysts said, 'My God, what do you do about control?' I said, 'What control? Don't have control, don't want control, if we had control we'd screw it up, you know?'"

The airline relies not on control, but on deep-seated core values and discipline for on-time performance. Organizational values help everyone within an organization see the world the same way. At SWA, those values help employees work together like a well-oiled machine, achieving levels of performance that are simply out of reach to other airlines. Guided by the same values, every SWA employee sees things the same way so there is little resistance or competition. The significant values at SWA that shape the character of the culture are *integrity, trust, mutual respect, inclusion, openness, excellence, courage, frugality, initiative, and fun.*[15]

The Tao of Southwest Airlines

Vision: Liberating people to fly—democratizing the skies.

Purpose: Total job security, profitability, and affordable fares.

Values:

- Integrity
- Trust
- Mutual respect
- Inclusion
- Openness
- Excellence
- Courage
- Frugality
- Initiative
- Fun

Integrity means treating others with uncompromising truth and sincerity. It means that you do what you promise you will do. Employees throughout SWA respect their top executives because they believe that whatever is communicated to them is the truth. "If it's bad, they tell you it's bad," said one flight attendant. Kelleher comments on integrity this way:

> *"I don't want to put out any advertising that's inconsistent with what we are and what we want our people to be. It's inconsistent if you advertise things that people know are not true or that you can't fulfill. It's the wrong message to our people. It's inconsistent*

if we behave one way at the general office but say you ought to do something else in the field. The texture, the fabric has to be a tapestry that all goes together—your advertising, your message to the field, your visiting the station in Los Angeles, your visiting with pilots in Orlando. It's all one thing, it's not a bunch of separate things; and they all have to be woven together beautifully for people to believe in it, for people to be motivated by it, for people to be inspired by it."

He adds:

"People in Washington have told me many, many times that they value Southwest Airlines because of its integrity. They have said, 'If you say you'll do something you'll do it. And if you don't say it, you don't do it and we can rely on that. And you watch out for the industry as a whole, not just yourself.' Well, if you ever get away from that kind of approach, it would be disastrous as far as Southwest Airlines' position is concerned. There's just a whole realm of different areas where you could seriously disadvantage Southwest Airlines if you tried to convert it to a different type of company."

Trust means that SWA knows their people are reliable and backs them up, even when they make honest mistakes. When Bob Montgomery, a property manager for SWA, made an oral commitment of $400,000 to the City of Austin for the preliminary design of a new airport he had no idea that the airline did not support a new airport in Austin. When word of the commitment reached Kelleher, he stood behind Montgomery's word even though the verbal agreement did not legally bind SWA. Kelleher explains: "If we give our word, it's our word and we keep our word. It doesn't matter whom it is that gives our word. On the other hand, I did say to Bob, 'Now pal, this is a fairly expensive lesson. A $400,000 lesson—I hope you remember it!'"

Mutual respect means that SWA employees almost always speak respectfully of their colleagues in other functional areas, regardless of position. In fact, "doing good for others" is the golden rule for all SWA employees. Kelleher elaborates:

"The title and position which you might occupy are really unimportant in and of themselves. It is the essential worth of the person and the contribution that they make that is the significant thing. If you run into anybody of exalted position and title, don't necessarily accept them as being a special person—many times, they don't have any [more] particularly desirable attributes [than anyone else]."

Inclusion means everyone is equal and executives are expected to do things they ask employees to do. Colleen Barrett comments: "Egalitarianism is one of our core values and it really enters into everything we do, whether it's communication or process or operations or anything else. People know that, so there's a very open forum of communication at all times—up, down, sideways, backwards."

Openness means being open to all ideas, even if they are not created at SWA. After reading the initial draft of this chapter, Kelleher was so open to some of the ideas expressed in the other stories that he said, "Let me do this. Let me peel off the Southwest part. I've read all of it and it's really kind of fascinating. I want to keep the other part, because there are a couple of ideas from Medtronic that I want to talk to Colleen about."

Excellence means being and doing your best. Hard work is an integral part of the SWA culture, and good enough is never good enough. The crusading spirit born of the airline's early struggle remains strong today, and employees are always on the lookout for ways to improve service and lower cost. For instance, an employee suggestion for removing the logo from the in-service trash bags now saves the company $300,000 a year.

Courage means the willingness to be boldly different, even if it means going against conventional wisdom. Under Kelleher's leadership, SWA became the first airline to forgo the hub-and-spoke system, disregard the notion of market share, focus on small regional airports, offer the lowest fares, and go ticketless. As a result, SWA is also the first airline to remain profitable since its inception and to offer the best return on investment for the past 30 years.[16]

Frugality means always looking for ways to reduce costs while offering better and better service. Kathy Mathews, a flight attendant I met on a flight from Austin to Phoenix, says, "We are very frugal. For example, we clean up ourselves whereas other airlines hire people to clean up." In addition, SWA does not subscribe to any airline reservation system other than its own, which saves $2 for every segment booked and millions of dollars every year.

Initiative means doing whatever it takes to get the job done, whether or not the task is in your job description. Johnny Bomaster didn't wait for a supervisor to give him instructions. He simply took the initiative of using a snowmobile to get to the grounded plane so he could inspect it. Similarly, SWA departure crews work closely together, with pilots sometimes helping baggage handlers load bags in an effort to keep flights running on time. Kelleher reflects on the reaction of new employees transferring from other organizations to their new found freedom:

> *"First of all, they are very suspicious when they arrive because they are used to a totally different environment and we just tell them, 'Say whatever you want to say, propose whatever you want to propose and be whatever you want to be as long as you're trying to be constructive and achieve the results that we're looking for.' And they think, 'This is a bunch of baloney, we're wary of this.' Then, after about 6 months, it's amazing what happens because we've had some people who said, 'Look, I just can't live in this environment. It's too loosey-goosey, it's too free, it's too touchy-feely, I just don't feel secure. I need more structure and organization.' And we say, 'That's fine. I guess we're just incompatible.' The other reaction you get is very interesting. I'm talking about people who've been with other businesses for some period of time. They finally say, 'It's for real, man! Now I can be what I've always wanted to be.'"*

Fun means making very hard work enjoyable. *Having fun* is a trademark of SWA. People at SWA are always having a good time, with humor and laughter flourishing everywhere. Customers love the lighthearted atmosphere. However, Ron Ricks points out, "It's not one of our core values just to have fun. It's one of our core values to make work fun. This is hard work and it is serious business."

These values encourage members of the SWA to take the initiative and be accountable for their actions. Unlike many organizations that only talk about values once a year at annual meetings, SWA constantly expresses its values in every action and decision. As a result of this constant focus on values, SWA employees have an exceptionally long "life" with the company. This is one of the key reasons that SWA maintains a substantial cash balance. It helps sustain the company and ensure job security during difficult times, such as the period after the September 11, 2001[17] tragedy. This attention to job security and employee continuity is crucial to SWA's success, allowing, for instance, front line workers to personally recognize a large percentage of their frequent customers. Such personalized customer service cultivates almost unheard-of customer loyalty that in turn contributes to job security.

From the Beginning

SWA is the envy of every other airline in the industry, but very few have been able to emulate this fun-loving airline's record performance or deep stability. Kelleher asserts that the spirit of SWA employees is the hardest thing for other airlines to copy or create:

> *"We recognize that the esprit de corps of your people is the hardest thing for a competitor to imitate. In other words, I always tell our people that the intangibles are much more important than the tangibles because your competitor can buy the tangibles, but they can't buy and easily create the intangibles."*

That "esprit de corps" is a deliberate strategy that the airline's founding members cultivated since the beginning. SWA has always hired people with the right attitude and values that fit easily into the culture of accountability, initiative, and caring. Colleen Barrett speaks of hiring for attitude and training for aptitude. At SWA, no amount of training or aptitude can make up for a lack of attitude. She tells every new group of pilots:

45

"You could have come to us with 22 letters of recommendation from top gun pilots, from the President of the United States, the generals, and all of that. We still wouldn't hire you if your attitude or behavior turned us off during the interview."

Jim Wimberly, Executive Vice President of Operations, adds that SWA hires people who put the needs of others in front of their own. In other words, the airline hires only those with a service mentality and fun-loving attitude, and trains them with additional professional skills.

The same cultural considerations hold true with companies that SWA acquires. When SWA acquired Morris Air in 1994, its decision was based in large part on the similarity of cultures between the two airlines. Morris Air used SWA as a role model, even going so far as to use SWA training films and values. Immediately after the acquisition, Kelleher brought a group of fifteen SWA employees to Morris Air with the goal of ensuring that the cultural integration would go smoothly. Kelleher warned his people:

"Now, we're going to visit a company that we have just acquired, but I want you to act as if they have just acquired us. I want you to listen and not talk. You may ask questions, but that's it. You may not hold forth, you may not lecture, you may not talk about how great we are because we are there to learn from them."

While Morris Air was a strategically sound acquisition, if the culture had not been a perfect match with SWA, the acquisition would not have happened. According to Kelleher, all other factors in the acquisition were secondary to the cultural aspect: "If that didn't work then nothing else was going to work."

New recruits at SWA are constantly indoctrinated into the SWA way—history, philosophy, the Golden Rule, accountability, discipline, operations, and more. Barrett points out that the SWA culture is so strong that peer pressure is a significant training influence on new hires. To emphasize the SWA way of life, she tells every new hire,

"If you are looking to become tremendously wealthy at Southwest, probably this is not the place that you want to be. But if you are looking for a cause to join versus just a company to work for, then we have got something that will set you afire."

From the early days, the company's officers worked hard to acknowledge and stay in touch with field employees. In fact, Kelleher instituted what he called a "Day in the Field," a concept he learned reading about China, in which executive officers spend the day out in the field working alongside regular employees. At 72, Kelleher acknowledges that it's getting harder to haul baggage, but he does it anyway. Such "Days in the Field" keep the SWA spirit alive not just in the field, but in the executive offices as well.

Yin and Yang

At the heart of SWA's success is the Yin and Yang of its culture: freedom and accountability fueled by trust. At SWA there exists a rare covenant between company and employees. SWA provides a meaningful cause, great freedom and flexibility, a fun atmosphere, and excellent benefits while its employees provide hard work, dedication and, most of all, accountability and responsibility for their own actions. In a world in which employees no longer expect companies to take care of them and companies no longer expect employee loyalty, such a bond of mutual trust is a rare and precious asset.

It's easy to see the many expressions of that trust everywhere in the SWA culture. For instance, the airline grants its employees great flexibility in creating their own work schedules. Within each employee work group, people can adjust shifts and days off, or trade work days with each other. In addition, employees have complete freedom to take action and make decisions to serve and assist customers and other employees. Kelleher recounts a story of initiative that delights him:

"I got a letter from a probationary agent at BWI and it was so funny. Now she's on probation for 6 months and she can just be fired, for whatever reason. So she writes me this wonderful letter,

and I had tears in my eyes. She said, 'Herb, you've always told us that it was OK to use our initiative as long as we're trying to do something good for the customers. Well, last night we had a plane that couldn't get from Baltimore to Islip, NY because of the weather, so I rented 5 buses to carry passengers to Islip from BWI. There wasn't anyone else here.' I wrote her and said, 'You're my heroine! You're my heroine! And do it again!'"

At the same time as it grants great freedom to its employees, the airline also has its disciplinary and educational side that helps to weed out employees who don't fit into the SWA culture. Those who cannot adhere to the strict discipline required to keep flights running on time are not encouraged to stay. All new hires are placed on a six month to one year probation, during which time they and the airline can decide whether they are a good match. Says Wimberly, "We're very strict in making sure that people who don't really fit in here, and they're probably not happy here either, don't stay. We don't hesitate in making those tough decisions and suggesting they go to work someplace else. And that typically happens during their probationary period."

In addition, employees are constantly educated on the impact of their decisions and actions. For instance, if an employee took the initiative to help customers but the decision had costly consequences for the company, SWA would invite the employee to the corporate eadquarters and explain the cost and impact of that decision. The goal is not to punish employees but to educate them and increase their awareness of frugality.

At the end of the day, the trusting culture at SWA serves as the bedrock of strong work relationships among employees, which minimizes the effect of alienation created by the division of labor. Wimberly describes the leadership group at SWA in this way:

"We're all friends first and we all have a common value and ethical system so there's not a large variation in how any of us would deal with the same problem with an employee. We always do our best to follow the Golden Rule—treat people the way we want to be treated. We do our best to live up to our mission statement, which says what we're committed to do for our employees."

This is the more intangible side of the airline's social capital which complements the hard discipline required to orchestrate SWA's complex daily operations.

To keep the family spirit alive, SWA celebrates—constantly. Every new employee at SWA participates in a full-day program called "You, Southwest, and Success," in which games, fun, and celebration are used to teach every newcomer "We believe in you," and to inspire every newcomer to achieve beyond their own expectations. When the SWA family loses a member, it mourns them by writing stories about them in the company's magazine Luv Lines. For instance, in his eulogy to an original vice president Jack Vidal, Kelleher dedicated an aircraft, naming it "Jack Vidal" so that "the spirit of Jack Vidal will always be flying with us and the spirit of Jack Vidal will always be watching over and inspiring us."

The spirit of acknowledgement and celebration is so strong in SWA employees that celebrations often occur spontaneously. For instance, when a pilot who had recently made a heroic one-wheeled landing appeared unexpectedly at the company's general office, every employee poured into the atrium to salute and acknowledge his efforts. Kelleher says, "It was bang, like that. Everybody poured out of their offices and went down there with no notice." The pilot, Roger Wayans, said "I came to see if I could get someone in the PR department. I don't write very well and I wanted to write some letters to all the people who helped out, the people on the ground, in the station. I wanted to write a letter to the crash, fire, and rescue squad that was there." He then added, "I just want to get to age 60 and retire without anybody noticing me." Kelleher responded, "It's too late Roger, it's too late!"

In 1990, SWA created an official committee dedicated to keeping the values, mission, vision, and philosophies as fresh and innovative as they were in 1971. The "Culture Committee," headed by Colleen Barrett, consists of people from every area of the company with at least 10 years experience with SWA. They exemplify the company's spirit of hardwork, fun, caring, and totally maverick way of doing things. Two of the key tasks of the committee are reviewing current strategic decisions to make sure that they conform to the values of

SWA and communicating SWA's values to members of its growing family. Many of the activities of this committee are incorporated into the normal celebrations throughout the company.

The most memorable event of the year for most employees is the Annual Awards Banquet. By far one of the most festive celebrations of the year, the banquet honors the dedication, loyalty, and extraordinary contributions of SWA's people. Besides honoring employees with 10, 20, and 25 years of service, the celebration highlights people who represent SWA's unique culture and spirit. In addition to the prestigious Founder's and President's Awards, the company creates unique awards each year to honor specific contributions.

At other celebrations, SWA honors employees with awards like Top Wrench, Top Cleaner, Heroes of the Heart, Creativity and Guts, and Training Excellence. Some wacky, offbeat awards, including Most Spirited In-Law and Hairdresser of the Year, accompany these standard awards. The Culture Committee created the Heroes of the Heart award to recognize those behind-the-scenes employees who never have direct contact with external customers. The winner is acknowledged on Valentine's Day, when employees gather for a celebration and the winner's name is painted on a special dedicated aircraft that carries the Heroes of the Heart insignia. The winner is featured in the company's regular *Luv Lines* magazine and the in-flight *Spirit* magazine.

Being Whole

One pilot recently shared his experience as a new member of the SWA family: "I was a pilot at another airline and decided to join SWA after I heard a talk by Kelleher. I was most surprised when I received a personal note from Herb on the birthday of my first baby!" Kelleher adds:

> *"There's nothing that takes place in our employees' lives that we don't recognize. If you have a baby, you hear from us. If you have a serious illness, you hear from us. If you have been gone from SWA for years because of illness, you hear from us about every 6 months or so."*

Once employees are part of the family, they are always part of the family. Can a company as large as SWA really be one big, happy family? Absolutely! Nothing less would produce the hardworking, fun loving, dedicated workforce that strives heroically on a daily basis to fulfill their vision of freedom in the skies. For employees, becoming an integral part of the SWA family not only gives their work meaning and fun, but it gives them the freedom to be who they are.

As a result, the division between work life and family life becomes blurred. Family problems become a part of the tapestry and culture of the airline. The company exerts itself to help employees with family problems, often taking the initiative without being asked. Says Kelleher, "We get thousands of notices about something serious that has happened to a family member. Everybody at Southwest Airlines pitches in instantaneously. That's the way we are. We get tickets for relatives to fly in when someone appears to be terminally ill—don't ask, just go do it."

SWA is probably the most emulated airline in the history of aviation. Why can't other airlines match SWA's performance? We believe that most airlines simply emulate the outer form instead of the essence of the SWA spirit. In fact, each year SWA used to offer a one and half day Culture Day and invite companies to learn about the SWA spirit. Most of the visitors want to learn the seven steps to success. But of course, as Ron Ricks says, "It's not seven easy steps to anything." Barrett adds, "These companies simply don't get it."

Sustaining the Dream

Dream the impossible dream! If there is one message in all the stories of this chapter, it is that for true dreamers nothing is impossible. The dreamers at SWA, Medtronic, and Grameen Bank smashed every mold, ignored every preconception, and denied every scrap of conventional wisdom in their quest to create a freer and more humane world. How many people could conceive of the idea that credit is a human right, that Frankenstein could be real, or that the masses should be liberated to fly? Clearly, dreamers are inspired in some special way when they encounter life events that others would consider normal or "just the way things are." Some force calls these dreamers to step forth and change what they see, create something above and beyond "the way things are." Most of us have been inspired in this way at some time or other in our lives, but few step forth with the vigor and spark of these dreamers. Few answer to the higher purpose that is always calling to us. By their actions, these dreamers not only show us how it is done, but also ask us whether we are willing to step up and create our own dreams.

What separates Herb Kelleher, Earl Bakken, and Muhammad Yunus from most ordinary dreamers is that while they have their heads in the clouds, they also have their feet on the ground. Not only do they clearly see the vision they strive to create, but they are also able to develop and nurture the means to create it. To manifest the dream, each has created his organization around its *soul*—the VPVs discussed earlier in the chapter:

- *Vision:* When people in an organization align to a shared vision, they unleash their passion to make a difference. At the Medtronic holiday party, the patients and doctors who tell their stories serve as constant reminders to employees that they are not just doing a job, but actually restoring people to full life. A shared vision provides a collective identity for the organization to move forward as a whole.
- *Purpose:* The destination is clearly stated and repeatedly communicated to every member of the

organization. The purpose guides the people in the organization to move in synchrony towards its vision. In the case of Grameen Bank, everyone strives to lift human society out of poverty by entending credit as a human right.

- *Values:* These form the concrete ethical guidelines or boundaries for employees and officers, within which empowered actions and decisions can occur. At SWA, while employees are allowed great flexibility in changing their schedules, they are required to show up on time, all the time.

Within the boundaries of the purpose and values, organizations can empower their people with the freedom to make independent decisions. To balance the equation, these organizations teach and cultivate accountability and responsibility. Within the Grameen Bank culture, the four values (discipline, unity, courage, and hard work) and the Sixteen Decisions form the boundaries within which workers and borrowers have the freedom to develop their own businesses and create financial freedom in their own ways. At the same time, the structure of the five person groups ensures accountability and responsibility. Freedom and accountability are thus the two sides of the same coin for an organization with Tao.[18]

Beyond creating the VPVs for others to share with, though, dreamers must do more. Dreamers are the sparks that set the dream afire, yet these dreams are massive and will take lifetimes to fulfill. As each new generation joins the dream, how do they keep the spark alive and fan the flames? What will keep the dream alive when the dreamers pass the torch to the next group of leaders? Medtronic, SWA, and Grameen Bank all seek to institutionalize the dream in different ways:

- *Celebrate:* Whether with noisy parades and parties, funky awards, impromptu gatherings, or joyful stories of recovery, these companies celebrate! They celebrate to remind themselves of their higher purpose and to acknowledge how their daily actions have changed the world for the better.

- *Back to the Beginning:* With the Mission and Medallion Ceremony, Medtronic officers bring every new employee back to the humble origins of the dream and the inspiration to restore people to full life. At SWA, new recruits are constantly educated by managers and peers alike about the airline's history and crusade to liberate the skies. Keeping the dream alive means that every new employee has to first experience the dream.

- *Dignity:* At Grameen Bank, each successful micro-loan creates a little more human dignity in the world. Both borrowers and workers are freshly inspired each time this happens, and more driven to seek out the next person to uplift.

- *Hire to Fit the Vision:* Rather than trying to force people into a certain mold, SWA hires only those people with the right attitude. Hiring to fit the vision ensures that the dream lives in every employee.

- *Cultivate Culture:* All of these companies cultivate their culture to serve a higher purpose. In fact, SWA dedicates an entire committee, the Culture Committee, to nurturing the culture and keeping the dream alive. These cultures create such a positive contribution to the dreams that we anticipate the development of Chief Culture Officers in many organizations in the near future.

No matter how an organization expresses its Tao, these great organizations show us that the key to living in Tao is to make a difference. Each of these companies seeks to improve the world condition in some major and very visible way. They pit themselves against impossible odds willingly and enthusiastically.

More importantly, the Tao that inspires these companies is all about freedom. Medtronic works to create freedom from pain or dysfunction in the body, and to free patients to once again live their lives to the fullest potential. Grameen Bank is on a mission to free the poor from society's shame and scorn, and to free the world of the image that the poor cannot be trusted. SWA seeks to create freedom in the skies so that more people are able to fly, travel, andexpand their horizons. It seems that the Tao of truly great companies are expressions of freedom and liberation from conditions that limit the world. These visions of freedom call to each of us, asking us to step forth beyond selfish desires and participate in creating a more wondrous tomorrow. It calls us forth to make a difference.

It is fitting to conclude this chapter with the following story:[19]

A young girl was trying hard to rescue thousands of starfish washed ashore by throwing them back to the ocean one at a time. She was stunned when a man stopped her and told her: "Why are you doing this? You can't possibly make a difference by saving all these starfishes."

She was deflated for a moment and then she bent down, picked up a starfish and hurled it back to the ocean with all her might. She then looked up straight into the man's eyes and replied: "Well, I made a difference to that one

II

The Art of Timing

"All of us, whether or not we are warriors, have a cubic centimeter of chance that pops out in front of our eyes from time to time. The difference between an average man and a warrior is that the warrior is aware of this, and one of his task is to be alert, deliberately waiting, so that when his cubic centimeter pops out he has the necessary speed, the prowess, to pick it up."
–Carlos Castaneda–

On April 27, 1994, the world stood back in awe as South Africans of all races stood in long lines to cast their votes in the country's first democratic election. Prior to that election, few could imagine that South Africa, bitterly divided between white power and black oppression, would become a symbol of hope to all nations. In a miraculous moment of perfect timing, all the necessary ingredients came together for the creation of the unprecedented Truth and Reconciliation process, which featured forgiveness and reconciliation between races rather than punishment and retribution.

Historically, the primarily black African National Congress (ANC) had been supported by the former Soviet Union, leading Western nations to support the opposing white apartheid forces. However, when Mikhail Gorbachev burst onto the world scene and brought the ideas of *perestroika* and *glasnost* to bear, the so-called "evil empire" of the Soviet empire began to disintegrate, along with its expansionist support of the ANC. As a result, Western nations could no longer justify supporting white apartheid South Africa.

As the dominant Eastern and Western nations began to withdraw their influence from South Africa, Nelson Mandela, imprisoned leader of the ANC, and F. W. DeKlerk, leader of the white apartheid government, both rose to meet the challenge of creating a peaceful future, seizing this single *cubic centimeter of chance* for reconciliation. DeKlerk had tremendous difficulty in persuading the whites that it was in their best interests to lay down their arms. It required great humility for DeKlerk to fight for a democratic process that would eventually vote him out of office.

But Mandela and other black leaders had a far more difficult time taming the fire of the blacks who demanded vengeance. After 27 years of imprisonment by the white government, though, Mandela stood as the perfect icon to preach and ask for forgiveness, creating the unforgettable process of Truth and Reconciliation.

Perhaps few could have predicted the outcome of the South African democracy, but leaders like Mandela and DeKlerk are not ordinary leaders. They rank among historical figures who seized the opportunity by letting go of their long held views and creating lasting values for their people. How can captains of industry develop the same ability to create better futures for their organizations?

When I first met Kanji Kobayashi, long time CEO of NEC, I asked him to name the most important decision he had ever made as the leader of his company. His answer was simple and straightforward, and spoke of a clearly envisioned destiny:

"When I took over as the President of NEC, I made the decision to phase out our business in nuclear reactors. It was clear to me then that the future of NEC must be in the emerging technology areas of computers and communication."

The acronym NEC stands for Nippon Electric Company. When Kobayashi assumed leadership of the company in late 60s, more than 50% of NEC's revenue came from its nuclear reactor business. Looking into the future, Kobayashi realized that the company's greatest potential for growth and longevity lay in the intersection of the computer and communication industries, industries still in their infancy. He took a huge risk by turning the company away from its existing energy business and focusing on the still uncertain futures of the two nascent industries. Kobayashi built the now famous C&C (computers and communication) roadmap, which identified competencies needed to exploit the opportunities that would emerge at the crossroads of both industries over a 30-year period (see Figure 2.1, an abbreviated version of the C&C map).

This roadmap identified three distinct technical and market evolution trends. Communications would evolve from mechanical cross-bar switching to complex digital systems, computing would evolve from mainframes to distributed processors, and components would evolve from simple integrated circuits (ICs) to very large integrated systems of ICs. The C&C map provided tremendous clarity and focus for the company and its employees. The map helped the company to anticipate the intersection points between the growth of the computer and communications industries, and proactively create products and services to serve those points of intersection. All of its joint ventures, alliances and licensing agreements throughout the three decades outlined on the map were carried out according to this vision.

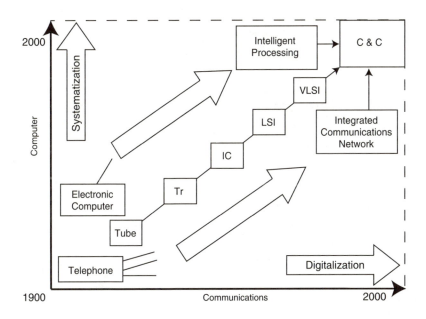

Figure 2.1 An abbreviated version of NEC's C&C Strategic Map.[1]

The map also defined NEC's *competitive space*, allowing the company to prepare products that took advantage of each new breakthrough in either industry and empowering the company to be first in new markets. Such a closely-defined area of competition kept the company on a focused path, preventing it from becoming distracted and jumping into unrelated industries. NEC, unlike the South Africans, did not wait for other sources to provide a perfect synchrony of events, but instead actively participated in creating its own future. The roadmap became the guidance system by which NEC could actually intercept its destiny.

NEC's roadmap is an example of the strategic principle, *"Think backward while moving forward"* advocated by my friend George

Kozmetsky, co-founder of Teledyne and long time Dean of the Graduate School of Business at the University of Texas. Kozmetsky explained his principle with the following diagram (Figure 2.2).

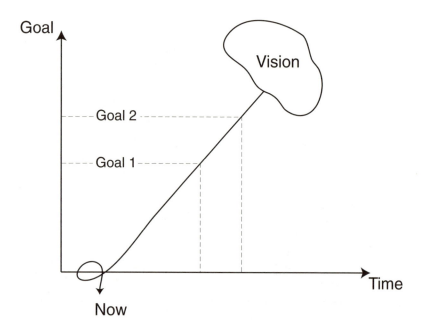

Figure 2.2 Think backward while moving forward.

The diagram suggests three important aspects of creating the future.

1. ***Know the End Game:*** The end game is the vision of the company. The vision, as discussed in Chapter One, is so far in the distance as not to be achieved in the near term but so inspiring that people never stop trying. The leader must keep the end game in mind and visualize possible paths to achieve it.

2. ***Establish Incremental Goals:*** With an end game in mind, leaders identify critical obstacles or requirements on the path to the future. To prepare for these key points, leaders establish incremental goals, such as

R&D projects or targets for acquisition, so they can be ready when the "cubic centimeter" of opportunity presents itself. Incremental goals are set in anticipation of clearly seen future barriers or opportunities as the company moves toward its destiny. These goals empower companies to actively co-create their future rather than simply reacting to outer events.

3. *Define the Competitive Space:* The strategic roadmap, developed as a result of viewing the future through different scenarios and creating incremental goals, helps companies narrow their focus to a limited competitive space. Within a well-defined competitive space, an organization can dedicate its full resources and attention, and act with great speed and agility. Except in cases of huge, unanticipated changes in the marketplace, the competitive space rarely changes. For instance, the Medtronic strategic map (Figure 1.3) clearly defines the boundaries of its competitive space as limited to implantable devices of many different types. This map keeps Medtronic's attention tightly focused on a huge and expanding, but specific marketplace.

While not all companies have developed an explicit roadmap to the future, almost all successful companies actively anticipate the future using the principle of "think backward while moving forward." Top leaders assume that that future is always changing and that tomorrow will be different from today, so they charge into the future rather than simply waiting for tomorrow to become today.

While the roadmap provides a clear overview of an organization's path to the future, the process of reaching that future is far from clear. In a world filled with uncertainty and change, leaders need ways to interact with the future so they can challenge their current assumptions and mitigate major risks along the way. Consider the 1973 oil price shock, when the price of gasoline sky-rocketed to impossible highs. Only Royal Dutch Shell (Shell) was emotionally prepared for the crisis, thanks to its scenarios planning group which had anticipated such a possible future. The group helped Shell prepare for unthinkable futures, propelling it from one of the weakest of the seven major oil companies to one of the strongest.

Shell's scenario planning approach, used over the last 30 years, assumes that the future is plural or that multiple possibilities exist in the future. This assumption is contrary to the traditional central planning efforts of the past, which focused on a singular future proceeding in a straight line from past to present. Most major companies now use scenario planning to create *future memories* and use these memories as guidelines for making decisions. For example, Paul Unruh, former Vice Chairman of the construction giant Bechtel, shared with me that using scenario planning allows Bechtel the flexibility and fluidity to move into any anticipated market with ease, when the window of opportunity opens.

Using scenario planning to create future memories enhances the reach and flexibility of the strategic roadmap, as shown in Figure 2.3.

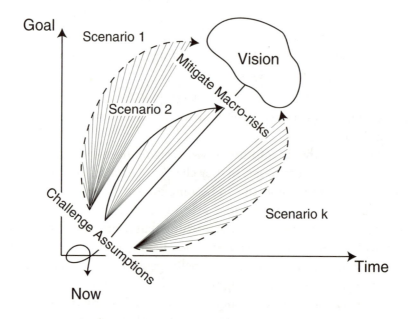

Figure 2.3 Enhanced strategic roadmap.

Almost every top company in the world uses some form of the roadmap above. Three companies, however, provide extraordinary demonstrations of the Art of Timing: Shell has refined scenario analysis to a practical mix of art and science; Intel uses Moore's Law and time pacing to track its progress toward the future; and Southwest Airlines (SWA) makes no long range plans but waits perched on the edge, ready to pounce when the cubic centimeter of chance arrives. These companies show us the three different approaches with which we can interact with the future:

- *Predict and Respond:* Shell uses scenario planning to predict the future and prepare its response accordingly, but in no way tries to interfere with the direction of the future.

- *Predict and Influence:* Intel uses Moore's Law (created by co-founder Gordon Moore) not only to predict future events but to actively influence the future of the entire industry.

- *Co-Create:* Rather than relying solely on scenario planning or a formula, SWA relies on its speed, agility, and wit to act when its cubic centimeter of opportunity arrives. SWA surrenders to a higher purpose and co-creates the future by living in synchrony with its destiny.

No matter the method, these three companies are always at the ready, perpetually eager and expectant for the arrival of the future. Let them show you how a company on a mission intercepts its destiny. Enjoy!

Royal Dutch/ Shell
Using Scenario Analysis to Create Future Memories

Royal Dutch/Shell (Shell) leads the world in the energy and petrochemical markets, the result of a merger in 1907 between two companies—Royal Dutch Oil Company of the Netherlands and Shell Transport and Trading of Great Britain. The Dutch company imported kerosene from Sumatra while the British company exported lamp oil to the Far East. Today, Shell owns more than 300 companies in over 100 countries around the world.

A cornerstone of Shell's success is its use of scenario planning, currently acknowledged as one of the most effective strategic planning tools and widely used by companies in a multitude of industries. Named by *Forbes* magazine as the "ugly sister" of the seven major oil companies in 1970, Shell began using scenario analysis early in that decade to help its managers make decisions. As a result, company leaders were aware of and prepared for the 1973 oil crisis, when prices skyrocketed. While other oil companies scrambled to react, Shell reacted swiftly to take advantage of the situation, clawing its way to the top of the heap. By 1979, the company had become one of the largest global oil companies and the most profitable—no longer the ugly sister.

Skirmishing With the Future

The U. S. Air Force developed scenario planning shortly after the end of WWII to develop alternative military strategies for the future. Herman Kahn, who developed an early version of this method at RAND for the Air Force, then began using scenario analysis as a tool for business planning. In the 1970s, Pierre Wack and other members of Shell's newly formed Group Planning division began using scenario planning, refining and popularizing the method until it became a standard business practice in the company.

In essence, scenarios are stories about the future that weave current trends, future barriers, potential breakthroughs, and other social, economic, and political factors together into an intelligible format that decision makers can easily grasp. At Shell, scenarios are used as a flexible common language that captures many different perspectives and rolls them into several storylines that define major pathways into the future. The stories then become different frames of reference or lenses for viewing the future.

Unlike crystal balls, scenarios are not meant to predict the future. They play the important role of helping decision makers broaden their vision and challenge assumptions. Without scenario analysis, managers tend to have a myopic view of the world and ask only short term questions such as:

- Will our competitor do this or that?
- Will the technology we use be obsolete?
- What will happen to us next quarter?

Scenarios force decision makers to take a much longer and broader view of the world, taking into account many more factors and influences. Scenario planning forces managers to ask a different set of questions:

- What technological breakthroughs will occur in significant industries, and how can we be ready to take advantage of them?
- What market niches will be created as a result of those breakthroughs, and what kinds of competition will that attract?
- What major impending political forces and trends might affect our future?

By answering these or similar questions, managers mentally and emotionally prepare themselves to deal with many possible future events. More importantly, scenarios force managers not only to question current assumptions about the future but to think of ways to respond to those possible futures. Scenarios help decision makers create a database of *future memories* that they can access when the future actually arrives.

When planners sit down to create scenarios of the future, they resemble explorers setting out on a journey of discovery. While the final destination—the vision—serves as a guiding beacon, the conditions are uncertain and the explorers must often change course when faced with new opportunities and unanticipated barriers. By making many simulated journeys into the future, planners have the opportunity not only to challenge their assumptions but also to highlight the major risks they may encounter. Like explorers marking and claiming territory, scenarios help planners benchmark major events in the future (see Figure 2.4). Effective scenarios force decision makers to explore not just the probable, but all that is possible, which helps them adjust their perceived destination and create maps to reach their vision. Scenario planning becomes a crucial tool for linking the corporate vision with short and long term strategies.

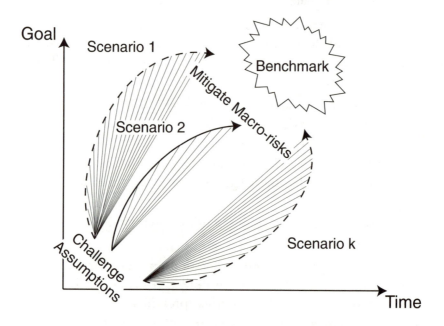

Figure 2.4 The application of scenarios.

For scenarios to be effective, the stories must include multiple perspectives and a broad vision. Therefore, the process of creating scenarios is a free and open process, focusing on collaboration and synthesis rather than the deep analysis used in the traditional central planning. At Shell, the process consists roughly of these five steps:

1. *Uncover the Key Frames of Reference.* The team highlights the reference points within the organization that are relevant to the strategic decisions being considered. These reference points include the company's vision and mission, along with industry trends, and drivers within the company that may create change in the future. This step helps leaders identify the types of strategic decisions that need to be made.

2. *Identify the Key Drivers of Change.* The team identifies social, political, and economic trends that might impact these assumptions over the relevant time horizon. The Shell team usually achieves this step by visiting places and organizations around the world to discover new breakthroughs or methods. The team also interviews well-informed people in various disciplines who are interested in exploring new intuition and sharing new insights.

3. *Use Workshops to Gather, Share, Test, and Link Ideas.* These workshops create a collective understanding about the key dynamics of change and their interaction, helping the team perceive possible relevant paths to the future. These paths become the basis of the scenarios.

4. *Craft the Stories.* The team usually builds two to four scenarios that integrate the insights and critical challenges that have emerged from the process.

5. *Test and Qualify the Scenarios.* The team uses simulation models and Shell's own data banks to refine the scenarios.

These stories create *future memories* for the Shell team, and give them a common basis and understanding from which to make strategic decisions today in anticipation of future events. A crucial factor that differentiates these scenarios from other types of visioning exercises is that these stories are deliberately relevant to the current context in which the company operates. These stories are not meant to predict the future. Rather, they are the tools with which the team can organize the possible future environments in which its decisions will be played out. The stories draw people into the future, helping them see the decisions they might make as well as the possible repercussions of those decisions. Scenarios give managers the information necessary to make knowledgeable decisions, with a reasonable awareness of both the risks and the rewards, in a world of uncertainty.

Shell's Scenarios Experience

Pierre Wack, Ted Newland, and other members of the Shell planning team began using scenarios in 1972 to explore the events that might affect the price of oil, which had been relatively steady since WWII. After creating and examining the scenario, the team realized that the Arabs had every reason to demand much higher prices for their oil. While Wack and the team could not pinpoint the exact moment when prices were expected to skyrocket, they anticipated that the Arabs would make their move sometime before 1975, when the current oil prices were due for renegotiation. Wack engaged Shell's decision makers in the scenario, letting them feel the potential shocks of such an event and telling them, "you are about to become a low-growth industry."[2]

As predicted in the scenario, the energy crisis and the predicted oil price shock exploded after the "Yom Kippur" war in the Middle East in October 1973. Of all the major oil companies, only Shell was prepared and responded quickly. By building scenarios around global economic and oil issues, Shell executives were already preparing to respond to events that most others in the industry considered unthinkable. While scenarios are not meant to predict the future, the insights often shock managers into opening their eyes, considering all the options, and creating positive responses.

With this first successful application of scenario planning, the Shell team continued to use this approach to rehearse the future. For over 30 years, Shell has used this method to develop scenarios for the entire organization, with some scenarios being more global and others being more focused. The stories that emerge from this method help Shell executives scrutinize the viability of their strategic decisions. In fact, according to Ged Davis, Vice president of Global Business Environment:

> *"The Shell Group Committee of Managing Directors decided that every Strategic Planning Unit must demonstrate robustness of strategy against both the Group's global scenarios and the supporting focused scenario work in countries and selected businesses."[3]*

In the mid-to-late 1970s, Shell developed two significant scenarios that greatly impacted the company's strategic vision. The first scenario, *Rapids*, was created in 1974 and anticipated the turbulence of the late 1970s, which was a period of transition and new challenges. *Next Wave*, the second scenario, provided an early glimpse of the 1990s global economy. In the words of Arie De Geus, the scenarios

> *"Helped to change the Shell corporate mind and opened our eyes for the gloomy messages of, respectively, a recession and a world of low prices. On these occasions, the message was absorbed without the messenger being shot. Such is the power of a strong, symbolic story."[4]*

Since Wack and the planning team created the first story depicting oil price shocks, scenario planning has gradually become a standard part of the Shell routine. All annual and capital budgets must be correlated with background scenarios, and Shell line managers must demonstrate that they have considered and planned for the future possibilities raised by the scenarios.

In the 1980s, Shell used scenarios to grasp global social and political developments as well as energy market dynamics. The scenarios considered topics such as the longevity of the Soviet Union, high oil prices in the early part of the decade and the subsequent collapse of prices. As the Cold War ended with the fall of the Berlin Wall in the early 1990s, the planning group explored the new shape of a more integrated world influenced by powerful forces. The first scenarios, created in 1991 and 1992, focused on the twin revolutions of *globalization* and *liberalization*, including the opening of markets with free trade and deregulation, and the emancipation of political systems with the free flow of information and new elections. Included in both of these revolutions were the technological breakthroughs that continued to grow in unrestrained leaps. The group constructed two stories about how the world might unfold as a result of these dynamics.[5]

The *New Frontiers* scenario describes the result when many poor countries successfully free themselves from autocratic governments and claim larger roles for themselves on the world stage in politics, economics, and culture. The scenario predicts that while this kind of liberalization is turbulent and painful to many established interests, it continues to occur because people believe that their own long-term self interests and prosperity are ultimately linked to the fate of others.

In the contrasting *Barricades* scenario, people resist globalization and liberalization because they fear the loss of what they value most, including jobs, power, autonomy, religious traditions, and cultural identity. Many economic and vested political interests feel threatened by liberalization and attempt to stop it. While some countries attempt liberalization, expectations are not met quickly enough and progress is slow. While many believe that liberalization will ultimately improve their lives, the promised improvement lies too far in the future and the required sacrifices are simply too great.

Both *New Frontiers* and *Barricades* presented logical, plausible, and challenging narratives about how Shell's business environment might evolve. Corporate leaders in Shell companies around the world used these scenarios as the grist for strategy workshops. These sessions empowered executives to discuss and act on the important opportunities and threats presented in the scenarios, including possibilities that were not previously on Shell's radar screen. In short, *New Frontiers* and *Barricades* helped the company skirmish with the future in a clear and focused way.

Following these two scenarios, the team created new stories for the year 2020. These stories added a new social dimension to the previous scenarios and focused on the social consequences of globalization, liberalization, and technology. The team produced two scenarios to model the social trends: *Business Class* and *Prism*. *Business Class*, symbolized by a briefcase, focused on efficiency and freedom of choice, whereas Prism, symbolized by a pair of glasses with rainbow lenses, depicted the multiple different ways that people see the world. In both scenarios people are the key challenges. These scenarios led Shell management to look carefully at its own diversity and put a new emphasis on inclusiveness.

Shell's most recent scenarios explore the energy needs, choices, and possibilities of the future to the year 2050. The *Dynamics as Usual* scenario presents an evolutionary progression in terms of a "carbon shift" from coal to gas, to renewable sources, or possibly to nuclear energy. The more radical *Spirit of the Coming Age* scenario digs into the more revolutionary environment of a hydrogen economy.

Decision makers at Shell consider scenario planning to be a cornerstone of their strategic decision making process that has a proven track record. This method has given Shell executives relatively reliable projections of future events well ahead of time. While critics charge that the stories offer no verifiable evidence of future events (in other words, the events cannot be proven until after the fact), the company nevertheless believes in the effectiveness of the scenarios. In fact, contrary to popular opinion, divination of the future was never Wack's primary goal. Peter Schwartz, one of the original members of the Shell Group Planning Team, says: "Pierre Wack was not interested in predicting the future. His goal was the liberation of people's insights."[6] Phillip Watts, Chairman of Shell, offers what is perhaps the best testimony and support for this process:

> *"We don't aim to pinpoint future events but to consider the forces which may push the future along different paths. Using scenarios helps us understand the dynamics of the business environment, recognize new opportunities, assess strategic options, and make long-term decisions."*[7]

In recent years, Shell has been using its scenario approach to tackle complex issues that seem to have no simple solutions and cannot be solved by a single institution. Scenarios offer a way to effectively work with multiple institutions, honoring their differences and broadening different frames of reference as a part of reaching resolution. In fact, Adam Kahane of the Shell team demonstrated the incredible power of scenarios in creating a common resolution among hostile parties when he assisted South Africa in making its transition to a democratic government.

South Africa's Flight of the Flamingos

In South Africa, during the period between 1990, when Nelson Mandela was freed from prison and the ban was lifted on the ANC and other black and left wing political parties, and 1994, when the first all race elections were held, a flurry of radical and miraculous events took place that helped the nation transition away from apartheid toward freedom. One of these events was the Mont Fleur scenario project, which was sponsored by a group of South African academics, business people, and activists.[8] They had heard about the Shell scenario methodology and wanted to use it to define a new future for their nation. Adam Kahane was chosen from Shell's strategy department to help them facilitate the forum. The group intended to influence the future of the country by developing a set of scenarios that described how events might unfold over the coming ten year period.

The forum consisted of 22 leaders drawn from organizations spread across the political map, including academics, ANC members, members of the old establishment, and businessmen. Kahane recalls the blessing of such a diverse membership:

> *"One of the good things about working with a group like this is that they can learn a lot about what is going on from listening to each other, and have somewhat less need than a corporate group for Learning Journeys and Remarkable Persons to help them see what they are not seeing. It was as if each of them had a piece of the larger puzzle picture of South Africa."[9]*

74

Using Shell's scenario planning method and guided by Kahane, the team came up with four scenarios:

- *Ostrich:* A story of the white government believing that it could avoid a negotiated settlement with the black majority, burying its head in the sand, and thereby making matters worse in the end.

- *Lame Duck:* A story of prolonged transition where the new government is hobbled by compromises built into the constitution and, because "it purports to respond to all but satisfies none," isn't really able to address the country's problems.

- *Icarus:* A story describing the results of a strong black majority government coming to power on a wave of popular support and embarking on a huge, unsustainable public spending spree that crashes the economy.

- *Flight of the Flamingoes:* A story about how the new government could avoid the pitfalls of the first three scenarios and gradually rebuild a successful economy.

According to Kahane, the *Icarus* scenario was the most unexpected and probably exerted the greatest influence. This scenario was created at a time when most leadership attention was focused on achieving a successful political and constitutional transition, not on economics. The *Icarus* scenario pointed out that the conventional tendency to redistribute resources away from rich whites to poor blacks would not create a sustainable solution for the country.

Once the scenarios had been written, the team organized a series of workshops with different political, business, and civic groups, where the stories were presented and the implications discussed. Kahane recalls one particular event:

"One of the workshops was with the leadership of the Pan Africans Congress (the PAC), a radical black political party, and at this meeting one of the members of the Mont Fleur team, who was the PAC's head of economics, presented the Icarus scenario. He said

'This is a story about what will happen if our rivals, the ANC, come to power. And if they don't do it, we will push them into it.' That provocation led to one of the most productive of all the workshops. Many years later, in 1999, when another member of the team was appointed to be Governor of the Reserve Bank, he said at his inauguration, 'We are not Icarus. There is no need to fear that we will fly too close to the sun.'"[10]

Kahane believes that economic wisdom and prudence of the post–1994 South African government has been influenced by the Mont Fleur scenarios, especially the Icarus scenario.

Co-Creating the Future

The Mont Fleur project has clearly made a lasting imprint on South Africa's social, political and economic transition. While the approach was basically transplanted directly from Shell's planning team, Kahane noticed that the effects were much different in South Africa. He says:

"Although the methodology of this project was the same as the one we used at Shell, the purpose was fundamentally different. The Mont Fleur participants were not, like corporate strategists, simply trying to adapt to the future as best they could; they had come together because they wanted to influence the future, to make it better. They were playing on a larger field. When you think about it logically, at least one of the reasons the future is unpredictable is because we can influence it. The team members didn't see themselves as detached observers, but as active participants; most of them had devoted their lives to fighting for a better South Africa. They were aware of how their own thoughts and actions had an impact of what happened around them—they were reflective."[11]

In other words, mere analysis lacks the force and purpose to create a desired future. South Africa's almost unimaginable transition demonstrates that co-creating a desired future takes passionate, active participation and the inspiration to serve a higher purpose.

Intel[12]
Leaping Into the Future with Moore's Law

I interviewed Gordon Moore twice, with each interview lasting about 90 minutes. During each interview, I felt as if I were surrounded by a Zen-like calmness because he was always in the present moment. He never took his eyes off me, never looked at his watch, and smiled the entire time. As the person who has had the most influence on Intel over the last half century, he certainly shatters the usual stereotype of the major corporate chieftain. With his sparkling eyes full of curiosity, he has maintained his scientist essence despite leading a large corporation for most of his career. When asked about some of Intel's successes, he usually credited his co-founder, Robert Noyce, or his successor Andy Grove. He is the epitome of a true leader (see Chapter 5).

Intel Corporation, the well-known corporate giant that launched the microprocessor industry, traces its lineage back to the very roots of Silicon Valley itself. Intel's co-founders, Robert Noyce and Gordon Moore, spent the early years of their career in the 1950s working for Bill Shockley, the acknowledged "grandfather" of Silicon Valley and founder of a successful fledgling semiconductor operation. As the semiconductor industry began to grow, Shockley grew increasingly paranoid and controlling, causing eight of the top scientists in his lab, the so-called "Traitorous Eight," to leave, Noyce and Moore among them . The "Traitorous Eight" eventually formed Fairchild Semiconductor and thrived until the company was bought out by its parent company, Fairchild Camera. Once again discontent, this time under the strain of Fairchild's East coast management style, Noyce and Moore struck out on their own in 1968 and launched Intel, a business dedicated to the development of integrated electronics, the core technology in microprocessors. Andy Grove joined Intel a year later, and together, these three gurus of technology guided Intel, driving the entire microprocessor industry into a new era.

Almost miraculously, Noyce, Moore, and Grove possessed the exact talents needed to navigate the then uncharted waters of the nascent integrated circuit market. Noyce co-invented the integrated circuit while Moore developed Moore's Law, the guiding force that helped Intel keep pace with its destiny. Then Grove, a scientist turned management guru, led Intel to dominate the PC industry.

Within the chaos of Silicon Valley, where every new idea generates at least one new startup (the "Silicon Valley Effect"[13]), Intel's leaders have always guided the company by an unfailing metronome that has helped the company keep pace with the explosive growth of technology—Moore's Law.[14] In 1965, Moore, then head of Fairchild Semiconductor Research and Development Laboratory, set forth his now famous law that predicted the pace of semiconductor advances. Moore's Law projects that the numbers of transistors on a semiconductor chip doubles approximately every 18-24 months as shown in Figure 2.5.[15] Reality has manifested according to Moore's projection every step of the way, leading the industry into a future where a single chip will hold one billion transistors—a far cry from Intel's first chip, the 4004, which had only 2,300 transistors. From the beginning, Moore's Law has been Intel's end game and the vision that has made the company the pioneering spirit of the industry.

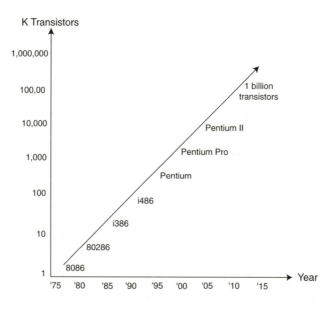

Figure 2.5 Intel's path according to Moore's Law.

Defining the Competitive Space

With Moore's Law as their end game and time clock, Noyce, Moore, and Grove set out to redefine the leverage in the semiconductor industry by defining and limiting Intel's competitive space. When Intel first entered the market, the semiconductor memory market was bound by certain factors. First, chips were not widely used and only about 10,000 computers (the primary target for ICs) were being sold annually. Second, manufacturers were creating custom chips for every application—a lengthy and expensive process. These limiting factors produced chips that were unique and difficult for competitors to steal, but also low in volume and profit.

Not content with the current state of affairs, Intel's founders decided to produce non-custom chips that could be sold in high volume but were complex enough to prevent imitation by competitors. Moore recalls,

> "We thought we saw an opportunity by putting a lot more value into the silicon itself by making a lot more complex chips. We set out to develop technology specifically for doing that. Semiconductor memory was the first product that, if you sold large enough volume, you could justify the design cost for a complex chip. Otherwise complex chips tended to be unique since they were made for computers and only about 10,000 computers were being sold a year. So the economics would not justify the advertising and design cost. That's how we really started."

Intel, under Moore's leadership, tried three different technology paths in an effort to develop the first high volume, complex chip. The first attempt, putting several chips in the same package, failed, while the second approach, a variation of the technology for making bi-polar transistors, turned out to be too easy to copy. The third one, however, silicon gate technology, produced the desired results. Intel was able to work around several potential technological issues and faced few competitors. In fact, it was seven years before Intel had a major competitor for this technology. Moore recalls how the silicon gate technology played a crucial role in the company's early success: "By luck, that technology was just right. Had it been more difficult [to produce], we would not have been able to tackle it as a startup, and if it had been easier, we would have had competition sooner. It gave us a really good start."

Silicon gate technology launched Intel into the memory chip industry and became the core technology behind several early products. In 1969 Intel introduced the first of these products, a 64-bit memory device called the 3101. A year later, it introduced the 1103, a dynamic random access memory chip (DRAM) that launched the semiconductor industry and propelled Intel from a mere startup to a successful venture in the early 1970s.

Keen to stay ahead of the pack, Intel later developed another highly successful product that remained a sleeper for a decade. The EPROM was another memory product that stored information semi-permanently and could be erased. Developers at Intel felt the EPROM would find a niche as a prototyping device for engineers, who could use it to program software before the code was permanently written to read-only memory (ROM). Because Intel executives felt the EPROM would attract only a small market, they priced it high. But it turned out to be an engineers' safety blanket and they bought it in droves. Moore recalls the economics of this sleeper product: "For at least 10 years our competitors did not appreciate the value of this product. It was our stealth product. It generated a major portion of our profit until the mid-80s, when the Japanese started to dump in this market and the price dropped 90% in 9 months."

As the memory industry became crowded with competitors, Intel leaders decided to take the company out of the memory industry and focus instead on microprocessors. Not surprisingly, the decision turned out to be crucial to Intel's later success and longevity. Noyce, Moore, and Grove have always had an unerring sense about the growth and future pathways of the technologies they created. At Fairchild, Moore oversaw the development of silicon and planar transistors as well as the first practical integrated circuits. Later, he led the effort to launch memory chips and microprocessors at Intel. All of these foundational technologies have played major roles in Intel's success. According the

Moore, Intel's leaders have always had an intuitive feel about technology that guided them to success:

> *"Making the right technology choices is the key. We've been very good at being in the mainstream and I don't know how much credit I deserve for that, but I'll take some. We have people running the company who are familiar with the details of this technology. Noyce was the first CEO, I was the second, and Andy Grove is the third. We have all been together for a long time, all Ph.D.s and we sort of grew up with the technology together. It's very valuable not getting off on the wrong foot. We have a good intuitive feeling of what's right and what's wrong as to which technology may get off to the wrong direction."*

Seizing Opportunities

Armed with the roadmap of Moore's Law and the well-defined strategy of producing only non-custom, high volume, high complexity chips, Intel leaders remained open to any technologies that fit the profile. The Busicom proposal is a perfect example. In 1969, Busicom, a Japanese calculator company, approached Intel about building custom chips for their programmable calculators (remember, at this time all chips were custom and produced in low volume). While Moore was not interested in developing custom chips, he was interested in creating a *computer on a chip* that could be used in a wide variety of applications, including calculators. Moore assigned computer scientist Ted Hoff to the project. Hoff eventually arrived at an innovative solution by separating the general-purpose logic processors from the program specific functions that are stored in ROM. The same logic processor chip could be used for almost any application while the ROM could be adapted to the specific application, thus creating the high volume "computer on a chip" Moore was looking for. It was called a *microprocessor.* Moore was excited about Hoff's solution because it was a general purpose product that could be embedded in everything from elevators to traffic lights.

Intel introduced its first 4-bit microprocessor, the 4004, in 1971. Following Moore's Law, the company quickly followed with the 8-bit 8008, then the more advanced 8080 in 1974. The 8080 caught the attention of fledgling computer enthusiasts like Michael Dell, Bill Gates, and Paul Allen, and ignited the PC revolution. Other competitors soon jumped into the fray and it was not until the Intel's introduction of the 386 chip that the company secured its place at the top of the heap. With the 386 chip (the industry's first 32-bit microprocessor), Intel executives decided not to second source it, instead keeping all the profit for themselves. Up to that point, it was typical for microprocessor manufacturers to create a second source, or backup manufacturer, for their chips to ensure that the quantity needed to meet the demand was available. Having lost great profit to second source companies with their 8082 to 8086 series chips, Intel scored big by keeping the rights to its 386 chip. Moore recalls this bit of history with great satisfaction:

> *"With our 8082 to 8086 microprocessor products (the one that IBM used in their AT), we licensed the product to all of our competitors based on the prediction of big volume. We gave it to AMD, Fujitsu, Siemens, and others for very little consideration, just the standard deal. But the volume never materialized, only a third of what our customers told us they wanted. We could have made it all. The net result was that we had given away profit in a whole array of products. So, when the 386, our first 32-bit microprocessor, was coming out, we decided that maybe we didn't need a second source. We tried to do it ourselves and supply everything our customers needed. We had an agreement with AMD that if they delivered certain products for exchange, then we would trade; but they never delivered their part so we did not have to give them ours. We just decided to go our own way."*

Once again the pioneer, Intel changed the entire economics of the industry by controlling the price and software on its 386 chip. The company copyrighted the chip's instruction set, which was closely tied to Microsoft's software, and patented everything else (or exchanged patents with others). When Compaq took the lead and used the 32-

bit architecture in their PCs, Intel assumed the dominant position in the industry. According to Moore, "The decision not to second source the 386 product was the single most important decision in our profitability of the last 10 to 15 years."

Strategic Inflection Point

Any successful company, like Intel, endures many crises throughout its life. When Intel started, it had almost 100% of the memory market. However, in the early 1980s, Japanese competitors almost broke Intel's balance sheet by flooding the market with high quality, low cost chips. Andy Grove recalled in his book *Only the Paranoid Survive*[16] that he asked Moore, then CEO, a question:

> *"If we got kicked out and the board brought in a new CEO, what do you think he would do?' Gordon answered without hesitation, 'He would get us out of the memories.' I stared at him, numb, then said, 'Why shouldn't you and I walk out the door, come back, and do it ourselves?'"*

Moore recalled that it was not a highly emotional decision for him because the economics were very plain. Occasions like these are what Grove terms *strategic inflection points*—points at which a company must face the potential of massive change or simply disappear into the annals of history. Moore's philosophy of constantly skirmishing with the future by experimenting with different technologies paid off, giving Intel the opportunity to leap into the microprocessor business when the memory market fell into a slump. Grove would meet such an inflection point once more when he became Intel's CEO. One morning, he was informed that IBM had stopped shipment of all Pentium-based computers because of a processor error. A rare error would occur only once in every 27,000 years of use. IBM had put Intel's credibility on line. Grove responded instantly. He pulled and replaced every Pentium chip on the market at the numbing cost of $500 million. In his book, Grove recalls that for the first time computer users, who were not even Intel's direct customers, demanded that the company's products be changed. The rules of the game had once again changed—overnight.

Intel's Fresh Fruit Business

Moore's Law consistently empowered Intel to anticipate and prepare for future events. Like measurements on a yardstick, the doubling factor of Moore's Law allows Intel engineers to set definite incremental goals for R&D and new product launches. For Intel, as well as other chip manufacturers, Moore's Law has several implications. First, chip manufacturers must, at the very least, improve their products to meet the doubling factor or face certain death at the hands of competitors who do meet those requirements. Says Moore,

> *"We started out with a roadmap based on a generation of technology every 3 years. The industry learned that unless they did that, they fell behind. So we changed that to every 2 years. It is very expensive and requires that a lot of things to be done. That's how the competition is won. A year's lead in technology was fantastic. Just a brief lead in technology is the difference between being highly profitable and not making any money at all."*

Moore's Law also dictates the economics of chip manufacturing. Since the life of a chip is extremely short, the price of that chip will drop dramatically over its lifetime. As a consequence, capturing high volume early becomes crucial, since initial manufacturing costs on each chip soars into the billions of dollars. Moore explains:

> *"If you look at the analysts' reports, they all say, 'Intel is cutting prices 40% on microprocessors.' We do that 3 times a year, but then we bring in new ones above that at the old price, and the average price hopefully increases or at least stays the same, but the price of a given product just plummets. I don't know any other industry where that happens. It makes for some really peculiar dynamics. Inventory rots. You put the thing on the shelf and the value decreases at the same rate. You never want to carry more inventory than you have to. It's kind of like a fresh fruit business."*

In 1992, the Semiconductor Industry Association coordinated the first efforts to produce the *National Technology Roadmap for Semiconductors* chaired by Gordon Moore. Like Moore's Law, the roadmap provides guidelines for the industry, and companies compete with these assumptions in mind, each trying to get ahead of the curve. These shared expectations have brought predictability to the once chaotic industry and created increased demand for semiconductor products.

Influencing the Future

Although every leader in the semiconductor industry is keenly aware of Moore's Law, few seem to capitalize on it the way Intel's leaders have. Intel veterans have historically sought to not only be ahead of the curve, but to define the curve itself since Intel has always sought to create its own future.

Noyce and Moore learned early on that customers were often reluctant to adopt new technologies, and that technology manufacturers must actively create and broaden the market to overcome this reluctance. At Fairchild, when Noyce introduced the first IC to the market, the volume was rock bottom. Engineers, used to measuring the performance of resistors, transistors, and capacitors separately, didn't know how to measure the IC's performance so refused to buy them. Realizing that there was no other way to overcome the resistance, Noyce resorted to price slashing, making the gutsy decision to sell the ICs for a dollar each (just the components on the chip cost more than a dollar to make). The ploy worked. When ICs became the cheapest method, customers began to buy.

At Intel, Noyce and Moore put the lesson to good use. Realizing that the decisions of PC manufacturers often hindered Intel's efforts to sell more chips, Intel executives began marketing to all kinds of end users, including engineering and purchasing departments and company CEOs. For instance, when IBM was reluctant to adopt the new 386 chip for its PCs, Intel started the "Red X" campaign, which showed a big red X over the 286 with the message, "Now, get 386 system performance at a 286 system price." IBM eventually bowed to customer pressure and adopted the 386.

Once company executives understood the vital importance of targeting end users, they began branding Intel products with the "Intel Inside" advertising campaign targeted at end users. The campaign ensured end users that Intel stood for reliability, quality, and performance. Intel leaders then extended their reach to include channel suppliers of PCs, including retail computer stores, direct order businesses, and resellers. To support these channels to better serve the end user, Intel created a team of Retail Managers to work with key retail and computer superstores across the United States. These managers work with channel distributors to tailor store displays to Intel processor-based PCs and provide sales staff with the latest product and technology information.

To help PC manufacturers and other companies with microprocessor-based products keep step with the acceleration of technology, Intel set up a team of Field Application Engineers (FAE) to provide technical support to the engineering staffs of these companies. The FAEs ensure that these companies are constantly ready to use the next generation of Intel products. Intel also created advisory boards in the U. S., Europe, Japan, and the Asia Pacific composed of key CIOs from leading companies. These boards meet quarterly to offer input and exchange information with Intel, providing suggestions and feedback on Intel products. For instance, at one point the CIOs wanted to reduce the total ownership cost of PCs, including purchasing price, maintenance costs, and upgrade costs. Intel responded immediately by forming "an industry initiative to drive down the total cost with technologies such as remote diagnostics and remote repair of PCs and servers."[17]

While Intel certainly has the advantage in understanding Moore's Law, Gordon Moore having created the law, the company nevertheless had to develop key management principles to keep pace with the projected acceleration. We identify some of these key principles below.

- *Invest in R&D:* Regardless of current prices or market conditions, Intel never reduces its R&D budget because new products that land ahead of the curve are the keys to success. According to Moore,

"One of my favorite things to say is that you never get well on the old products. You have to keep developing new products through the recession. If you look at our R&D budgets you never see a single dip in it, in spite of profits going up and down and revenue bouncing around. With the old products the price goes almost to zero and it never comes back up significantly. You have to have a whole new family of products when the business gets better in order to get well."

- *Use Minimum Information:* Unlike the university research lab model employed by IBM and Xerox PARC, Intel's researchers never try to fully understand any new technology. Instead, they focus on speed and time-to-market, using the minimum information necessary to create a new product. As a result, Intel's conversion rate of research projects to new products is extremely high.

- *Outsource Equipment for Speed:* At Fairchild, Moore learned that any business on the cutting edge can only move in a limited number of directions at once. Intel adopted the policy that the company would never produce its own equipment: "We decided that we would not even develop the equipment ourselves. If we developed the equipment, we'd give it to our suppliers. Our strategy was to move as fast as we could."

- *Take Risks:* To land ahead of the curve on a consistent basis, Intel executives learned to take big calculated risks. In fact, Moore recalls that the Board accused him of "betting the company" every single year. He doesn't see it that way, though:

  "That's the hardest value to get people to understand. In this industry, which changes so fast, you have to try significant things all the time,

try new things, have new ideas. If you stay with the old things that worked, you'll be obsolete in a short period of time. It's a high risk business."

- **Develop a Problem Solving Culture:** Intel maintains a very open culture in which no one hesitates to question anyone else. According to Moore,

  "We are interested in solving problems—that's what we do for a living. We like to hear about problems and people don't get beaten up for bringing problems to the table."

  To encourage its 80,000 employees to take initiative, Intel practices "applied responsibility." If an employee sees a job that needs to be done and no one is doing it, he or she steps up and does it. Honest mistakes along these lines are accepted. Says Moore,

  "I guess one thing a leader does is remove the stigma of mistakes. People who are afraid of making mistakes all the time just don't try anything."

- **Strategic and Operational Planning:** To synchronize the entire company to the same vision and goals, Intel has adopted a highly organized strategic and operational planning process. Strategic planning occurs twice a year, in April and November. At the April meeting, leaders set the company's strategic goals for the next three to five years, while any mid-course corrections are made at the November meeting. The corporate strategic objectives are then published and posted throughout the company. To link strategic and operational plans, product line business executives develop their business plans directly from the strategic objectives, converting strategic plans into concrete product road maps. These plans are then merged into yearly operational plans in the 4th quarter of each year. Finally, Plan of Record reviews are held quarterly to review overall profit and loss, progress on key programs, action plans, and budgets.

These principles have been developed over the last 40 years under the consistent and vigilant guidance of Intel's three initial CEOs: Robert Noyce, Gordon Moore, and Andy Grove. Such principles allow the company to detect *strategic inflection points* early, even if they can't pin down the precise timing. Noyce and Moore were the indomitable captains of the company's early years. Today, Grove is Intel's Chairman while Craig Barrett, another Intel veteran, is CEO. Under such steady leadership and guided by an unerring roadmap, Intel continues to pioneer the industry and lead the pack.

When Moore's Law Hits the Limit

As of this writing, Intel is aggressively developing new manufacturing plants for flash memory and investing in over 500 companies to exploit new technologies. As the limit to growth in the computer and communications markets is still a long way off, Intel is banking on Moore's Law to carry it into its next meeting with future destiny. Yet some critics argue that Moore's Law will soon hit its limit, either because technology will advance faster than the law predicts or because semiconductors will eventually saturate the entire known market. When asked about such limits, Moore smiles and says,

"I have no idea and that's a concern as it's not far away. When the technology gets totally leveled, there will still be a lot of design work to do. But no industry can continue growing at several times the rate of GNP forever. I used to end my talks with a slide that shows two curves. One is the growth of the world GNP and the other is the growth of the semiconductor industry. They intersect around 2020, in which the whole world is a semiconductor. Obviously, this can't happen. So, I think like any industry, there will be some maturing. There are a lot of complexities, opportunities and niches. Electronics is a fundamental technology."

Southwest Airlines[18]
Strike With the Force and Alacrity of a Puma

"Look at my wife's mother, whom I dearly love. She was born before the Wright brothers flew their flight at Kitty Hawk, so during her life you have the first powered flight and the first person landing on the moon. You also have the advent of the automobile in America, the communication revolution, and you could go on and on. That all happened in one lifetime. I don't think someone in 1901 or 1902 would have believed you if you said, 'Now let me prepare you for the automobile, powered flight, television and more.' So readiness is my word. You've just got to be ready."

–Herb Kelleher–

Readiness is indeed the word at SWA. Unlike Intel and Royal Dutch Shell, SWA makes no long-range plans. Instead, the company relies on its crusading vision and simple solid strategy, plus the agility of 35,000 individual employees dedicated and empowered to bringing that vision to life. According to Kelleher, long-range planning is impractical in the highly unpredictable airline industry. Says Kelleher,

"In this environment, where capital assets travel at 540 miles an hour, it's just silly to sit around and talk about whether we're going to a city 10 years from now. You might have five other airlines that went into it during the interval, three of which went into bankruptcy."

To keep pace with its planes, SWA sticks to its plan: delivering rock-bottom fares, providing total job security, and maintaining profitability by offering primarily short haul, point-to-point and frequent flights (3,000 per day). That plan is so clear and concisely stated that the airline wastes no time wandering down first one road, then another. Kelleher states,

"This is what we are, unless we decide to change it. This is fundamentally what we are going to do, how we're going to do it, and apart from that, we just want to be able to move quickly."

At SWA, moving quickly means giving employees the freedom to make any decision necessary to serve the customer, while also asking them to be accountable for their individual actions. With each employee perched on the edge of readiness every single day, SWA is able to "strike with the force and alacrity of a puma."

Skirmishing with the Future

Just because SWA executives do not engage in traditional long-range planning does not mean that they are unaware of the forces in the marketplace. Having clearly defined their competitive space—providing the best service *and* the lowest fares in a specific market niche—SWA leaders are constantly skirmishing with the future to keep pace with their destiny. To stay sharp and focused, they ask questions like the ones below.

What are some scenarios of the future?

Like Royal Dutch/Shell, SWA constantly creates future memories, albeit much more informally. Within their clearly defined competitive space, SWA executives continuously test multiple future scenarios. According to Kelleher,

> *"Vision is saying, 'I think in the next 10 years this may possibly happen, and this may possibly happen, and this may possibly happen' and preparing a scenario for each for how you're going to respond. We do that all the time. If regional jets come in, for instance (that's a recent theory), what are we going to do? How are we going to respond? Do we have to respond?"*

SWA chooses three to six of the major possible scenarios that might happen in the future and creates contingency plans for each. None of these plans, however, go into effect. They are simply ready responses that allow the airline to move with speed and efficiency and prevent it from being blind-sided by future events.

How can we learn about our future from past history?

Kelleher is a military buff and a great fan of history. Following the old adage that "history repeats itself," he relies on historical events to benchmark and predict future events. He also believes that a solid education teaches people not just to respect history, but to use it. Being able to recite historical events is not enough. One must use history to see "how trends appear, how they manifest, and how they wind up." From that fundamental understanding, Kelleher often overlays the past on the future, saying, "Well, I see something going on here that is very similar to what happened in the Peloponnesian War. I think this is where it's going." In SWA's early years, Kelleher decided to shift the airline away from such heavy dependence on the Dallas-Houston route, which at the time provided the airline with 50% of its revenue. Comparing the situation with the European phase of WWII, Kelleher saw the similarities:

> *"I wanted to put Southwest Airlines in a situation that was more like a war in the Pacific because I didn't want anybody to be able to come in and knock us off as they did to Braniff at DFW because you've only got one anchor point. If they are going to get us, I want them to have to go island by island, atoll to atoll, with a firefight on every one. So they'll have to come get us in Albuquerque. They'll have to come get us in Phoenix. They'll have to get us here, there and a thousand other places. You cannot overthrow or destroy Southwest Airlines by simply attacking one vulnerable point. It's not a Maginot Line. I think that type of synergistic thinking and reasoning is very helpful."*

What are our competitors about to do?

Kelleher points out that many organizations are too internally focused, more intent on institutional regularity than on the outer conditions of the market. He adds that these are also the organizations that usually fail. Kelleher keeps a sharp eye on SWA's competitors. He constantly asks, "What are our competitors doing? What are they thinking about doing? You know, you have to be able to pick those things up without someone just saying, 'This is what I'm going to do.' It's the little hints, the things from a speech that someone gave."

How can we distract our competitors from what we're doing?

Kelleher, an avid student of Sun Tzu's classical *The Art of War* text, not only keeps a close eye on his competitors, but also carefully camouflages his own intentions. For instance, when SWA gets ready to expand, everyone in the airline industry pays close attention. If SWA sends its facilities crew to a particular airport in a given city, word spreads instantly throughout the industry, and other airlines mobilize their resources to compete. To confuse and distract his competitors, Kelleher once sent his facilities staff to six different airports at once. He recalls, "We were going here, we were going there, and we were going someplace else. We were going to do this and we were going to do that, just to confuse everybody, and waste their time, their effort and their thinking."

Kelleher played the same tricks when SWA entered the California market and began competing head-to-head with PSA. To camouflage his intent, he entered phony fares in the reservation system, fares that were much higher than SWA intended to charge. When PSA called to check up on SWA fares, they received false information. Kelleher recalls what happened next:

> "We held a press conference and in the press conference I just ripped up the press release and said, 'These damn fares must have been conjured up by our Chief Financial Officer. That person doesn't know how to charge passengers, and actually our fares are going to be half as much.' Well, of course, PSA got the biggest shock. We had to rewrite a lot of tickets, but PSA was way off in what they were charging."

Kelleher banks on his ability to stand in his competitors' shoes and know their personalities and predictable methods for making decisions. Kelleher himself, on the other hand, is anything but predictable. He attributes his unconventional nature to his Irish heritage, "Most people have predictable personalities rather than unpredictable personalities. The Irish tend to be more unpredictable, I think, because they drink so much!"

Does an opportunity fit the SWA strategy?

Before SWA decides to move into a new city-pair, the executives carefully consider how the new city-pair will fit into the existing network of flights. Kelleher explains, "You put that piece into place and you know it's going to work because the other five pieces are already there."

SWA also developed a formula for appraising the amount of traffic in any given market within a period of a year based on frequency, service, and fare stimulation factors. Kelleher explains:

> *"If you go into a market with four flights a day, and you charge exactly the same fares, just this service addition will stimulate the market. Then on top of that there is the fare stimulation, which is a much more powerful factor. And if you reduce the fares by 50-60%, then you get an enormous amount of stimulation. Fundamentally, we can produce a prediction of how much traffic will be produced within the city-pair at the end of a year, and how much of that traffic we will carry."*

Note that these two factors, more flights and reduced fares, act synergistically to produce a compound effect. When SWA adds more flights, it stimulates more people to fly. The airline then reduces fares which, together with the increased flights, generates a tidal wave in the new market. For example, Kelleher mentioned that traffic in the Baltimore-Providence market increased by 800% in the first year that SWA entered the market.

Other factors that are not necessarily or easily quantifiable also enter the equation. For example, if SWA thinks another airline is "hungrily eyeing a city," it might want to enter that market first, pushing other city-pairs further down the priority list. Another consideration is whether a city is flourishing or just starting to prosper. Kelleher elaborates:

"Sometimes we may go into a city before it's near its peak because we want to be on the front of the wave instead of on the back of the wave. Although we sometimes have elements which are not easily quantifiable, we will ultimately have quantifiable predictions for any given city-pair market."

Kelleher is very proud of the formulaic approach he helped refine for SWA. In fact, the formula has become so refined over the years, by consistent research and trial-and-error, that SWA can make precise predictions with 95% accuracy, with errors generally falling on the conservative side. Says Kelleher, "We can look at any city-pair market and tell you, within 5%, exactly what the traffic will be with a given fare and frequency of flights."

SWA uses scenarios to create future memories and precise formulas to evaluate any new market. The airline's consistently high performance over the years pays tribute to the success of these synergistic levels of planning.

Do the economy and the culture support a growth opportunity?

When it comes to expansion, Kelleher carefully monitors SWA's bottom line, always following the philosophy of "managing in good times to do well in bad times." Unlike other airlines, SWA has never been required to borrow on a long term basis to buy a specific set of airplanes or support a particular expansion. Instead, if needed, the company uses a short-term line of credit and its profitability to finance growth opportunities.

In terms of growth, Kelleher is cautious and patient, often moving much slower than the financial community demands. Others have often pressured SWA to expand faster, proclaiming, "You've got the financial strength to do it. You've got the low cost and you can charge the low fares," but Kelleher has always bided his time and waited for the perfect opportunity, the cubic centimeter of chance. He explains one of the limitations he places on the airline's growth:

"We only want to bring a certain number of new people into our culture each year. If we have 20,000 people and bring in 10,000,

*do you think we can have the same culture? So there's that
limitation that we recognize in our expansion."*

When SWA does expand, though, it moves with lightning speed
and without hesitation. For instance, when US Airways pulled out of
the California market SWA swiftly stepped in. Kelleher recalls,

*"I just said, 'Let's get six more airplanes, and I want one in each
of those cities in one month.' We took over California. We went
from 1% to 52% of the entire California market within a year
and a half. Why should we have to sit around and analyze it and
study it? If it doesn't work, you can always stop it."*

Co-Creating a Better Future

Always poised to move quickly, Kelleher patiently waits in full
readiness for the perfect opportunity to arrive. While he monitors
almost everything in the airline industry, from analysts' reports to
speeches by executives of competing airlines, he nevertheless follows
his own unpredictable nature and intuitive feel of the marketplace.

Ready to follow him into any situation or battleground are the
SWA employees. Filled with the "Southwest Spirit," they seek their
own ways to help SWA maintain its innovative atmosphere and creative
impulses. At one time, SWA and Continental were paying their pilots
the same wages, but SWA pilots were willingly flying 75 hours a month
while Continental's were only flying about 42 hours per month. The
dedication of the SWA employees empower the airline to remain lean,
speedy and agile. Says Kelleer,

*"If your people's stars are aligned [with your purpose], then they
are much more productive."*

Like other companies, SWA uses the tools of the trade to skirmish
with the future, including scenario analysis, defining the competitive
space, and influencing the future. Unlike other enterprises, though,
this airline moves under the auspices of a higher purpose, which lifts
its every action to an entirely different and much grander level. While
others seek to co-create a more profitable future, the leaders at SWA

seek to co-create a better future in which more people are free to fly, more employees have job security and the company earns a solid profit. Profitability, expansion, and return on investment are all normal concerns of healthy businesses. At SWA, these are the natural end results of co-creating a better future and striving to make a difference.

Mirror, Mirror on the Wall
The Value of Time

"To realize the value of one year, ask a student who has failed his exam;
To realize the value of one month, ask a mother who has given birth to
a pre-mature baby;
To realize the value of one week, ask an editor of a weekly newspaper;
To realize the value of one day, ask a daily wage laborer who has ten
kids   to feed;
To realize the value of one hour, ask the lovers who are waiting to meet.
To realize the value of one minute, ask a person who has missed the
train;
To realize the value of one second, ask a person who has survived an
accident;
To realize the value of one millisecond, ask the person who has won a
silver medal in the Olympics."
—Anonymous—

Most managers devoutly wish for a magical mirror that tells them what the future holds so they can prepare for tomorrow, today; so they can be ready at a second's notice to leap on that cubic centimeter of opportunity. As the techno-driven world spins ever faster, leaders are often at a loss for direction. In the "dizzying disorientation brought on by the premature arrival of the future" predicted by Alvin Toffler in *Future Shock*, the traditional reponse of working harder and being more efficient is no longer a sufficient solution. The awareness of the trends and forces that will shape tomorrow's world and the ability to arrive in that world first make all the difference.

Royal Dutch Shell, Intel, and SWA all look deeply into the mirror on the wall, each fathoming different futures and fashioning unique responses. When Shell looks into the mirror, it sees a myriad of possibilities wrapped into a few succinct stories. Shell narrows a multi-faceted view of the world, as seen through the eyes of its customers, advisors, competitors, and socio-political leaders, down to two or three major trends. From these factors, Shell plans how it will respond to future events, but rarely seeks to change or influence the world itself. Shell sees how it fits into the futures predicted by its well-orchestrated scenarios.

When Intel looks in the mirror, it sees the pioneering role it plays in the semiconductor industry. Guided by a detailed roadmap, Moore's Law, Intel's leaders have successfully navigated the hazards and stayed the course, choosing the right technologies to intercept the next curve on the map and actively developing the market for their products. Faithfully following the path projected by Moore's law, Intel acts as the trailblazer, demonstrating Moore's Law and beyond, creating ever faster and more intelligent microprocessors for the world to consume.

When SWA looks in the mirror, it sees itself creating freedom for millions of people who wish to fly. Constantly inspired by its vision of a freer world, the airline is always ready to create the desired future. Guided by the vision to free the skies, Kelleher and company rely on agility, wit, and the crusading spirit of the SWA employees to respond with speed and innovation to any barrier or opportunity that presents itself.

What can leaders learn from Shell, Intel, and SWA? These three companies demonstrate that great leaders are always looking for the inevitable signs of change that are synonymous with the future, and the roles they will play in those changes. Whether leaders choose emotional detachment or active, dynamic transformation, they must prepare and skirmish with the future. To skirmish with the future, leaders must start with a roadmap.

Creating a roadmap to the future is somewhat akin to stepping into a time machine. The leader must move far and fast into the future to visit the organization's ultimate vision, then travel methodically backwards on the time track until he arrives back in the present, carefully observing possible major obstacles and opportunities along the way. He must think backward while moving forward. To create the roadmap, the leader must possess the double-vision necessary to hold the organization's dream close to his heart while walking the daily path to destiny with stability and surefootedness. Every opportunity or obstacle he sees with his future vision must then be planned for and dealt with in present time in the form of incremental goals. In today's marketplace, many leaders are myopic and shortsighted, driven only by quarterly reports, while others are dreaming visionaries lacking in practical, daily guidance. Great leaders, though, move with fluid grace back and forth along the time scale, leaping nimbly between visioning and implementation, equally skilled in both.

Once the leader has created the roadmap, the next step is to define the level of active participation or co-creation to play in shaping the future. Regardless of the level of emotional commitment, for a company to intercept its destiny, its employees must be open to listening to and observing the forces in the world that are already in motion so that they can respond readily. They must be perched in that edgy balance of relaxed readiness. A company can thus seize opportunities at the exact right moment, appearing, as the great Wayne Gretzky does, not where the puck is but where the puck will be.

As companies create their future, waiting for their *cubic centimeter of opportunity* to pop up, they come to understand the meaning of Richard Feynman's oft-repeated wisdom,

"The best way to predict the future is to invent it."

III

The Art of Leverage

A Sense of Goose[1]

"Have you even wondered why geese, when heading South for winter, fly along in 'V' formation? Consider what science has discovered about the reason they fly that way. As each bird flaps its wings, it creates uplift for the bird immediately following. By flying in 'V' formation, the whole flock adds at least 71% greater flying range than if each bird flew on its own.

When a goose falls out of formation, it suddenly feels the drag and resistance of trying to go it alone, and quickly gets back into formation to take advantage of the lifting power of the bird in front.

When the lead goose gets tired, it rotates back in the wing and another goose flies point. Geese honk from behind to encourage those up front to keep up their speed.

Finally, and this is important, when a goose gets sick or is wounded by gunshot and falls out of formation, two other geese fall out with that goose and follow it down to lend help and protection. They stay with the fallen goose until it is able to fly or until it dies; and only then do they launch out on their own or with another formation to catch up with their group."[1]

−Anonymous−

During the Three Kingdom era (220-265 A.D.), General Kung Ming battled the army of Wu across a river. One day, the officer in charge of the front line reported the bad news to Kung Ming that his army had run out of arrows. Undaunted by the news, Kung Ming noted that the weather had been foggy in the mornings. After some thought, he suggested borrowing some arrows from the enemy across the river. The next morning, he launched an armada across the river in the fog toward the enemy camp, each boat filled with straw men dressed as soldiers. Predictably, the enemy shot waves of arrows at the straw men, which in the fog, looked like actual soldiers. By midmorning, Kung Ming's navy returned with tens of thousands of arrows—gifts from the enemy.

Consider Samsung, the well-known Korean electronic products company. While it had developed a reputation in the recent past as a company selling "me-too" products at low prices, today its products are not only chic and cool, but of extremely high quality. In fact, in the digital economy Samsung has grown so much that it now competes directly against top companies, including Nokia and Motorola in the cell phone arena, Intel in the flash memory market, and Sony in the big-screen TV industry. How did Samsung leap forward so quickly?

Sung Lee, President of Samsung Austin Semiconductor, shared a story about the Chairman of the Samsung Group, Kun Hee Lee. Bent on launching Samsung into the big leagues, Chairman Lee took issue with the number of defects in the company's cell phones. To make his point, he collected every defective Samsung cell phone and threw them into a huge pile in front of the telecommunications building. Then, with many engineers looking on, he lit the pile, creating a huge bonfire. Many of the engineers present were so shocked that they cried, watching as their labors of love—the cell phones—burned to ashes. The quality of the company's phones went up dramatically afterwards. Lee, though, didn't stop there. He continued to press the issue by rigorously testing the phones, dropping or even throwing them on the floor. Lee understood that he could gain effective results by leveraging his engineers' pride. By 2003, Samsung passed Motorola in overall global cell phone revenue.

Neal Kocurek, co-founder of Radian (a top environmental company) has a reputation as "Mr. Gets Things Done," and is another great leader who was able to successfully leverage his company's resources. During an interview, he shared one of his management secrets, called *muscle-building*, which is a process of leveraging his company's internal strength.

Kocurek holds regular meetings with his vice presidents, with the goal of assessing their organizations and leveraging their strengths. For instance, in one meeting, Jean, a vice president, stood up and discussed her organization's strengths and weakness with the collective group. When she discussed a weakness in her organization, she reported the action steps taken to correct the problem. She also listed the people she felt were capable of replacing her should something happen to her. The discussions were interactive and lively, empowering participants with knowledge of each person's strengths and weaknesses, and allowing them to make helpful suggestions to the speaker. For example, one vice president might suggest trading personnel to mutual advantage or offer new strategies for handling organizational weakness. Kocurek concludes:

> "To go through that organization this way would take four to five hours. But they all learned Jean's organization, personnel, strengths and weaknesses, everything. Each one of them, because of the discussion, comes up with a list of things on how to strengthen their organizations—different things for different folks."

Kocurek's muscle building method is based on open communication that provides mutual support and leverages the strength of each department to support the others. In short, Kocurek teaches his people to operate with much the same results as geese flying in formation, with each vice president taking point and others offering support and gaining leverage.

If today's CEOs had as much sense as geese, they would strive to leverage other parties—customers, partners, employees, and competitors—to achieve their goals with greater ease and efficiency. They would also avoid un-leveraged frontal assaults, knowing that these are expensive even if they are successful. Leverage should be the key principle behind any strategic decision, demonstrating Archimedes' oft quoted phrase:

> "Give me a lever long enough and a place to stand, and I will move the earth."

Points of Leverage

Kung Ming, Lee, and Kocurek demonstrate how companies can find and use long levers to achieve great results with minimum effort by leveraging different aspects of their environment (see Figure 3.1).

There are two major categories of leverage: internal and external. Internal leverage includes new business models, workforce cohesion, cost structure, processes, and proprietary technology. External leverage focuses on customers, suppliers/partners, competitors, market conditions, and government regulations and policies. In the previous cases, Kung Ming leveraged his enemy's predictable shooting response to gain arrows, while Lee leveraged on his engineers' pride, and Kocurek leveraged the internal strength of his company through open communication in muscle-building sessions.

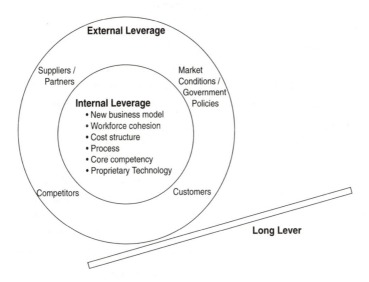

Figure 3.1 Where to leverage?

The Process of Leverage

Kung Ming's strategy of borrowing arrows from his enemy represents the high art of leveraging; a sly approach which reduced casualties and achieved the desired goal. Kung Ming understood that the only place to get arrows quickly was from his enemy. He also correctly predicted the behavior of the enemy soldiers, knowing they would shoot at the least provocation. His straw men created a lever with which he could redirect his enemy's resources to his own use. Kung Ming's leveraging process can be distilled into three major steps:

1. Identify the force or resources that you need in your environment without prejudice. In other words, do not distinguish between friend or enemy, inside or outside the company, when locating the needed resource.

2. Understand the predictable patterns that exist in and around the players that affect the resources or force.

3. Create a channel or new space to redirect the force or resources for your own advantage.

In other words, *the fundamental principle of leverage is to achieve maximum effect with minimum effort.*

Plenty of modern day masters leverage resources from their environment to transform their weaknesses into advantages. Consider Microsoft, the prince of leverage. Bill Gates and Paul Allen, cofounders of Microsoft, were inspired by the first microcomputer kit, the Altair. They envisioned "a computer on every desk and in every home"[2] and built Microsoft to leverage this vision by providing software for all these computers (step one of the leveraging process). Anticipating the explosive potential of the PC industry, which was non-existent in 1975, Gates and Allen revolutionized the software licensing industry. Rather than following the industry norm and licensing Microsoft's software to a single hardware vendor at high price (step two), Gates and Allen licensed the software to all computer makers at a low price (step three), which vastly increased their available market.

Then, Gates snapped up the rights to an operating system, called the "disk operating system" or DOS, and persuaded IBM to use DOS instead of the predominant system in the market. With IBM on its side, Microsoft gained instant credibility by leveraging IBM's reputation. With DOS, Microsoft was able to leverage all the software developers by integrating their products, including bestsellers such as Word and Visual C++, into its operating system. Both DOS and Microsoft's next generation operating system, Windows, launched the company that would become the largest software company in the world.

By 1995, however, Microsoft recognized that it was lagging behind competitors in the Internet tidal wave. When Microsoft proposed to partner with Netscape, the dominant player that held more than 90% of the market, Netscape refused. Microsoft then leveraged the power of Windows' dominant position and its own financial strength to crush Netscape (the process is well documented in various documents of the anti-trust lawsuit of *United States vs. Microsoft*). Throughout its evolution from tiny start-up to industry dominance, Microsoft has cleverly and consistently followed the three-step process of leverage outlined above.

The Market Inflection Point[3]

Pierre Omidyar founded eBay, then called Auction Web, in his Silicon Valley town house on Labor Day 1995. His premise was that the Internet formed the perfect medium for buyers and sellers to meet. Within eight years, eBay became an Internet legend, valued at more than Sears, Kmart, and J.C. Penny combined. In 2003, more than 30 million people bought and sold over $20 billion in merchandise, spread over almost 20,000 categories; and more than 150,000 entrepreneurs make their living selling items in eBay stores. In fact, eBay is already the largest auto dealer in the world, selling more vehicles than the top U. S. dealer, AutoNation.[4]

eBay is an undisputed master of leverage, bringing all the forces of leverage into convergence to create a tidal wave of market growth. These new forces can be grossly categorized into four major categories: *a valued-center business model, an innovative market strategy, product/ process innovation, and cost and delivery efficiency.*

Value-Centered Model: Omidyar built eBay not just as a shopping site, but as a full-blown community. By including e-mail addresses, Omidyar allowed users to communicate directly among themselves to solve each other's problems. The community can also share information via eBay's message board. Omidyar wanted his corner of cyberspace to be a place where people could form real connections with each other. Plus, he wanted it to operate according to the moral values he subscribed to in his own life: people are basically good, and given the chance to do things right, they generally will. As eBay grows into a teeming virtual community of 30 million, it is governed by its own laws through the feedback system, set up by eBay, in which buyers and sellers rate each other on transactions. This virtual community also has something akin to a bank in eBay's PayPal payment-processing unit, which allows buyers to make electronic payments. Members of the eBay community have 24/7 access to every sale, every trend, and every regulation in the eBay world—a world of utter transparency. Through eBay, a whole new medium of exchange is opening up which provides value to all concerned: buyers, sellers, and eBay.

Innovative Market Strategy: In eBay's democratic marketplace, an individual seller with few resources can compete on an equal footing with the largest corporations. eBay creates a global market that allows anyone to compete on an equal basis, providing a degree of economic independence heretofore impossible to people in countries such as China or Guatemala—countries rich in native wares, but lacking in resources. Today, those people need only an Internet connection to compete. This transformational power is the most remarkable aspect of the eBay story.

Product and Process Innovation: eBay, more than any other dotcom company, has fully harnessed the potential of the Internet by connecting 30 million buyers and sellers around the world. By moving goods and services from people who value them less to people who value them more, eBay has increased the "social utility" of these items, making people, as a whole, happier than they would have been without the goods. eBay has permanently changed the way commerce is conducted.

Cost and Delivery Efficiency: eBay thrived because Omidyar built both a vast commercial crossroads and the large community that always comes with it. By leaving the selling up to individuals, Omidyar has kept eBay completely "virtual." However, unlike Amazon.com's one-to-many style, eBay's transactions are many-to-many. It is an amazingly efficient model for building community and facilitating connections between people.

eBay is on a path of seemingly unlimited growth. Its CEO, Margaret C. Whitman, describes it as a *dynamic self-regulating economy.*[5] In fact, what is behind its growth is a little known pattern of leverage called the *market inflection point.* When the major forces of leverage—including a value-centered business model, innovative marketing strategy, product/process innovation, and cost and delivery efficiency—converge all at once, a multiplicative effect is created as shown in Figure 3.2. The effect of a market inflection point is to spur major new market growth while simultaneously dropping the price of products or services drastically.

A Journey into the Land of Leverage

In this chapter, we will introduce you to three masters of leverage: Wal-Mart, Dell Inc., and Southwest Airlines. Their stories illustrate how masters leverage every part of their environment to achieve peak performance in profit, time-to-market, customer share, productivity, quality, and more. These masters share a common trait: when they enter a new market, they create a tidal wave that simultaneously spurs the market to unprecedented levels of growth while drastically reducing prices. In other words, although these companies each dominate different industries, they all reached the top of the heap by bringing the forces of leverage into convergence and creating a market inflection point.

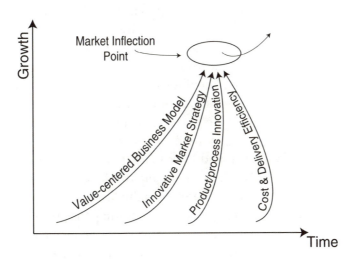

Figure 3.2 The effect of the market inflection point.

Wal-Mart
An Agent for Customer

Sam Walton stumbled into the retail business when he got a job at J.C. Penney after graduating from college. Having been bitten by the retail bug, Walton opened his first Ben Franklin 5-and-10 franchise in Newport, Arkansas. He then went on to open the very first Wal-Mart store in Rogers, Arkansas in 1962; the very same year that Kmart, Woolco, and Target opened their first stores.

Never one to stand on ego, Walton leveraged his competitors, customers, associates, and partners, learning everything he could from them. In fact, he spent much of his time at his competitors' stores, gleaning retail secrets on pricing, display, and merchandising. During Wal-Mart's early days, Kmart became his role model:

> *"I was in their stores constantly because they were the laboratory, and they were better than we were. I spent a heck of a lot of my time wandering through their stores talking to their people and trying to figure out how they did things."*[6]

But Walton did more than just learn from Kmart, he leveraged the strength of their marketing department. In the 1980s, when Kmart was aggressively advertising weekly specials to pull customers into its stores, Wal-Mart refused to get into an advertising battle but offered similar specials. In addition, some Wal-Mart stores began posting Kmart's weekly specials at the front of their stores, promising to match or beat Kmart's prices. Knowing that Wal-Mart had the same merchandise at the same or lower prices, customers flocked to Wal-Mart stores. With this simple, clever maneuver, Wal-Mart turned Kmart's own strength against itself.

Later, after Walton toured Price Club, founded by his friend Sol Price, he founded Sam's Club, leveraging the already successful Price Club formula. In fact, in his autobiography Walton tells how he was caught by Price Club security guards for recording the prices of various items and the arrangement of different types of merchandise. He walked through Price Club recording everything he saw!

While Wal-Mart certainly delights in leveraging their competitors, it's not above also leveraging its own people. When Walton visited one of his stores in Crowley, Louisiana, he was surprised to be greeted by an elderly gentleman at the door. It turned out that this particular store had a history of problems with shoplifting, and the greeter was stationed at the door to discourage such activity. At the same time, though, the presence of the greeter created a perfect customer service interface. While it was unlikely that these elderly greeters could actually physically stop shoplifters, their presence seemed to have a marked effect in reducing shoplifting. Walton was so impressed with the idea that he insisted every Wal-Mart store have greeters. After 18 months, he was able to wear down all internal resistance to the idea, and greeters became the norm in Wal-Mart stores. With this practice, Wal-Mart is able to further reduce cost by discouraging shoplifting, pass the reduced cost on to customers and enhance its customer service image.

Because of Walton's constant learning and savvy ability to leverage every part of his environment, Wal-Mart stores are some of the most productive in the industry and provide the best return on equity. For example, over a 30 year period from 1972 to 2002, Wal-Mart's annualized return was 25.97%, second only to Southwest Airlines.[7] Says Walton,

"Most everything I've done I've copied from someone else."[8]

In the Beginning: Small Town Strategy

Wal-Mart developed it's so called "small town strategy" almost by accident. Walton's wife, Helen, refused to live in a city with more than 10,000 people after they were forced out of the lease on their Ben Franklin 5-and-10 franchise. They ended up in Bentonville, Arkansas, a town of only 3,000 people. Although at the time, people believed that discount stores needed a town of at least 50,000 people to support them, Bentonville's tiny population turned out to be a blessing for Wal-Mart in its early years. Walton recalled the use of the guerrilla strategy:

"We could really do something with our key strategy, which was simply to put good-sized discount stores into little one-horse towns."

This early edge provided the company an opportunity to refine its methods before moving into more competitive markets. It turns out that small town America had a huge thirst for discount stores. In the 1960s, as people began to move their families into the suburbs, they often had to drive up to 50 miles to larger towns to pay reasonable prices for items they purchased regularly. When Wal-Mart moved into town, these people were delighted. They paid lower prices, shopped during convenient hours, had ample parking space, and were greeted by friendly staff. The Wal-Mart experience was so memorable that people easily bypassed the traditional variety store competitors, which offered 45% markups, scarce selection and limited hours.

During its early years, Wal-Mart had time to refine its small town strategy because Kmart would not consider opening stores in towns with less than 50,000 people, and Gibson's avoided towns with populations of 10,000 or less. While other chains disdained these tiny towns, Walton saw an opportunity to leverage small towns to build his business. Knowing that a head-to-head competition with the other chains would cut deeply into Wal-Mart's then tiny balance sheet, Walton simply dropped his business off the radar screen of his potential competitors and focused on the three step leverage process described in the introduction.

1. He located the resources he wanted: customers.
2. He identified the predictable patterns that affected the customers he wanted. In other words, other retail chains didn't want small town customers, but small town customers thirsted for discount stores that offered good value in terms of price and selection of merchandise.
3. Finally, he directed those customers to his stores by offering them low price and satisfaction.

By using the three-step leveraging process at the company's inception, Walton was able to firmly establish Wal-Mart's presence in the marketplace.

With this strategy in mind, Walton was willing to bring Wal-Mart into towns of 5,000 or less. In these small towns, Wal-Mart pursued the strategy of saturating a market by *spreading out, then filling in*. When the company moved into a new area, also called "spreading out," it would locate all its stores within a day's drive of the distribution center, with all stores under the control of the district manager. Wal-Mart would then begin *filling in* the area around the distribution center with stores, town by town, county by county, and state by state, until the market was saturated. In addition to allowing Wal-Mart to spread quickly and thoroughly through any given market, this strategy also saved on advertising expense. While other retailers put out weekly circulars, Wal-Mart was able to get by with a single monthly advertisement because their stores were so well known and convenient.

While competitors like Kmart focused on gaining market share in one large city after another, Walton patiently built his small town strategy by getting out in front of the expansion and letting the population build outward to Wal-Mart. In other words, Walton built stores where no stores existed, cleverly avoiding any competition, and waiting for the population to grow. By leveraging small towns, Wal-Mart was constantly building stores for the future.

Although Wal-Mart is now the leading retailer, it keeps its small town spirit alive by *thinking small*. Thinking small became a way of life for Walton, even an obsession. For decades Walton worked hard to keep his company simple, streamlined, and grass roots. He listed six ways for Wal-Mart to continue to *think small*:[9]

1. Think one store at a time.
2. Communicate, communicate, communicate.
3. Keep your ear to the ground.
4. Push responsibility—and authority—down.
5. Force ideas to bubble up.
6. Stay lean, fight bureaucracy.

By thinking small and keeping its original small town strategy, Wal-Mart is able to expand quickly, repeating its successful formula over and over and stamping out stores in cookie-cutter fashion. Because of its decades of experience in small towns, there is no market too small for Wal-Mart. The company need only decide the size of the store and the location based on the kind of potential a community offers. The twin strategies of *saturation* and *building ahead of the growth curve* still continue to serve Wal-Mart well.

An Agent for Customer

Wal-Mart is a valued-centered company that is thoroughly focused on customer value. Walton's secret of successful retailing is to give his customers what they want. Early on, he learned that customer loyalty was a myth in retailing. Customer loyalty does not exist because customers shop for the lowest prices among retailers offering standard service. So Walton focused on low price, leveraging the consumer's desire for a good deal. He said:

"When customers think of Wal-Mart, they should think of low prices and satisfaction guaranteed."[10]

But, he also knew that customers wanted more than just low price, they wanted everything. Customers seek a wide selection of high quality merchandise, friendly service, convenient hours, many locations, and more. That's why Walton insisted that Wal-Mart associates consider themselves agents for the customer. Store managers are constantly finding ways to please customers or top the competition. The same is true at company headquarters. Personnel from the head office spend about four days per week in the field, visiting with customers or employees in Wal-Mart stores or doing reconnaissance in competitors' stores. Every Saturday, the staff gathers for a morning meeting. The collected data from the week's fieldwork is reviewed and analyzed, and the management team makes necessary corrections in merchandising and advertising. The Saturday meeting preps the company for the coming week and gives them a two-day jump start on the competition.

Other Wal-Mart employees are equally diligent in their efforts. Wal-Mart buyers, for instance, are always told to negotiate on behalf of their customers, which makes them tough and demanding, but also fair. Buyers leverage not just their own attitudes, but also Wal-

Mart's giant size to negotiate the best prices from suppliers. In the stores, Wal-Mart associates are trained to be extremely courteous and highly knowledgeable, and are given the latitude to take the initiative on behalf of customers. For instance, Wal-Mart pioneered the concept of "a store within a store," which empowers the managers of different sections of the store to fully participate in creating a place that enhances customer value.

Only a visit to one of Wal-Mart's weekend management meetings in Bentonville, Arkansas can offer a true picture of this company's dedication to providing customer value. Hundreds of people usually attend this meeting, not just associates but also their families. Among the many festivities is the Wal-Mart Cheer, which Walton used to lead:

> "Give me a W!
> Give me an A!
> Give me an L!
> Give me a squiggly ! (every one rolls their hips)
> Give me an M!
> Give me an A!
> Give me an R!
> Give me a T!
> What's the spell?
> Wal-Mart!
> Who's number one?
> THE CUSTOMER!"

While the meeting is festive and loud, the leadership team manages to communicate a huge amount of information and bring the group into consensus. However, the most telling insight into how well Wal-Mart delivers customer value is the huge tote board that constantly tracks the amount of money Wal-Mart has saved for its customers throughout the year—a number that never stops growing! Wal-Mart's guiding principle is its slogan "Always low prices!" and Walton constantly took steps to ensure that the entire company stayed true to this vision.

In Wal-Mart's early years, big retailers like Sears failed to acknowledge the discount chain as a primary competitor until far too late in the game. The disdain of Sears and other major retailers, who refused to buy into the discount chain store model, helped Wal-Mart gain a foothold in the industry and expand quickly. Walton truly believed that his dedication to creating value for his customers helped Wal-Mart leapfrog its competitors. While other retailers were still reaping the benefits of huge markups, Wal-Mart rapidly convinced huge hordes of customers that cheaper was indeed better.

While the retail giant is clearly interested in customer value, it's also interested in providing value for its employees, suppliers, partners, and shareholders. For its associates, Wal-Mart provides a stable employment with a "family-like" culture as well as personal and professional growth. Wal-Mart's profit sharing is outstanding, and the company primarily promotes from within. For its suppliers and partners, it provides a large, steady source of demand at an acceptable overall profit. Finally, its shareholders have been amply rewarded by its consistently high return of more than 25% over the last 30 years.

Merchandise Driven

True to his early roots at J.C. Penney, Walton remained a merchant at heart. He was always merchandise-driven, keeping a keen eye on merchandise that would sell, quickly getting rid of anything that did not sell. Walton always put merchandising managers in charge of the stores, firmly believing that they knew best the mix of items that would sell in each particular area. Walton constantly reminded his managers to listen to and support the merchandisers in the stores.

Merchandising was so important that he placed a merchant in charge of each department within the stores as well. With its concept of "a store within a store," Wal-Mart treats these merchant managers as the leaders of their own businesses, with the authority and power to maximize customer value. In many cases, these departments have annual sales figures that exceed the revenues of many original Wal-Mart stores. These merchant managers are flooded with information from headquarters that helps them make informed decisions, including cost of goods, freight costs, profit margins, and their store's ranking relative to every other store. Managers are also rewarded for excellent performance with bonuses and performance incentives.

To be merchandise driven, Wal-Mart senior management strikes a fine balance between autonomy and control. While Wal-Mart has certain standard store procedures, department heads have the primary responsibility for ordering merchandise, store managers are responsible for promoting merchandise, and buyers shoulder great responsibility for deciding which items the store will carry. Wal-Mart employees experience much greater levels of freedom in making decisions than people in most other retail chain stores.

Wal-Mart's merchandising strategy evolved through Walton's passion of picking and promoting particular merchandise, and his willingness to experiment. He said: "I suspect I have emphasized item merchandising and the importance of promoting items to a greater degree than most any other retail management person in this country." As a result, Wal-Mart stores would, from time to time, buy an incredible amount of a single item and dramatize it by making it grandly visible in the store. Walton used to say one could sell anything if it is hung from the ceiling. In general, Wal-Mart stores feature only few brands and offer strong volume discounts. What makes Wal-Mart successful is the breadth of selection. Every category is represented. By allowing store managers the freedom to experiment with different items, Wal-Mart stores become a moving target, with each store manager choosing merchandise to suit the specific customer base. That's why Wal-Mart stores are more productive. For example, a 1995 study[11] showed that sales per square foot at Wal-Mart were $297 compared to $211 for Kmart and $195 for Target.

Cost and Delivery Efficiency

Frugality is one of Wal-Mart's key cultural elements, the result of Walton's early experience in running small town stores. Walton firmly believed that if he could control his expenses, he could afford to make a lot of different mistakes and still recover. One of Walton's trademarks was his old pick up truck, which he frequently drove to work. To that end, Wal-Mart stores and offices are always designed with frugality in mind. The cost advantages are further clarified with Wal-Mart's distribution systems.

Wal-Mart's distribution system is the best in the industry. In fact, Wal-Mart leads the pack in terms of investments that help the company operate at peak efficiency. We break its distribution system down in terms of its hardware, process, software (or information technology), and people.

Hardware

The core of the Wal-Mart operational system lies in its mechanized distribution centers around the country. Each center is located within 350 miles of all the stores it serves, and is a megalithic building with the equivalent of 23 football fields of floor space filled to the roof with merchandise. Every item is bar-coded and tracked. On one side of the building is the shipping dock with loading doors that can handle more than 30 trucks at a time. The other side of the building is the receiving dock, which has up to 135 doors for unloading merchandise. To keep merchandise moving through the building efficiently, all the routes within the building are guided by lasers, which direct boxes to different areas: incoming, outgoing, or temporary storage. Keeping in mind that Wal-Mart's operations are in motion simultaneously in more than 30 centers around the country, one gets a glimpse of the enormity and complexity of its distribution systems.

As Wal-Mart stores stock more than 80,000 items, with more than 85% of their inventory being directly replenished by the distribution centers, the gap between a store placing an order and receiving the goods averages less than two days, 50% less time than Wal-Mart's competitors. While Wal-Mart certainly saves time and is flexible with this procedure, its cost savings are phenomenal when compared to the model used by most retail stores that contract third parties to deliver merchandise. Wal-Mart stores never have to rely on the vagaries of third party vendor to get their products. To further ensure utter reliability, Wal-Mart purchased its own fleet of trucks, the largest in the country.

Process

Wal-Mart is the first retail company to restructure its entire supply chain, negotiating agreements with partners who could meet the company's stringent speed, cost, and flexibility requirements. The company began experimenting with these relationships with Proctor & Gamble (P&G). Today, P&G ships products to Wal-Mart based on daily demand information from Wal-Mart's computer system, information that is provided in a continuous round-the-clock flow. When P&G's trucks arrive at Wal-Mart distribution centers, the goods are often "cross-docked," which means they are moved directly from the incoming dock onto outgoing Wal-Mart trucks, which deliver the products directly to the stores. On the back end of the process, P&G generates both the order and an invoice for immediate payment, completing the transaction for both parties.

While both Wal-Mart and P&G had to restructure their logistics processes, this philosophy of "supplier as partner" has benefited both companies. Wal-Mart gets the speed, delivery efficiency, and cost savings it demands, and P&G gets continuous demand data, which allows it to plan its manufacturing schedule and monitor which products are selling and which are not. Wal-Mart and its supplier partners jointly examine the logistical processes, from the time of manufacture to the point of sale, to determine how to achieve maximum efficiency and savings.

Wal-Mart pioneered this new form of inventory management, in which it manages *information* rather than inventory. Information creates additional value for Wal-Mart, its customers and its partners. Normally, customers receive value when the goods are delivered, and because each Wal-Mart store is able to track the shipment of various types of merchandise in detail, they are able to keep almost all items in stock all the time. This constant availability becomes a value that customers come to rely on. Since information flows faster than inventory, Wal-Mart is able to make quick decisions and reduce the usual bureaucracy associated with logistics. Information is cheaper and can provide value earlier than inventory.

In addition to its partnership with P&G, GE, and others, Wal-Mart's distribution centers also make *customized* deliveries to meet the needs of its stores. Every six months, a store can decide which of four delivery plans it prefers. In addition, Wal-Mart also offers accelerated delivery for certain stores, with shipments arriving within 24 hours. These are simply examples of the constant improvements Wal-Mart makes to its distribution process, reflecting Walton's long-established desire to improve something everyday.

Information Technology

Wal-Mart's most significant investment for increasing its efficiency is its use of information technology. Beginning in the late 70s, Wal-Mart executives began planning ways to increase the capability of the information system while still maintaining control. In 1983, they launched their satellite system, at a cost of $24 million, for interactive communication among all of its stores, distribution centers, and the general office. Walton, while neutral on the technology investment in the beginning, was delighted that he could get real-time information that he could act upon instantly.

To say that Wal-Mart's investment in information technology is massive is an understatement. By 1992, the company had invested $700 million in its information systems. These investments provided Wal-Mart with key competitive advantages. Wal-Mart keeps a 65-week rolling history of every single item stocked in its stores or in Sam's Club stores. At any moment, executives and store managers can pinpoint the exact date an item was bought, the quantity purchased, the number sold, and the days it took to turn. From this information, buyers and merchandisers extrapolate customer preferences, hot-selling items, and new trends. No vendor knows more about how its products are doing in stores than Wal-Mart. This is the key competitive advantage Wal-Mart enjoys from its investment in the information technology.

People

It is important to note that while technology, process, and hardware have all been significant to Wal-Mart's success, it is the dedication of

Wal-Mart's people that continue to make the difference. For example, Wal-Mart truck drivers consider themselves "ambassadors" of the company and willingly work beyond the call of duty to ensure that the merchandise they carry is delivered on time, as expected. The people throughout the distribution system believe that their primary jobs are to take care of the customers in Wal-Mart and Sam's Club stores.

The Wal-Mart Effect

People often accuse Wal-Mart of destroying the home-town flavor and uniqueness of mom-and-pop shops in the towns it enters. But, as Walton confessed, the fault really falls on the shoulders of those shopkeepers who refuse to change their retail model to better serve customers while insisting on their standard 45% markups. When Wal-Mart enters a new market, it brings all the leverage it has accumulated to bear on that market: a value-center business model, a small town mentality of always thinking small to make things better, a merchandise driven strategy that fulfills customers' needs, and its cost and delivery advantages. When these forces of leverages converge, it produces the *Wal-Mart Effect*—prices go down and volume goes up as shown in Figure 3.3.

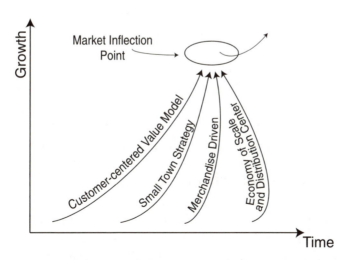

Figure 3.3 The Wal-Mart Effect.

Dell Inc. [11]
The Direct Connection

Michele Moore, former Vice President of Corporate Communications at Dell, Inc. (Dell), shared a great story about Michael Dell with me. When she flew from California to Austin to interview for a position at Dell, she sat next to an older gentleman flipping through some charts on Dell. Curious, she asked him many questions about Dell, finally asking him, "How do you interview with a 23 year-old CEO?" The gentleman replied, "Treat him as you would any other CEO, because he is very, very bright." She later discovered that the man on the plane was Bob Noyce, inventor of the integrated circuit and co-founder of Intel. Michele continued to marvel, after she retired, at Michael Dell's ability to retain the competitive spirit of a start up even as Dell expanded to a world-class company. She also remained impressed with his personal humility, despite his youth and wealth.

Michael Dell learned the benefits of the direct connection—bypassing the middlemen—at a tender age. As a young boy, he collected stamps. Wanting to sell his stamps, he discovered that he could circumvent the auctioneers by issuing his own product catalog called "Dell's Stamps," which he advertised in Linn's Stamp journal. Getting people in his neighborhood to consign their stamps with him, he was able to earn $2,000. More importantly, he learned firsthand the rewards of eliminating the middlemen.

When he was 16, Dell got a summer job selling newspaper subscriptions for the Houston Post. He was directed to make "cold calls" as a way to attract new customers, but he soon found a better way. He discovered that people who were about to get married or buy a house would most likely subscribe to the paper. He went after these "high potential" customers with personalized letters, and managed to earn $18,000 that year, a sum that exceeded his high school teacher's salary.

When personal computers (PCs) began coming out on the market, Dell fell in love. He began helping people upgrade their computers in Houston, Texas, again bypassing the middlemen, the computer stores. When he arrived in Austin to attend the University of Texas, he intended to study pre-med, but his upgrade business just kept growing. His parents, having got wind of his aspiring business, visited him in Austin to help him set his priorities in order. When his father asked him, "What do you want to do with your life?" Michael answered, "I want to compete with IBM!", thus setting his course in life clearly.[12] In 1984, he founded PCs Limited in Austin, a business that built custom PCs for its customers, eliminating the dealer channel, along with the reseller's markup, and the risk of carrying large inventories.

In this story, we explore the leverage points of the Direct Model (DM) that empowered Dell to expand the company into a multi-billion dollar enterprise aimed at capturing 40% of the world market share.

The Direct Model

Located in the heart of Texas, Dell transformed the PC industry with its pioneering DM. Surprisingly, this model is not new. In fact, mainframe and minicomputer manufacturers originally sold their computers directly. However, because of the expenses involved with direct sales, most of these companies sold high end products directly only to their best customers. But Dell is direct all the way. Dell's DM orients the entire business, from manufacturing and sales to listening to customers, toward delivering what customers want. At the core of Dell's business is the build-to-order strategy. When customers order PCs from Dell, their order is routed through a credit check, then directly to the manufacturing floor. The custom PC is then built, tested, and shipped to the customer, who receives it five business days after placing their order. Dell's DM places the customer at the epicenter of its business.

Ultimately, Dell extended the reach of its DM to tap the power of the Internet as a sales channel. In 1996, the company began taking orders over the Internet and their success in this medium quickly became legendary. In the first quarter of 1997 alone, the online business captured $1 million in sales. By the second quarter, Dell sold $2 million via the Internet. By early 2002, Dell logged between $60 and $70 million per day in sales through this channel.

Over the years, Dell's success has inspired competitors such as Gateway, Compaq, and IBM to emulate the DM, but none have been nearly as successful. In fact, Compaq and IBM have largely abandoned the direct approach. What Dell's competitors failed to notice is that the DM is not simply a product distribution model at Dell; it is a theme that aligns all of the company's business units and people. In other words, at Dell every person, whether an outside customer or another Dell employee, is considered a customer. For instance, Dell's IT division has almost no central staff members. Almost all IT personnel report directly to a business unit, such as manufacturing. Similarly, Dell University is structured so that its different departments report to and serve different business units, with the University's budget coming from those business units. The survival of each department depends on the satisfaction of each of its customers—the various Dell business units. In summary, *Dell's DM aligns all of Dell's resources towards the customer.*

In addition to leveraging all of its internal resources to satisfy its customers, Dell's DM also exploits competitors' assets, namely their distribution network. Consider the early competition between Dell and Compaq. Compaq's distribution network added time and cost to the selling process. More importantly, since Compaq did not have direct access to its customers, it was forced to rely on imperfect information from its distributors and make wild guesses about customer preferences, building products far in advance of sales. In an industry where the price of materials and products drops weekly, wrong guesses penalize companies with high costs. Dell's DM takes advantage of Compaq's long cycle time and slow distribution network to gain market share.

More importantly, Dell was able to stand Compaq's distribution network on its head. How? If Compaq imitated Dell by pursuing a 100% DM, it would probably be abandoned by its partners. Instead, Compaq chose a hybrid model, selling direct as well as retaining its distribution network. The result was disaster. Dell used its DM to transform Compaq's partners, originally assets, into liabilities. A true judo master, Michael Dell summarizes his philosophy of leverage:

"Understanding the profit pool of you industry—where your competitors really make money—can open your eyes to new opportunities. Think of a competitor that has high market share and is very profitable in a specific part of the market. Then think about how compelling it would be to exploit that strength as a weakness."[13]

Build to Order (BTO) Strategy

The foundation of Dell's DM is its BTO strategy, which is based on the philosophy of market pull or demand rather than the traditional approach of Build-to-Forecast, which pushes products into the market based on forecasted figures. Two key aspects are required for a successful BTO strategy: *process focus* and *mass customization.*

At Dell, process is paramount to success because it is Dell's internal processes that enable the company to offer customers such speed and flexibility. Within the company, all processes are constantly scrutinized and enhanced. For example, the company's process of translating a customer order into a custom-built PC is nothing short of astonishing. When a customer places an order, an immensely complex yet highly efficient process is triggered, which orders parts from suppliers, prepares software to be downloaded, and launches the manufacturing process. The sales order actually contains all the information necessary to begin the manufacturing process. The amount of time from customer order to manufacturing is almost nil, thanks to Dell's highly automated BTO infrastructure.

Dell's DM is based on one-to-one relationships with the customer, since the company builds only the products selected and specified by the customer. By design, Dell is able to meet every customer need precisely. But that's not enough. At Dell, it's no longer acceptable to simply meet customer expectations. It's not even good enough to delight the customer, since these are often one-time goals that are fulfilled as soon as the customer's order is fulfilled. Continued success is the result of knowing the customer, which means Dell has to know enough about each of its customers to constantly add value.

Knowing the customer means Dell can design new products, new services, and new pricing schemes that constantly meet and exceed customer expectations. Dell achieves this through creative use of their information systems as well as through their people. Their information systems assemble, store, manipulate, and report the most detailed information on each customer. Their people creatively use this information to immediately respond to changing market conditions, changes from competitors, and changes in customer preferences. Internally, Dell is always examining its share of the market within a particular customer account. Michael Dell likes to ask questions such as:

"If we have say 99% [market] share of the Ford Company, the question we ask is, 'How do we improve the customer satisfaction in order to get that additional 1% share?'"

Knowledge of the customer produces different solutions and services for each customer segment. When Dell first began aggressively wooing new consumers while also introducing customized support to some of its largest long-term accounts in the late 1990s, the services required by each were very different. For example, "relationship" accounts such as GE, Boeing, and GM find value in Dell's quality, predictability, and the consistency of delivery. On the other hand, consumers find value in Dell's lower total cost. Michele Moore, former Vice President of Communications, described it this way: "Transaction customers are one-time buyers with a need for a high volume of relatively low-value support. But customers who buy repeatedly from us require a low volume of high-value support." Today, Dell's consumer business has matured to a point where a large percentage of its customers are repeat users who don't necessarily require a high-volume of support. Also, Dell has greatly expanded its "relationship" support offerings.

Market Strategy

Dell relies on two key strategies to enter markets: *segmentation and technology standardization.* To truly provide customized solutions for the masses, Dell's organizational structure, which reflects its customers, is structured by market *segmentation*. In the 1990s, Dell had three major segments: large and medium-sized companies, educational and government organizations, and small business and consumers, each with its own distinct sales organization. In late 1990s, Dell enhanced its customer segmentation approach by creating complete business units around different customer types, each with its own sales, service, finance, IT, technical support, and manufacturing capabilities. "Whenever we see a group of customers emerging, we create a segment to serve them better," says former Dell CFO Tom Meredith.

Dell's segmentation approach allows it to truly understand customer needs and proactively meet those needs at the right time. Michael Dell summarizes:

"Most of the companies in this business segment themselves by product. We do it by customer. Every segment is about a $1 billion business, with a shared set of products and a mandate to use the Direct Model. But at the same time, the people in that segment know the products which relate to their customers. And the segment has growth and operating margin targets as well as service level targets which are relevant to them. And we have found that a segment can be much more responsive to the customer because of the basic learning that takes place."

The technology *standardization* strategy basically identifies markets that are near commoditization, meaning that the primary technology within the market is being standardized. This strategy leverages the people who have found innovative ways to use technology. In fact, Dell has a very small R&D budget compared to other technology companies. For example, HP's one billion dollar R&D budget for its Printer division in 2003 is more than Dell's entire R&D budget.[14] However, Dell applies its R&D budget toward enhancing its processes, technology optimization, and product designs rather than creating new technology. Then, with the efficiency of its BTO technology, Dell strikes just before the market reaches the point of commoditization. This applies not only to the PC markets, but also to geographic markets as well. In recent years, it has also ventured into the services market as a natural leverage of Dell's IT infrastructure, which is readily available to its best customers. This strategy is depicted below in Figure 3.4.

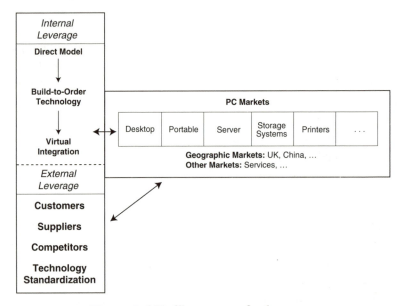

Figure 3.4 Dell's strategy for leverage.

Management Principles at Dell

Dell managers speak of a few key management principles that are fundamental to Dell's DM. These include:

- Drive for customer value.
- Exchange inventory for information.
- Focus on velocity, value, and volume.
- Embrace constant change.
- Understand the criticality of coordination.

Drive for Customer Value

Dell's business processes are driven by what the customer wants, not by what the internal managers want to provide. The BTO strategy is based on "market pull" as compared to the traditional manufacturing strategy of pushing products to market. At Dell, every product is built when and only when a customer asks for it. Customer value is derived from the company's fast response time, from the lower costs provided by its inventory management approach, and from the ability to give the customer exactly what is asked for, with predictability and consistency, by customizing every product built. The "Customer Experience" initiative is another example of being customer-centric, enhancing the customer experience at each contact point.

Michael Dell says he launched the "Customer Experience" initiative in May 1998 to leverage the DM to "deliver the best possible customer experience across all points of contact with Dell." He added,

> *"There are countless stops along the way where employees behind the scenes make day to day decisions that affect the customer. Each of us owns part of the customer experience because everything we do ultimately touches the customer. At Dell, a complete customer experience should never end. Strategically speaking, this affects all employees all the time in everything we do. This initiative will keep all of us focused on the most important people outside Dell— the customers. Our customers should be treated like VIPs."*

To measure the success of this initiative, performance goals were clearly outlined, and managers targeted three key metrics to evaluate the progress of the company, with each metric to improve by at least 15% during the year. The metrics were:

- *Order and Delivery:* The percentage of orders shipped to the customer by the targeted date.
- *Installation and Operation:* The percentage of customer calls to technical support which require a part dispatch within 30 days of the invoice date.
- *Service:* The percentage of on-site service incidents resolved by a Dell Service Partner within the target time frame.

By constantly driving toward better customer value, where customer interests are expanded to include stakeholder value, Dell has built barriers to entry by increasing switching cost. For example, customers with Platinum Accounts have web pages that give them access to Dell's operational systems. They can check on orders, configure systems, and manage their inventory directly on Dell's systems. These types of services increase the value to the customers, which increases the costs associated with switching to one of Dell's competitors.

Exchange Inventory for Information

At the heart of Dell's success is its strategy of exchanging inventory for information. Rather than keeping costly inventory on hand at Dell, in a warehouse, or at a retail outlet, Dell keeps only information about customer orders, needs, and forecasts. The manufacturing department predicts the number and types of orders it anticipates, alerts suppliers of needed parts, and increases the staff to meet demand. This gives Dell several distinct advantages. First, information is easier to store, and costs less to keep. Second, information is easier to move and, when necessary, discard. Inventory is costly to store, move and discard. Finally, mistaken information is easier to correct than mistaken inventory. Dell managers have designed their systems to minimize inventory and maximize information. As soon as demand forecasts change, information about the change is easily shared with the rest of the organization and partners, helping the company stay in sync with its high-speed business.

The early and wide use of Internet at Dell is a natural outgrowth of this principle. Scott Eckert, VP in charge of the initial Internet operations, explains:

"The Internet is useful because of the richness of customer information and the possibilities of integration. For example, the configurator tells us what a customer bought, but it also tells us what other choices he or she looked at. We can then build a database of information about the choices our customers are making, which allows us to analyze price elasticity. If a customer looked at a Pentium II and a Pentium system, then bought the less expensive Pentium system, we assume the customer bought the best 'processor

for the price' and therefore we would have information telling us that, for this customer, the Pentium II system was too expensive relative to the Pentium system. We've never had this kind of information about what customers evaluated but didn't choose."

Focus on Velocity, Volume, and Value

As Dell exchanges inventory for information, they increase their velocity, or the rate at which their business processes occur. Velocity is a critical focus for Dell management. To manage the changing requirements of their customers and the changing technology critical to their products, Dell must be able to respond with the speed of a cheetah. This is termed velocity at Dell.

As velocity increases, the volume of business increases. This volume is dependent on the amount of information Dell can obtain or access, store, and process. The ultimate result of velocity is value to customers, shareholders, and employees. For example, the velocity of their inventory turns is multiples of their competitors', which translates directly into a large volume of supplies from suppliers. This gives Dell the opportunity to negotiate favorable agreements with suppliers simply because its volume has grown faster, in a shorter period of time than its competitors' volume. This ultimately translates into value for Dell customers.

Time is a key value at Dell and the compression of time adds value for all stakeholders. For customers, it's lower cost. For stakeholders, higher returns. And for suppliers and partners, it's a larger volume of business. Finally, employees get larger profit-sharing bonuses. As the velocity at Dell increases in all their business processes, time is further compressed, and value continues to increase.

Embrace Constant Change

While virtually every business knows that the business environment is in a constant state of flux, Dell managers are more keenly aware of the factor of change than almost anyone else. They take it for granted that the only thing they know about their future is that it will be different from the present. This assumption has significant implications for how the company is organized and managed, and further highlights the emphasis on velocity. To better handle constant change and the increasing velocity of change, Dell managers intentionally create change. Tom Meredith, former CFO, says: "We create the order and discipline needed to purposely spark innovation within the desired time frame."[15] By driving the changes themselves, Dell managers have greater control and are less likely to be blind-sided.

Dell managers identify potential new strategies as early as possible, and reinvent their processes to meet those strategies. For instance, when Dell entered the Internet market, the company had to reinvent its DM to allow customers direct access to its information systems. Dell transformed itself again when it stopped seeing itself as just a hardware manufacturer, and began embracing the vision of a hardware integration and distribution system. Keith Maxwell, former Senior Vice President of Operations, described this vision, "We sell solutions, not systems." As the competitive environment shifts yet again, with other PC manufacturers targeting Dell as a primary competitor, business units are increasing the acceleration of reinvention. Each business unit continues to evolve, gaining ever deeper knowledge of its customers.

Understand the Criticality of Coordination

Coordination efforts at Dell are extensive. The top management team meets monthly, quarterly, and ad hoc to discuss everything from strategy and new product development to alignment, empowerment, and optimization. In an organization that moves as fast as Dell, empowerment is critical. However, coordination is the ingredient that helps prevent people from working against each other. To keep all elements of the organization moving in the same direction, while at the same time responding to changes and movements in the environment, coordination between individuals, business units, and geographical segments is critical.

At Dell's rate of growth, such coordination is almost an impossible challenge. Aggressive communication is part of an overall coordination effort to keep people aligned. Although *time pacing* helps cultivate a culture of speed and a sense of urgency that keeps people moving with a general rhythm, good management systems, which include performance-based incentives and monitoring measurements, provide general guidelines for making decisions most beneficial to all stakeholders in the long run.

Virtual Integration

Dell's DM has evolved to automatically involve customers, suppliers, and other stakeholders in its business processes. For example, on the manufacturing floor suppliers unload directly onto the floor, rather than into inventory storage areas because they are viewed as partners in the manufacturing process. At the other end of the line, UPS trucks wait to deliver completed goods to end-users. They, too, are partners in this operation.

Another example is the order processing cycle. Forecasts for new systems are based on orders, and are sent to the partners to assist them in their planning. Meredith called this an *ecological* approach, where all entities involved in the process are informed of issues relating to the process. A more traditional *holistic* approach, on the other hand, keeps most of these issues internal, passing on to external partners only the information needed to satisfy an organization's requirements. An *ecological* approach forces the entire partnership to focus on the customers' needs whereas a *holistic* approach would force the external partners to focus on Dell's needs and Dell to focus on customer needs. Through an *ecological* approach, the boundaries between Dell and its customers are blurred. Even customers are included at Dell, since through the company's website, a customer is able to access significant parts of Dell's IT infrastructure.

Relationships with suppliers are critical to make the BTO concept work. Suppliers know what parts are needed when the order is taken, and emergency messages are sent to them if previously unanticipated supplies are needed. Short cycle times are possible because the suppliers are included in the process. Similarly, delivery vendors are part of the process. Their shipper provides logistics services that go beyond simply picking up the package and delivering it to the customer. They may actually stock components, such as monitors. When a system is ordered, Dell alerts the shipper, who begins the process of shipping the required components to customers, resulting in delivery of all needed system components at the same time. Finally, even the customer is part of the process. New web technology has enabled Dell to offer its customers access to the systems that help them configure their desired purchase. Customer orders over the web have added significantly to sales, further pushing the direct marketing model.

The whole of Dell's business model results in *virtual integration*— the business is stitched together with all of its partners as if they all belong inside the same company. In so doing, Dell is able to integrate the different pieces of a 21st century electronic organization—customer focus, supplier partnerships, mass customization, and just-in-time manufacturing. Dell is able to achieve a tightly coordinated supply chain, which is traditionally achieved through vertical integration, as well as precisely serve its customers' needs. By bringing all players together, traditional boundaries and roles in the value chain are blurred as shown in the shaded areas of Figure 3.5.

Figure 3.5 Virtual integration blurs traditional boundaries.

Virtual integration and connectivity with customers means that the customer has built organizational and technical connections with Dell's IT infrastructure and vice versa. The cost to the customer of switching from Dell involves decoupling from Dell's IT infrastructure, which is much more costly to most than the savings to be gained from a competitor with slightly lower per-unit costs. As Dell continues to focus on increasing value through its virtual environment, such as the Dell Plus integration service and automatic software installation on the factory floor, it increases Dell's distribution capability and raises switching costs for the consumer.

The Dell Effect

We summarize the advantages of the DM here:

1. Dell eliminates middlemen or resellers, which are part of the traditional distribution model. This empowers Dell to pass the savings to the customers in the form of lower costs. It also allows Dell to understand customer needs firsthand and adapt to market changes more quickly than competitors. The DM gives Dell the opportunity to constantly *take the pulse* of the customers, hence providing the right solutions at the right time.

2. Dell builds computers directly for customers, not for inventory. This means that the company does not waste resources building systems that may not reach customers, does not need staff to move inventory around the world, and does not spend time managing and tracking inventory or reworking systems that become obsolete before purchase.

3. Dell practices just-in-time manufacturing, with vendor trucks pulling up to one side of the plant to unload parts and delivery trucks pulling up to the other side of the plant to load finished systems. Vendors' delivered parts do not become the property of Dell Computers until they are unloaded, which takes place as frequently as every few hours. Such a practice provides Dell with tremendous cash flows, since customers pay Dell upfront but Dell is not required to pay vendors until 40 days after parts are unloaded. Dell gains the equivalent of a 40 day float. In other words, by paying up front, customers finance the bulk of Dell's operations.

4. Dell works closely with its strategic partners. The DM model is based on the "supply on demand" principle to fulfill customer orders. While traditional manufacturers push their product to market, such as

during the Christmas holidays, Dell's demand-supply management uses market pull to reduce resistance. As a consequence, Dell has reduced its suppliers from hundreds to about two dozen, according to Maxwell, which represent 98% of all the materials used. When an order is made, Dell alerts these strategic suppliers. As a result, the transformation cost (or cost of transforming raw materials to finished products), as a percentage of revenue, can be driven lower and lower.

5. Dell's information systems connect the entire company, routing orders to the next step in the business process and eliminating waits, backlogs, and losses that a less automated system may experience.

6. Virtual integration increases barriers to entry and switching costs. Dell creates barriers to entry and high switching costs as it operates in an increasingly virtual environment. Meredith explains:

> "I would rather plan in a non-physical world because it will create huge barriers to entry, huge switching costs, and massive competitive advantages for us. The basic infrastructure for the non-physical world consists of speed (time), intangibles (knowledge), and connectivity. The advantage is increased because these objects can be manipulated more easily than their physical counterparts."

These advantages add up to a very beneficial bottom line for Dell.

Normally, technology companies in a high-end market without standardization will mark up gross profit margins up to 60%. However, when Dell enters the market, it typically lowers the price by approximately 30% while trying to quickly build up a 20% market share. Therefore, Dell creates a convergence of several forces: technology standardization, a new business model (DM), product innovation such as speedy implementation of new technologies, and cost and delivery efficiency. It usually drastically accelerates the process of commoditization, spurring rapid growth in the market. We refer to this phenomenon as the *Dell Effect* as illustrated in Figure 3.6.

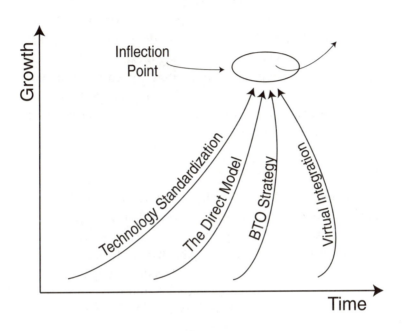

Figure 3.6 The Dell Effect.

So far, the Dell strategy has worked extremely well despite some hiccups along the way. One hiccup was the development of a family of desktop and workstation computers in 1989, code named Olympic. It was a major flop. The technology was developed without much customer input and was based on "technology for technology's sake," although some technologies developed through the Olympic project proved useful in later products. The Olympic fiasco reminded Dell to put customers back at the center of its model. Another hiccup was Dell's entry into the storage system market. Unlike the PC and server markets, there were no standard storage technologies. Its acquisition of the ConvergeNet Technologies in 1999 was not successful since ConvergeNet's complex technology did not fit Dell's commodity-oriented model. However, Michael Dell's conviction that *all technologies will commoditize over time* is manifesting in the storage systems area, and its partnership with EMC, the industry leader in this market, seems to be producing excellent results.

The question now is whether Dell can apply the DM to the service market. Kevin Rollins, Dell's President, thinks so. He believes that the DM is not just about producing inexpensive boxes, but is a key principle to keeping Dell intimately connected with its customers. This intimate relationship allows Dell to continue delivering precisely what customers want at a lower cost than its competitors. Time will tell.

Next Step?

What's next for Dell? Scott McNealy, CEO of Sun Microsystems, once talked about Dell this way: "Dell doesn't make computers. They're not in the PC industry any more than Safeway is in the food manufacturing business."[16] On the other hand, Michael Dell considers Dell to be a broad computer systems and services company. This means that his competitors are not only in the PC industry, but also include other service giants such as IBM, EDS, and HP. Dell summarized the key leverage points of his approach in 1998:

> *"You actually get to have a relationship with the customer. And that creates valuable information, which, in turn, allows us to leverage our relationships with both suppliers and customers. Couple that information wit technology, and you have the infrastructure to revolutionize the fundamental business models of major global companies."[17]*

Southwest Airlines[18]
Think Small

Before the tragic events of September 11, 2001, Southwest Airlines (SWA) was the sixth largest airline in the U. S. Only one year later, SWA was "valued at $10.8 billion, more than all the other majors combined,"[19] and is currently the most profitable airline in the industry, expanding its routes and hiring people while the other top five airlines either filed bankruptcy or faced massive losses. As of August 5, 2003, SWA became the largest airline in terms of originating passengers carried (6.5 million pm).[20]

Perhaps what is most revealing about SWA were Kelleher's thoughts right after the tragedy. Kelleher recalls:

> *"The first thing on my mind, quite honestly, was the well being of our crews and our passengers. Are we getting the airplanes down safely? Do we know where everyone is? Are we taking care of them? The second thing was, just instantly, this is an economic catastrophe which is going to have widespread effects for a long time to come and survivability is going to depend on cash. So cash is king! Forget profitability. Get all the cash that we can, so we went out and borrowed a billion dollars because I figured this was going to be a war of attrition. Whoever had the most cash could last the longest."*

Kelleher's genuine concern for his people and for SWA's ability to survive are the twin pillars of his success. His concern for people led to a *value-centered culture* that has always provided job security for employees. This establishes a collective identity for the airline's 36,000 employees, bridges the divide of work and family and creates principle-based relationships.

The concern for survivability led to its unusual *market strategy*, marked by unpredictability and patience; its *service mentality* and long term partnership with all of its extended families based on inclusion; and finally, *low cost, flexibility, and speed*, leverage points that have propelled SWA to become the most successful airline today.

Kelleher summarizes his whole philosophy of leverage in two words: *"Think small."*

A Value-Centered Culture

We mentioned in Chapter One that SWA is one of those rare companies that has a strong collective identity because of the vision, purpose, and values (VPVs) shared among its people. The shared VPVs are the basis for the airline's unusual close-knit and family-like culture, which provides three aspects of leverage: the power of collective identity, efficiency derived from bridging the work and family divide, and effectiveness in practicing principle-based relationships.

The Power of Collective Identity

It is almost impossible to find an employee at SWA who works mechanically by rote. SWA employees are on a mission to liberate the masses to fly. From flight attendants to back office workers, each of SWA's 35,000 employees strives to help not only the customers but also each other. It is a place where people are gathered together for a clear purpose that is beyond survival and shared by all. At SWA, organizational social capital is totally enmeshed in interpersonal relationships so that people work together to co-create a meaningful future. SWA's powerful collective identity as crusaders is a powerful motivator for peak organizational performance. SWA employees willingly work more hours than employees in the same position in other airlines and accomplish more, too. For instance, SWA flight attendants clean the plane after each flight rather than relying on costly third-party cleaning crews. Why? Because the employees of SWA have a tremendous trust that their efforts will be rewarded by the airline's leadership. Ron Ricks, Vice President for Government Affairs, sums up the situation:

> *"I think that the people in management in Southwest Airlines, following Herb's lead, understand that we are stewards. It's not our company, it's not our money. We are managing this enterprise and taking care of people's money. We're taking care of people's education for their children; we're taking care of people's retirement.*

We're taking care of people's livelihoods and there's a tremendous responsibility that goes with that."

An organization with a strong collective identity helps every single person in the organization align his or her personal purpose to the organization's higher purpose. SWA's crusader identity channels everyone's energy in the same direction, creating a tidal wave that the airline leverages against its competitors. While other airlines may offer standard service, few can offer the enthusiasm, innovation, and utter joy that SWA employees display everyday on the job.

High Performance from Bridging Work and Family

While a strong collective identity gives employees extra motivation, it also allows employees to fully maintain their individuality. At SWA, the management team is interested in the whole person, which includes a person's family and personal issues. Kelleher likes to tell people at SWA that: "You can be whole. You don't have to be fragmented. You don't have to be segmented. It's the whole person we like, it's the whole person we hired, it's the whole person we want to give freedom to and that's it." The principle of *wholes within a whole* is a true characterization of the airline's trusting culture.

Because the management at SWA is very aware of the whole person, it is the recognized leader in the airline industry for its scheduling flexibility, allowing front line employees to trade shifts and juggle schedules to meet family obligations without sacrificing work commitments. Since employees must use their workplace relationships to negotiate schedule trades, both workplace and family relationships are strengthened. Kelleher sums it up this way:

> *"We really exert ourselves to help out with family problems. In other words, we exert ourselves to help employees with problems they have outside the workplace unconnected with work, but we also exert ourselves to help their families."*

Because employees see the airline demonstrating its caring all the time, work is no longer just work. Working at SWA is like working for one's extended family. Many companies talk abot employees as an extended family, but at SWA it's really true. The result is a high-performance workforce that competitors are hard-pressed to imitate.

Effectiveness from Principle-Based Relationships

In employee relationships, just as in family relationships, heated arguments and disagreements flare up, which is no surprise given the heavy time and schedule pressures under which SWA employees constantly operate. To maintain a high level of performance while still caring for employees' personal needs, SWA created a set of *Basic Principles* for guiding relationships:

1. Focus on the situation, issue, or behavior, not on the person.
2. Maintain the self-confidence and self-esteem of others.
3. Maintain constructive relationships with your employees, peers, and managers.
4. Take initiative to make things better.
5. Lead by example.

An excellent example of how these principles are put into practice is the method SWA uses to resolve conflicts between employees. Whenever such conflicts arise, SWA leaders bring all involved parties together for a face-to-face session. Conflicts are resolved with open and honest communication. While bringing employees together who are often assigned to different SWA locations around the country can be time-consuming and require a great deal of effort, it also creates a strong bond among employees. Ron Ricks summarizes the effects of principle-based relationships:

"Time and time again the standard is, 'What the best thing is for our employees, shareholders, and customers?' If you have that framework, what's the right thing to do, then it makes the decision-making process a lot easier. You don't have internal politics or being afraid to express yourself. You just have to step out there and express yourself. Time and time again what I think Colleen has done such a magnificent job of is recognizing employees' contributions. So in terms of the popular culture within the

company, so to speak, there are all these success stories where people are celebrated, recognized, and rewarded so that that serves as a lesson to other employees that that's the kind of behavior we want you to emulate. It's not just, 'Thank you very much...'"

As a result of practicing principle-based relationships, SWA has had very few labor problems throughout its history, even though it is the most unionized workforce in its industry. It also has the most productive workforce in the airline industry with its pilots flying more hours than pilots from any other airlines. In fact, SWA employees are so interested in on-time performance that pilots have been known to help ground crews load luggage. Pilots in other airlines, on the other hand, are prohibited from crossing their job boundaries. SWA mechanics can change an airplane tire faster than their counterparts at other carriers.

Market Strategy

SWA's strategy for entering new market can be characterized by three fundamental principles: filling in, unpredictability, and patience.

Filling in

With its low cost structure and precise formula, SWA can go into almost any new market, with sufficient density, and be profitable. However, it actually spends the bulk of its expansion resources on existing routes in order to build a solid foundation every step of the way. Kelleher explains:

"We always take care of what we have before we venture into new territory. In other words, we always survey our existing markets. For example, we may say that the load factor of that market is too high. We may not be serving everyone as we should, especially Fridays and Sundays. Many airlines in this situation will raise fares. We don't, we increase flights. There is another factor, if you look at any city-pair market, there is very little temptation for another carrier to come in on the basis that the market is underserved. We don't leave any holes where somebody might say

'Gee, that market might need more flights' for we make sure that market is saturated. We are constantly adding flights and reducing fares. So a lot of our airplanes are used for that purpose. And as a rule of thumb, with some variability from year to year, approximately 75% of our incremental capability is used to serve our existing routes. And only 25% is used to go into new cities."

In this sense, SWA and Wal-Mart share a striking similarity in using the "filling in" marketing strategy. Wal-Mart, as shown earlier, always fills in all the markets within one day's reach of its distribution center while venturing into new territory with care.

Unpredictability

Being Irish, Kelleher likes to swim upstream. By getting the first SWA plane off the ground, despite rampant legal battles, Kelleher already beat the odds, but there's more. Unlike almost any organization today, SWA has managed to offer its employees complete job security. To stay nimble and ahead of the competition, Kelleher keeps a sharp eye out for his competitors' predictable patterns of behavior, especially their reactions to certain types of information he releases to the media. Kelleher gives an example of the way he thinks: "This is the way he thinks about it. Everybody in the analytical community thinks tht if we do this we're going to be jumped. Mm-mm. We're not because he doesn't regard this part of his territory as sacred."

In general, Kelleher tries to put himself in other people's shoes as a way to anticipate their strategic moves. He says,

"Putting yourself in other people's shoes is very helpful. Now let me see, if I were running his company what would I be thinking about, what would I be focusing on, what would I be planning? It's just an enormous process…the process is very difficult to define because it is a process, an ongoing process and one which never should come to an end. It's not like a project. It's not like you say, 'We're going to build this and we're going to finish it next Thursday.' It's just something that tumbles on endlessly. It's totally dynamic and if it's not dynamic it's nothing."

In this process, Kelleher realized that most people have highly predictable personalities, which makes his job easier. Other people, however, have a much harder time getting a bead on Kelleher, who jokes that his Irish personality and love of drink makes him hard to predict. He adds,

"Many places it's been helpful to us because they have tried to predict us based on the way they think, and it had nothing to do with the way we think. I'll give you an example. When other airlines all threw us out of the computer reservation systems, all the travel agents had to write out tickets—handwrite tickets. The American Society of Travel Agents came to me and said, 'This is just a horrible situation. You've got to get back into these computer reservation systems' and I said, 'No, we're going ticketless. If we don't have tickets you don't have to write one.' Then I said [to myself], 'How do we do this?' But we did do it."

Patience

SWA has learned not to expand faster than its infrastructure and culture can tolerate. Unlike other airlines, which are driven to capture market share, SWA knows that its expansion is limited by its ability to maintain a value-centered, principle-based culture. In terms of expansion, SWA is also concerned about how each new city-pair will fit into the overall network, not just the earning potential. Kelleher explains the basic reason SWA can be patient:

"We're talking about new cities, OK? Over the years we have evolved a formula, which predicts exactly what kind of traffic we're gonna get at the fare level we're going to offer, from the flights we're gonna fly. You know that the fares are going to be 50 or 60% lower on average. It's not quite the strain that you otherwise might have, because you basically can say that any one of these cities we go into is going to be successful. It's a question of ranking them in terms of opportunity cost, but if you go in with 50-60% lower fares, better service, more frequency for people's convenience,

and people that are more welcoming to passengers, I think you're going to do OK whenever you enter them."

Service Mentality

When SWA enters a city, it increases the number of flights, and as it gets additional passengers, it cuts fares further. These two factors create a synergistic effect resulting in a dramatic increase in the number of customers who want to fly. Kelleher emphasizes that an additional, less tangible, factor also contributes to the skyrocketing number of passengers—SWA's excellent service quality. He explains:

> *"I am talking about the attitude of our people. You cannot discount that. It is not quantifiable like other factors, but it is there and exceedingly powerful. That's what I call the third force [in addition to more flights and lower fares]—excellent customer service, not just on-time performance, but a welcoming attitude and hospitalable quality on the part of our people."*

SWA is legendary for its service, which is known to be fun, kind, and loving. The leadership at SWA constantly communicates to employees that happy, satisfied and loyal internal and external customers are at the foundation of their job security. Kelleher illustrates this point with respect to internal customers with an example:

> *"We ask our finance department, 'Do you know who your customers are?' The rest of Southwest Airlines. You are a service department. If you treat somebody badly in maintenance, and maintenance communicates that to someone who is repairing an airplane, that's not a good thing for Southwest Airlines. So we want you to hire the way everyone else hires. We want you to hire people who are affirmative, outgoing, having the capability of enlisting themselves in something beyond themselves, and it's just as important that you do it in the accounting department as it is that we do it with the flight attendants."*

In fact, Colleen Barrett likes to say: "SWA is a service company which happens to be in the airline industry." Is it any wonder that customers always get extraordinary service from SWA?

A Company of Families

SWA is well-known for being a company of families. At SWA headquarters, the walls are filled with mementos of employees at various company events. These mementos help people relive their fondest memories at SWA and lift their spirits. They also provide a glimpse of SWA's primary value of *inclusion*. SWA is an inclusive place to work, not only for the SWA family, but for its extended family members including its vendors and partners. Colleen Barrett, the unofficial *Chief Culture Officer* and the inspiration behind this inclusive philosophy, elaborates:

> *"This is something I'm really very proud of. I really brag on this a lot, because I think it's so important. The spouses of our employees, when they talk about Southwest, will almost always say 'we.' My son would say 'we.' He's never worked at Southwest. You know, there is that warm partnership—the partnership from the heart versus the partnership from the pocketbook."*

Barrett goes on to describe how many people who do contract work for SWA tell her that they would rather work with SWA than just about any other company because the employees are fun, efficient, and productive. Says Barrett:

> *"It gives you a great sense of pride. It doesn't have anything to do with me. They love our people, they love working with these people. We get that a lot of places. We have all kinds of people that work for us as contractors in one way or another and then they want to come on board. They take huge cuts in salary to do it because they want to be really part of the group as opposed to sort of an outsider looking in."*

In fact, the feeling of inclusion is so predominant at SWA that the airline rarely needs to conduct formalized customer surveys or studies. SWA customers and passengers feel so proprietary about the airline that they readily volunteer suggestions and ideas without any prompting from the airline. Customers also provide immediate feedback when something isn't to their liking, and they know they will get an immediate response. Barrett describes SWA's unique relationship with its customers:

> *"I think because of the kind of operation that we have, we're almost a commuter airline so people live on our airplanes. It's not a matter of someone flying us maybe every six months. They know our operation as well as we do, and when that happens we are faces with names—we aren't just airline people or employees. So if they see something that they don't like or if they question some new process or procedure, I mean they feel very proprietary about it. Whether they are shareholders or not they are very free to express their opinions and they know they will get an answer."*

Although the SWA workforce is heavily unionized, represented by such traditional unions as the Transport Workers Union, the International Brotherhood of Teamsters, and the International Association of Machinists, its labor relationships are some of the most successful in the airline industry history. The key reasons for such harmony in these relationships, which are often marred in other companies by hostility and wariness, are mutual trust and respect. Whenever SWA negotiates with the unions, management always tries to put as much money on the table as possible. However, SWA always resists offering special perks and favors, choosing instead to focus on the fairer "profit sharing" method to distribute its gains. Ron Ricks has this to say about the issue:

> *"Herb and the other senior leaders here in the company, including Colleen and Jim Parker and Gary Kelly, our Chief Financial Officer, knew that the profit sharing plan was a cornerstone of our corporate culture, share and share alike. Win, we all win. Lose, we all lose. The traditional labor union approach to pension*

*plans is you lose, I win. You win, I win more. It doesn't matter.
There is no correlation between the success of the enterprise and
the bottom line as far as the individual is concerned."*

While the negotiations are not always harmonious, the respect
and trust have always created mutual satisfaction. Jim Wimberly,
Executive Vice President of Operations, commented on the airline's
mostly smooth labor relationship:

*"But then they are part of our family, too. A lot of our unions are
led by and created by employees. Our pilot union is not affiliated
with any national union; all the elected officers of our pilots union
are pilots, our co-workers. Same with our dispatcher's union, same
with our flight instructor's union. You're all dealing with your
coworkers so you don't have that same antagonistic relationship.
Even with national unions like the Teamsters or the Transport
Workers Union or the Machinist Union, basically we try to have
the same kind of relationship with their leadership as we do with
our fellow family members, even though they are not employees."*

In fact, SWA gets along with its unions so well that it has had
only two strikes i its entire history, one lasting three days and another
lasting just three hours. Says Wimberly, "That goes back to Herb.
Herb treats the union with the same respect, the same care he has for
a Jack Welch versus someone who delivers his newspaper everyday.
He has that same kind of connection, the same kind of relationship
with the union leadership that he does with employees."

SWA proactively builds partnerships with suppliers, such as airports
and FAA's Air Traffic Controllers, demonstrating the same inclusive
loyalty that it does with its employees. For instance, SWA only buys
Boeing 737 jets for simplicity in fleet maintenance and staff training.
SWA enjoys such a close relationship with Boeing that the airline
jointly developed the 737-700 model with Boeing, and is usually the
first airline to launch new Boeing 737 models. SWA pilots regularly
visit Air Traffic Controllers, bringing them hamburgers and talking
with them to develop the personal relationships that are crucial to
communication on the job. With any of the airports it flies to, SWA

strives to work with airport personnel on issues that are mutually of interest. For example, Kelleher shared with me that after the September 11th tragedy, the airline spent millions purchasing security machines and increasing security staff to ease the traffic flow at airports, without knowing whether the federal government would reimburse it.

The stories of the SWA inclusion principle in action are endless. By integrating its suppliers, unions, airports, and even Air Traffic Controllers into its extended family, SWA effectively extends its sphere of influence over its entire value chain, including all the people and organizations that support it in delivering ever better performance.

Low Cost Structure and Speed

A few years ago, when SWA entered the Albuquerque-Phoenix market, Kelleher predicted that the fight with another airline in the area would be short and sweet. "There's no way. They can't afford to fight this battle," he said. SWA had such a strong balance sheet and such low overall costs that the other carrier simply could not compete and faced little alternative but to leave the market. Statistics show the advantage of SWA's low cost structure. For example, its cost per seat mile is 7.5 ¢,[21] lowest in the airline industry for equivalent stage length, and its aircraft spend an average of 10.9 hours per day in action,[22] the highest in its industry.

The top leaders at SWA share a philosophy that it's absolutely imperative to have a quick response capability. Kelleher gave an example:

> *"On one occasion, another carrier had put in a fare that was an entirely new fare—a new type of fare in the industry. We were trying to decide how to respond to it so I had everybody come in at 8 o'clock and we sat down and one of the participants said: 'Well, it will probably take us, you know, two weeks to study it and think about it, so forth and so on.' My response was: 'Well, I've ordered lunch and I've ordered dinner, and we're not leaving this room until we reach a decision.' It was made two hours later at 10 o'clock. In other words, my experience is that the best decisions are normally made quickly. The worst decisions are those that you*

agonize over, that you spend years studying, and many times the opportunity to do anything is really gone."

He sums up by saying, "If we are quick, if we are low cost, if we have a strong balance sheet, then we're ready to do anything that pops up at anytime. And we do leverage that."

Think Small

Kelleher likes to quote Winston Churchill, who said, "Remember, success is never final." On many occasions, he has tried to instill a sense of urgency in SWA employees, reminding them not to take success for granted. In one of his key speeches, he provided many examples of people who took things for granted and suddenly found themselves at the bottom of the heap. One of these examples is the race for the America's Cup, which the U. S. had won for 101 years. Having had such a long winning streak, the U. S. team took success for granted. They lost that year. Kelleher believes that while it is hard to get to the top, it is even harder to stay there. He said: "The biggest threat to our continued success is for us to take it for granted. There is no more dangerous point than being successful."

Kelleher believes that the bigger a company gets, the harder it is to fight the bureaucracy and preserve the original entrepreneurial spirit. For example, at SWA the management structure is restricted to five layers between frontline employees and CEO. Kelleher summarizes his philosophy of always being alert and utilizing resources efficiently by saying:

*"Think small and act small, and we will get bigger.
Think big and act big, and we will get smaller."*

Put it another way, when you think small, you must leverage. A good example is that SWA has always been a contrarian airline. For example, it was the first airline to forsake the spoke-and-hub system, it uses only one kind of airplane, it prefers smaller regional airports such as Love Field or Midway, it has no assigned seating (first come, first serve), and it does not serve meals. By promoting efficiency, cutting costs everywhere, and keeping things simple, SWA is able to turn its airplanes around in less than 25 minutes and keep its fares low. By being non-traditional, SWA transforms its competitors' assets, suh as large fleets of mixed airplanes, the spoke-and-hub system and big airports, into disadvantages.

"Think small" has been the guiding philosophy at SWA over the last 30 years. Thinking small keeps the temptation to rapidly expand infrastructure and personnel at bay. Other airlines, unable to think small, have failed time and again to emulate SWA's successful formula. Consider SWA's legendary 25 minute average turnaround time, compared to industry standard of 55 minutes. This 30 minute difference alone represents a savings in investment of about $5. billion for SWA.[23] This number is calculated by a savings of 1,350 operating hours fro approximately 2,700 turnarounds per day. With about 12 hours of operating time for each aircraft per day, this savings is the equivalent to 112 Boeing 737-700 planes at a cost of around $50 million.

For other airlines to emulate SWA, they would have to renounce several industry standards, including the spoke and hub system, assigned seating and substantial distribution of tickets through agents. Additionally, they would have to adopt a philosophy of simplicity, including a uniform aircraft fleet. Most importantly, though, they would have to move to a freedom-oriented (instead of control-oriented) culture, which would leverage the employees' initiative to "do the right thing" to satisfy customers. In other words, they would have to tear everything down and start building from scratch. Few have the courage to do that, and courage is what SWA has had from the very beginning.

The Southwest Effect

The philosophy of thinking small has led to the notion of the *Southwest Effect*, coined by the U. S. Department of Transportation,[24] which characterizes the net effect when SWA enters a market: fares are reduced by an average of 65%, and passenger traffic is increased by at least 30%. This is a result of bringing together the multiple forces of a value-centered culture, a market strategy of fillng in, legendary customer service, and low cost structure and speed to create a tidal wave which results in the Southwest Effect (see Figure 3.7).

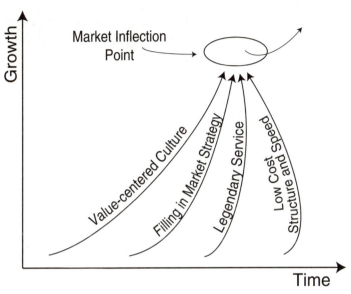

Figure 3.7 The Southwest Effect.

Kelleher explains:

"We have gone into markets which are considered too small by traditional measures. And we have improved the traffic by 800% within one year. The Providence-Baltimore route is an example of this. It was a city with 100,000 passengers and by the end of the first year, it produced more than 800,000 passengers. In many cases, the market does not look viable for additional services based on historic passenger traffic. But with the enormous stimulus we bring, we can tell that it is a much bigger market than it was thought to be. Let me give some extreme examples. We have increased a market as much as 1200% and in one case 2,000% within the first year. In the case of Baltimore-Cleveland, it was about 1,200%. But Baltimore-Chicago was about 2,000%. While these are outliers just to give some examples of what can

happen, a 300-400% increase in traffic in any given city-pair market is not at all unusual when we go into it."

Kelleher and the people at SWA are always looking for resources, both internally and externally, to leverage so that the minimum effort will yield the maximum effect.

Finding the Long Lever

The stories of Wal-Mart, Dell, and SWA discussed in this chapter bear great similarity to each other. All three started from nothing, all have become the best and most profitable companies in their respective industries, and leverage has played a crucial role for all of them. Internally, each has a unique value-centered business model that aligns employees and processes/technologies to its goals. Externally, each is virtually integrated with customers, suppliers, and partners. Furthermore, all three companies are able to leverage their competitors' assets, transforming those assets into disadvantages.

Their strategies follow the same three basic steps discussed in the introduction:

1. *Identify what resources you need and where are they in your environment, regardless where they are located.* Dell understood the disadvantages of having middlemen: less profit, delays, inability to predict customer needs accurately, and greater inventories. Dell was able to leverage the middlemen of their competitors, however, to great advantage. Similarly, SWA understood the disadvantages of having the spoke-and-hub system, and leveraged the point-to-point system to its advantage.

2. *Understand the predictable patterns in and around the players that affect the resources.* Although major airlines have challenged SWA over the years, even going so far as setting up separate divisions specifically designed to compete with SWA, Kelleher has remained successful by leveraging SWA's low cost structure and efficient delivery process. Similarly, competitors of Dell and Wal-Mart may try to copy the outer form, but remain unsuccessful in distilling the essence of these masterful companies.

3. *Create a channel or new space to redirect those resources for your own use.* When some Wal-Mart stores began

posting Kmart's weekly specials at the front of the stores, promising to match or beat Kmarts weekly deals, Wal-Mart successfully leveraged Kmart's advertising assets—turning it to Kmart's disadvantage. Customers shopped at Wal-Mart instead.

The business strategies of leverage described in this chapter are very much akin to standard military strategies. For example, when Wal-Mart focused on rural America with communities as small as 5,000 people, it was practicing the principles of guerrilla warfare by taking unoccupied territories. Dell, on the other hand, was flanking IBM and Compaq with the new business model of going direct. SWA just wanted to start an intra-state airline but was immediately attacked from all sides by its competitors and forced to stay grunded for four years before making its first flight. But when it did take off, it adopted both the guerrilla and flanking approaches by using small regional airports and offering low fares. All three companies, however, were relentless in defending their turf, constantly skirmishing with themselves to improve efficiency and lower costs. When opportunities arose, they never hesitated to attack a competitor's weakness head-on, using concentrated forces to overwhelm the opponent at any single point to gain increased market share, especially during economic downturns. Table 3.1 provides a summary of some military principles and leverage points.[25]

	Defense	Offense	Flanking	Guerrilla
Principles	To block competitive moves; to attack self.	To attack the weakness of others; focus on a narrow front.	Surprise; uncontested area; fast follow up.	Start with a small, unoccupied niche.
Leverage Points	Internal strength; relationships.	Internal strength; relationships.	New model; new technology; new market.	Not on radar screen of others.

Table 3.1 Military strategies and their leverage points.

These companies are masters of leverage and they share some common characteristics:

1. They understand that knowing the customers is the foundation for creating value. All forms of leverage are deployed for delivering value to customers and other stakeholders.

2. They maintain a deep, singular focus on their business model.

3. They stay on the offensive all the time, using different strategies as they evolve.

4. They look for leverage everywhere.

5. They are willing to experiment—always sharpening their swords.

6. They are patient but quick to enter new markets when opportunities present themselves.

7. They have the courage to be contrarians—they are more interested in doing the right thing than fitting in.

These characteristics have empowered the best companies to bring multiple forces of leverage together in new markets. They create a tidal wave effect, a *market inflection point*, when they enter a new market, which greatly spurs additional growth in the market while also drastically reducing prices. These companies have value-centered business models and cultures that create value for customers first, and then for all other stakeholders. They also have innovative market entry strategies. For Wal-Mart, it's the small town strategy, while Dell waits for technology standardization. SWA's formula focuses on city-pairs and network traffic. For all three companies, constant innovation, low cost, and efficient delivery systems are the cornerstones of their conservative, "think small" business models. While these forces are different for different companies or industries, the essence is the same.

The Art of Leverage often dictates making choices that are drastically different from what is expected. These leaders have all committed themselves to very different paths through their distinct new business models, their convictions, their focus and their willingness to act. They all face uncommon criticism and challenges as they evolve to greatness. It seems fitting to end this chapter with the following verse from Robert Frost's poem *The Road Not Taken*:

> *"I shall be telling this with a sigh*
> *Somewhere ages and ages hence;*
> *Two roads diverged in a wood, and I—*
> *I took the one less traveled by,*
> *And that has made all the difference."*

IV

The Art of Mastery

"As it acts in the world, the Tao
Is like the bending of a bow.
The top is bent downward;
The bottom is bent up.
It adjusts excess and deficiency
So that there is perfect balance."
—Lao Tzu—

Cycling legend Lance Armstrong began making world-class championships a habit at the tender age of thirteen when he won the Iron Kids Triathlon. Later discarding the running and swimming aspect of the triathlon in favor of pure cycling, he went on to become a major contender until he was literally forced off his bike in sheer pain during a training session in October 1996. Tests later revealed that Armstrong had developed advanced testicular cancer, which had already spread to his stomach, lungs, and brain. While doctors offered little hope of recovery, Armstrong's wife knew better. She hung his bicycle in front of his bed so he could see it every waking moment. Armstrong miraculously recovered, driven by the sheer will to ride again. He went on to win the most grueling endurance test in the cycling world—the Tour de France—a stunning five times in a row.

While Armstrong undoubtedly trains hard, 4–8 hours a day in rugged conditions much of the year, his mastery comes not primarily from his physical stamina and mental discipline, but from his heart. His depth of character and incredible fairness, balanced with a tough competitive spirit, shows through in all that he does. For instance, when one of his major competitors, Jan Ullrich, lost control of his bike and slid 20 feet down into a roadside ravine during one stage of the 2002 Tour, Armstrong simply waited until Ullrich was back on his bike before proceeding.

What defines Armstrong as a master in a field of many winners is his pursuit of *inner perfection* rather than outer achievement. In this race against the ultimate competitor—himself—he is engaged in the never-ending pursuit of balance and discipline, of "the edge." Lance Armstrong illustrates that a master is measured not by his external achievements, but rather by the inner passion of his heart and the stillness of his mind.

Mastery—the very word evokes scenes of samurai warriors, Zen monks, and Aikido fighters emerging from the mists of time. For many of us, mastery can seem a distant concept that is reserved for the elite among us, unreachable to "the rest of us." We see mastery in action in our sports heroes and in movies. We may have even tasted mastery ourselves, in a highly inspired moment here or there—on the golf course, in business, or in life. But when we try to define mastery as a working, active principle by which we can guide our lives, we often come up short.

It is fitting that entire books dedicated to the subject have failed to define mastery in concise terms. Mastery, like Tao, cannot be neatly captured and dissected by words and phrases, but must instead be tasted, sampled, and experienced, then stored in memory as an internal yardstick.

A Metaphor

Like much esoteric knowledge, mastery is best glimpsed through metaphors and examples. Borrowing a metaphor from the movie Hero,[1] in which the Emperor of Chin discovers the three ascending levels of swordsmanship, gives us an insight into the Art of Mastery:

Level 1—Sword and Man are One: The warrior has perfected his bond with his sword. Wherever his thoughts take him, his sword automatically follows. At this level, the swordsman's body is in sync with his sword. The swordsman at this level is often victorious.

Level 2—Sword in Mind, No Sword in Hand: The warrior no longer needs a particular sword to triumph, any tool will suffice. He has learned to use his mind as the sword. This leads to victory under almost any conditions.

Level 3—No Sword in Hand or Mind: The warrior has achieved true mastery, through which he "wins without fighting," the highest form of Sun Tzu's art. This ultimately creates win-win resolutions for all parties involved.

These three levels of mastery in swordsmanship illustrate increasing degrees of balance for the swordsman. At the first level, the swordsman's body is highly balanced with his sword. This level of intimacy is demonstrated by some of the best professional sports players, such as Michael Jordan with basketball and Tiger Woods with golf. Artists and musicians have similar experiences. Witnesses recall legendary cellist Pascal Casal being so weak that could hardly get out of bed during his last years. However, whenever he sat in front of his cello, he was transformed into a different person, sitting erect and gracefully drawing sweet music from his cello. He became one with his cello, possessing full awareness of himself and his cello. Clearly, these masters have tremendous discipline, but they also have talent, a key ingredient that elevates masters beyond mere winning.

At the second level, the swordsman is detached from his weapon, viewing it as only an expression of his mind. This level of proficiency was exhibited by the legendary samurai Miyamoto Musashi. Born in 1584, Musashi has long been revered in Japan as Kensei, or "Saint of the Sword." One of his most notorious battles, which took place on Funashima Island, was with the equally famous swordsman Kojiro. The tale tells of how Kojiro, fighting with his famous and historical long sword, was nevertheless defeated by Musashi, who had as his only weapon a wooden sword carved from an oar during his two hour boat ride to the island.

Wisely choosing not to become attached to any particular weapon, Musashi is famous for his philosophy, "One should have no preference of the weapon to be used."[2] He was also dedicated to the path of sword and willing to give his life in discovering its truth. As such, he was able to attain the state of "void," a state in which he achieved a sharp awareness not only of his own balance in body, mind, and emotion, but also his environment and opponent. In this state of heightened awareness, freed of all mental and emotional burdens, he flowed with the forces of nature, guided by pure instinct. In the purity of the void, he knew his opponent's every move, blocking each move before it was even initiated. On the attack, he followed the path of least resistance and struck at his opponent's fatal weakness. Musashi was known for his ability to apply the right force at exactly the right time and place—precision without apparent effort.

At the third level, the swordsman's awareness rises to connect with his ultimate purpose (his Tao) and he operates in total harmony and balance with nature. This level of mastery transcends the ordinary physical, mental, and emotional realms and stretches into the spiritual realm. This is the wisdom of Sun Tzu, the ancient legendary Chinese military strategist, who taught that "the best strategist wins without fighting." This philosophy demonstrates Sun Tzu's ability to see any situation in its entirety, in its wholeness. Seeing the whole stretches a person's awareness to include all possibilities, allowing new possibilities, not available with traditional thinking to arise. While military strategy deals with disharmony, Sun Tzu sees a level beyond mere conflict resolution, a level at which conflict is altogether unnecessary. Win-win solutions, unavailable within the confines of conflict resolution, are the mark of true masters. Indeed, for Lance Armstrong to wait for his archrival Jan Ullrich to recover from his fall before proceeding, raises the competition beyond the sense of conflict. The Tour de France becomes a platform for Armstrong's own inner perfection. Masters at this level simply *surrender* to their Tao.

Both Musashi and Sun Tzu achieved what is considered impossible at the lower levels of awareness, reaching ever finer dimensions of physical, mental, emotional, and spiritual balance. At each level of mastery, the bar is raised and a new dimension of balance is added. Most professional managers today have excellent training and discipline, but operate at the level of "sword in hand but not in mind." In other words, they work with some basic managerial principles and discipline, but lack an overall vision or strategy.

Doing the Fosbury Flop

The journey to mastery is never ending. Consider the journey of athletes in the high jump competition. Over the last century, the standard for high jumpers has consistently risen. In the early part of the 1900s, the high jump record stood at just over 6 feet. By 1990, that record had been raised to over 8 feet.[3] Between 1900 and 1990, innovative high jumpers introduced three radically different techniques, each one a vast improvement over the previous one. The last one, the Fosbury Flop, was originally ridiculed by critics who felt the technique looked sloppy and undignified, but the results were stunning. The introduction of each new technique caused the entire high jump world to shift to a new paradigm, always with a slight pause as athletes struggled to adjust themselves to the new world order. Each new technique pushed the sport to a new level, where it reached a plateau and gained maturity until the next technique was introduced.

Similarly, top organizations constantly strive for the next Fosbury Flop. Leading companies consistently see and leap to the next plateau, pausing to regain their balance as they prepare themselves for the next leap. Always, awareness and balance are the cornerstones of these great leaps.

Organizational Mastery

Mastery, as discussed above, requires both balance and a continuous drive to "raise the bar." Great masters reach a Zen-like state where everything achieves perfect synchrony. We believe that masterful companies constantly push the envelope, walking an aggressively fine line between calculated risk and utter failure, always poised in precise balance. Athletes achieve mastery by stretching their bodies, minds, and emotions to the limit while maintaining balance. As they continue the journey, they inevitably embark on a quest for internal perfection and begin the development of their spiritual dimension as illustrated by Lance Armstrong. Similarly, organizations must stretch and seek balance in the equivalent areas of infrastructure (people, resources, and capital), learning capacity (processes, knowledge and operational efficiency), and culture while simultaneously developing their spiritual component (see Figure 4.1).

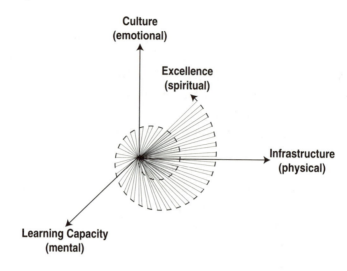

Figure 4.1 Organizational balance.

Companies on the leading edge continuously push for balanced growth and development in all three areas, but the development along each axis must be balanced and synchronous with growth in the other axes lest the whole corporation wobble and fall. For instance, companies that seek market share by rapid physical expansion without scaling up their learning capability and culture to match ultimately spin out control like helicopters with unbalanced rotors.

People's Express Airline perfectly demonstrates the results of rapid growth along a single axis. In its haste to compete with the more established airlines, People's Express pushed for rapid physical expansion without developing the foundational culture and process necessary for such growth. Founded in 1980 to provide low-cost airfare to travelers in the eastern United States, People's Express became the nation's fifth largest carrier within a short five years. Its low fares attracted more and more passengers and the airline expanded quickly, adding flights, planes, and hundreds of new employees. At that rate of growth, however, the company lacked the time and resources to provide the necessary training, cultural indoctrination, or processes to meet its mushrooming growth. As a result, customers went elsewhere, becoming tired of long wait times, poor customer service, and lack of on-time service. Texas Air Corporation eventually took over People's Express after it lost $133 million in the first half of 1986. While People's Express may have tasted the thrill of success momentarily, its rapid growth upset the delicate balance required to achieve mastery and serious financial consequences soon followed.

It should be noted that corporate growth should not only be carefully balanced among the three axes of infrastructure, learning capability, and culture but also within each axis. For instance, along the infrastructure axis, managers must weigh long-term capital investments against short-term tactical gains. The same is true of the mental aspect. For example, should the company focus on less disruptive incremental process improvement or more radical transformational changes?

Culturally, companies like HP have struggled to manage the delicate equilibrium between empowerment and alignment. For instance, early HP executives adopted a policy of openness and empowerment, giving division leaders complete authority over the kind of products to bring to market. While this policy produced fresh and innovative products early in the company's history, it became problematic as the company grew. As HP blossomed into forty separate divisions, company executives realized that many divisions were producing competing products, which confused customers and cut into HP's bottom line. While division leaders were certainly empowered with authority, they lacked the discipline and coordination to act in tandem with other division leaders. Because HP executives favored freedom and empowerment over balance, they were unable to maintain their place in the sun.

Achieving Mastery

To achieve mastery in the business world, leaders must understand how to keep their company in balance while, at the same time, push the limits of possibility. While it is possible to start anywhere, an organization usually begins by building up its physical stamina, similar to the way that athletes train. Later, the company must also develop its emotional and mental functions to reach the delicate balance required for optimum performance. Like individual masters, the path to the different levels of mastery requires different elements at each stage:

1. *Discipline and Talent:* An organization has to work hard to excel, but discipline alone often produces only the "sword in hand but not in mind" effect. An organization must have talented people with discipline in order to build a solid foundation for excellence.

2. *Passion:* An organization's people must be fired up by an internal passion for what they do. They must be bonded by a strong covenant with the company, which ties them into a united force many times more powerful than the group of workers who are organized but passionless. In this way, an organization usually achieves the level of where "sword and man are one."

3. *Wisdom:* As an organization begins its quest for internal perfection, its people develop a collective wisdom, transcending from knowledge to intuition, to move to the level of "no sword in hand, but sword in mind."

4. *Surrendering to Tao:* When an organization is living in Tao, it transcends into the spiritual dimension where it is synchronized with its destiny, winning in the material battlefields of the market, but not guided by them. When a company surrenders to its Tao, it seeks to improve the world and strives to make a difference.

Consider General Electric (GE), the company Thomas Edison founded more than 100 years ago. When Jack Welch took over the reins of the company in 1981, it was the 11th largest company in the U. S. with approximately 440,000 employees and a market value of $12 billion.[4] However, despite the outward success, GE was steadily decaying under the weight of its nine-layer hierarchy, deep functional boundaries, and high costs, all which created exceedingly low productivity of only one to two percent. GE, once the crowning glory of American industry, had become a slumbering giant, joining the ranks of General Motors and IBM in the late 1970s. In other words, the company lost its mastery and was only a mechanical version of its former spirit.

Undaunted by these inauspicious circumstances, Welch leapt to the challenge and transformed GE into a lean, agile, global company of the 21st century. He first defined a new vision for GE:

1. Become number one or two in every market GE serves.

2. Integrate diversity.

3. Erase boundaries.

He pursued this vision by first making GE physically fit, reducing its levels of hierarchy, cutting costs, and shedding non-performing businesses. With this ruthless push, he began awakening the sleeping giant, restoring it back to its original, lean fighting form.

Shortly after, he launched an ambitious ten-year cultural revolution called *Workout*, aimed at changing GE's traditional inward focus. *Workout* had the following objectives:

1. To build trust.

2. To empower employees.

3. To eliminate wasteful work.

4. To establish a new paradigm for GE.

The people chosen to participate in *Workout* were those who faced the daily problems within the organization. The program was based on the assumption that those closest to the problems were best able to solve them. *Workout* was more than just a problem-solving process; it was an attitude changing program that applied to all levels of the organization. It was a cultural revolution, the largest experiment in corporate American history. As it neared completion, Welch started the Six Sigma program to make GE much more productive through process transformation. Six Sigma improved product quality, driving all but 3.4 defects per million "parts" or "events" out of a product, process, or service. The Six Sigma process used data to determine root causes of quality problems, and then proceeded to eliminate one cause after another. It involved many initiatives conducted at all levels of an organization under trained professionals.

By the late 1990s, GE had shed many of its former core divisions and began aggressively pushing into new areas, such as financial services. In parting with many of its former core divisions, GE detached itself from its sword, moving from the level where "man and sword are one" to the next level where it held "sword in mind but not in hand." In other words, GE had learned to use its swiftness and cunning as its sword, becoming capable and willing to move into any market that served its aims.

By 1999, Welch had restored GE to its former position as master of its trade, a global company with #1 ranking businesses in 10 world markets and a market value that soared to nearly $300 billion. At the same time, the company's workforce shrank from 440,000 people to just 260,000, with productivity at consistently over five percent.[5] Figure 4.2 depicts the GE transformational process under Welch's leadership.

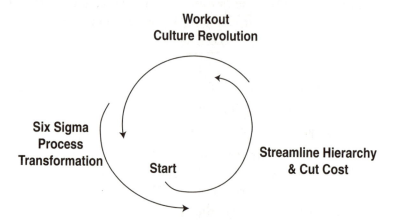

Figure 4.2 GE's transformation under Jack Welch.

The Journey to Mastery

Companies like GE, Intel, and Medtronic demonstrate that mastery comes in many forms. While there is no generic formula for mastery that can produce success for every company, it seems that the ascent up the ladder of mastery requires first discipline and talent, then passion, wisdom, and finally the willingness to surrender to Tao. Therefore, it seems that companies that maintain the balance between infrastructure, culture, and learning capability, while at the same time striving to expand and improve each component, are walking a well-traveled path toward mastery. The masterful leaders of great companies seemingly follow these three levels of mastery with consistency, demonstrating that these three levels can indeed be used as guideposts on the journey.

To start you on the journey to mastery, we offer you three very different, yet masterful organizations: Singapore, the tiny nation that transformed itself from a third-world island to an advanced nation in less than 40 years; the ULCA Bruins, the college basketball team that won 10 national championships under the guidance of legendary coach John Wooden; and Southwest Airlines, the largest, most profitable and fun-loving airline in the United States. We have selected these widely differing organizations to illustrate that, despite the diversity among them, they nevertheless reach mastery through similar processes. Enjoy!

<u>Singapore</u>[6]
Thinking Schools, Learning Nation, and
Gracious Society

The first time I visited Singapore in 1980 as a consultant to the Housing Board, I was impressed by this tiny nation's goal of having more than 70% of its people stay in housing projects. These projects, financed by individuals and their employers, empower young Singaporeans to move into apartments that they own, in drastic contrast to the rest of Asia where housing costs began to soar out of control in the late 1970s. Today, more than 90% of Singaporeans own their own homes under the auspices of the housing project.

Singapore is well known for its miraculous economic development, but this busy cosmopolitan city is far more than an economic nexus where East meets West. It is a gathering place of proud, strong, and hardworking people who have raised themselves out of the swamp of indigence, and who continually reinvent their nation in anticipation of changing world conditions. In 1879, British writer Isabella Bird sought to capture the essence of Singapore when she said, "How I wish I could convey an idea, however faint, of this huge, mingled, colored, busy, Oriental population." Bird's description, in my opinion, still holds true today.

Singapore's rate of economic development is nothing short of astonishing. The tiny island nation began as a third world country with a per capita GNP of less than US$320 in 1961. By the end of 2002, Singapore had transformed itself into an advanced developing nation with a per capita GNP of approximately US$37,000[7]; 115 times its original GNP and on par with that of the U. S. During its four-decade long economic journey, Singapore has focused on building a harmonious, politically stable, and well-regulated location for doing international business. Consistently rated as one of the top ten business environments in the world and one of the best places for offshore manufacturing, Singapore demonstrates that size does not limit the creation of wealth.

A city-state of more than four million people, Singapore is ideally located at the crossroads of international air and sea trading routes in the Asia-Pacific, one of the most dynamic areas of economic development in the 21st century. Singapore's current strategy is to become the "Grand Central Station of the global economy," acting as the central Asian hub for tourism, manufacturing, communication, and finance. Playing the role of business architect for its customers—both local and multinational corporations—the Singaporean government helps companies develop and grow their businesses in international markets, using Singapore as a home base. Says George Yeo, Minster of Trade and Industry,

> *"If the world is a network and you need to plug in at the most convenient point where the bandwidth is greatest, it would be Singapore. We are your most convenient plug-in point in Southeast Asia."*[8]

When Singapore began the process of economic transformation, however, the situation was much less ideal. Because of its tiny size, Singapore could not use other developing nations as a blueprint for growth. It lacked the advantages of most other industrialized nations, such as raw materials, large home markets, well-developed industrial skills, or strong education systems. In fact, Singapore's only major resources were its location and its people, who had a strong desire for transformation. With an indomitable spirit, tremendous investment in its people, and an unstoppable desire to be the best, Singapore has traveled a journey that most thought to be impossible. From indigent swamp to prospering economic hub, Singapore demonstrates mastery of international trade and economics. Throughout its spectacular journey, Singapore has always managed to push the leading edge of economic development, constantly driving itself to the next plateau of development, from bare survival to turnkey industrial parks, then to a learning nation and now, toward a gracious society.

From Bare Survival to International Presence

When Kuan Yew Lee became Singapore's Prime Minister in 1959, he became the leader of a mosquito-infested swamp filled with indigent people living in crowded housing crammed amidst pig and chicken farms. Faced with a complete lack of natural resources, little infrastructure and a poorly developed educational system, Lee realized that Singapore's people were his best and only resource. Philip Yeo, Executive Chairman of the Economic Development Board (EDB), eloquently restates Lee's view:

> *"If you have no natural resources except your people and your skill, you have to compete in those terms."*

In the beginning, the Singaporean work force was so poorly educated and lacking in any real skills that the government could only set a goal of full employment. So in 1961, it set the goal of achieving full employment in labor-intensive industries. In short, the government hoped to gain a foothold in the international markets by offering the cheapest labor around. Singapore faced considerable difficulty, however, when it lost its membership in the Malaysian Federation and the British decided to close their naval bases, reducing Singapore's economy by a drastic 25%.

By 1965, though, Singapore's economy had recovered and was starting to grow. At the same time, throughout the late 1960s and 1970s, Singapore faced greater competition from neighboring countries like Malaysia and Indonesia, which were beginning to offer even cheaper labor. By then, Singapore had attracted a solid group of multinational corporations from the U.S., Japan, and Europe, which had relocated their manufacturing facilities to Singapore. But with increased competition from nearby countries, Singapore felt the need to leap to the next plateau by focusing on more capital-intensive, high tech industries and providing more value-added services beyond just labor.

In 1986, Philip Yeo, the newly appointed chairman of the EDB, was charged with upgrading Singapore's labor, infrastructure, partnerships, and business landscape to the next level. While other leaders may have been daunted by the enormity of the task, Yeo possessed the same intrepid adventuring spirit of all Singaporeans and leapt to the challenge. Here are just a few of the initiatives tackled by the EDB:[9]

- Attract multinationals and also develop local capabilities in new industry clusters such as semiconductors, chemicals, and biomedical sciences.
- Create joint ventures with Indonesia, India, and Vietnam to build industrial parks (and even a beach resort in Indonesia), which allows Singapore to offer its multinational customers turnkey manufacturing solutions with professional management and the least expense.
- Upgrade the labor force by increasing the number of graduate engineers and expanding the technical education sector.
- Promote information technology, telecommunications, publishing, and other supporting industries, thus expanding Singapore's service offerings to multinational clients.
- Develop joint ventures with multinational and local companies to create industry clusters and develop Singapore as a business and information hub.
- Promote industry to undertake more and more R&D activities in Singapore.

By the late 1980s, Singapore was secure in its new position as an international business architect. Multinational companies, attracted by the nation's upgraded labor force, corruption-free government and efficiency, relocated their regional headquarters, R&D centers, and marketing divisions to Singapore and moved their manufacturing operations into the industrial parks managed by Singapore. Having gained a new sense of security and balance in the world of international commerce, Singapore prepared itself for yet the next level: the knowledge economy.

Thinking Schools, Learning Nation

Having expanded its sphere of physical influence by joint venturing with neighboring countries, Singapore next turned its attention to developing a presence in the more intangible sphere of the knowledge economy. When Lee assumed power in 1959, he immediately began to instill in Singaporeans an obsession for learning. He recognized that education would be the key to raising the nation's population from poverty to prosperity. He also realized that to stay ahead of its competitors, Singaporeans could never stop learning. He explains:

> *"The quality of a people determines the outcome of a nation. It is how you select your people, how you train them, how you organize them, and ultimately how you manage them that make the difference."[10]*

The mission of Singapore's Education Service is "to mold the future of the nation by molding the people who will determine the future of the nation. The Service will provide our children with a balanced and well-rounded education develop them to their full potential and nurture them into good citizens, conscious of their responsibilities to family, society, and country."[11] Using the slogan, "learning to think, thinking to learn," the Singaporean government recognizes the importance of education as a basis for creativity as well as for developing an environment for the multi-disciplinary thinking necessary to fully embrace the knowledge economy.

The Raffles Girls School is one of five "thinking schools" in Singapore. Students at this school come from the top 3% of elementary schools in the country. Located at the center of town, the school sits in a quiet corner with abundance of space, a premium in Singapore. When I visited the school one afternoon, a group of teenagers was working with their partners in Canada on a zoology project. Mrs. Carmee Lim, principal of the school, told me that in order to develop leadership skills in their students, the school was breaking away from the traditional Asian "forced duck feeding" approach. Teachers encourage students to express their feelings, which is atypical in Asian societies, and foster teamwork.

The Raffles School has total autonomy in hiring its teachers and designing its curriculum. For example, instead of the traditional five-day week, the school uses an eight-day week, with students focusing on one specific subject such as math each week. The teachers are constantly learning new ways to be more effective, and many of them are sent abroad for short periods to study the "best practices" in education that stimulate creativity in students. These efforts have paid off. Singaporean students are leaders in the fields of math and science. In fact, the Third International Mathematics and Science study in 1999 ranked Singaporean students first in math achievement worldwide and second in science. Carrying that leadership to the University level, Professor Hang Chang-Chieh, Deputy Vice Chancellor of the National University of Singapore, strives to manifest his vision of making his university world-class by creating joint ventures with top-notch universities such as M.I.T., Harvard and Oxford.

In addition to these aggressive educational programs, Singapore also borrows and recruits world-class talent from other countries. Prime Minister Goh Chok Tong elaborates:

> *"The ability to attract world class talent is directly related to the future survival of Singapore."[12]*

To attract such talent, the government sends its elementary school principals to Malaysia and other countries to woo top students from those nations, offering scholarships as an incentive. The goal is to bring top students to Singapore as early as possible, increasing their chances of fitting into the culture and staying for life. High school recruiters sent to capture top Chinese talent follow the slogan, "Get them before they decide to go to Beijing University!"

At the industry level, the A*Star Agency for Science, Technology, and Research leads Singapore in the transition from a manufacturing nation to a knowledge nation. The Agency focuses on promoting science, engineering, and biomedical research, and relentlessly recruits top talent in these fields from around the globe. Philip Yeo, as head of the EDB and A*Star, leads Singapore's most recent biomedicine initiative and has recruited well-known scientists such as Alan Colman of Scotland, one of the scientists who developed Dolly, the cloned sheep; Professor Yoshiaki Ito, a world renowned stomach cancer specialist from the Kyoto University of Japan, along with his research team; and Edison Liu, director of clinical research from the U. S. National Cancer Institute and currently the executive director of the new Genome Institute of Singapore. To date, more than $1.8 billion have been committed to this aggressive initiative. The physical centerpiece of this initiative is the Biopolis, a two million square foot integrated R&D complex that provides a common environment between public and private sector researchers through the concept of "cohabitation."

As it continues to recruit foreign talent, the government is also trying to cultivate domestic talent. A*Star currently offers $286 million in scholarships for students to pursue PhDs in biomedical science at home and abroad, in exchange for their promise to work in Singapore for up to eight years. In addition, by offering tax holidays and other incentives, Singapore has had great success in attracting drug manufacturers, including well-known companies such as Merck & Company, Pfizer, and Schering-Plough. As a result of this intensive push into biotech, Singapore's pharmaceutical production increased by about 50% in 2002, to $5.56 billion, and is well on track to reach the government's goal of $7 billion by 2005.

To encourage these pharmaceutical companies to build R&D centers as well as manufacturing plants in Singapore, the government offers to pay up to 30% of the cost of building research and development facilities. Well-known industry giant Eli Lilly, along with 29 other companies, have accepted the offer. Another company, Novartis, is also building its Institute for Tropical Diseases in Singapore.

Singapore is so successful at cultivating foreign talent that it has become a micro-version of the United Nations, with one foreigner for every six people. The foreigners tend to be white-collar professionals rather than laborers, since Singapore focuses on borrowing the necessary brainpower to lead the knowledge economy. In the 1990s, foreigners contributed 41% of the nation's GDP, with 37% coming from white-collar professionals. To maintain the steady rate of recruitment, the government is also considering lowering the income tax rate from 25% to 20%. These and similar initiatives have catapulted Singapore to the next plateau, and prepared them to compete with any nation in the knowledge economy.

Strive to Be the Best

"We dare to dream" is the often-heard slogan of the Singaporean people. Like all Singaporeans, Philip Yeo is obsessed with being number one. He outlines his thinking this way:

> *"Nothing is wrong with being in the number two position, but that is not the point. The issue is about desiring to be and working at being number one. It is a mindset, a competitive spirit, not so much the absolute position we actually achieve. If we are satisfied with being number two, we will gradually slip to the 3rd position, the 5th position, then 10th and 20th and so on. Similarly, if we are presently number one and we take it for granted, we know for sure that someone will overtake us."*

The World Bank ranks Singapore as the country with the highest per capita income in the world in terms of Purchasing Power Parity. However, as Singapore becomes more prosperous, with a higher standard of living, its cost also goes up. In order to sustain this top position, Singapore must go beyond cost competitiveness and enhance the overall value it delivers to its customers. As such, Singapore consistently invests in the infrastructure that it perceives its customers will need in the near future, including the areas of education and training, technology, and innovation. This strategy has succeeded beyond all expectation. Data supplied by the EDB shows that between 1985 and 1997, the annual manufacturing investment commitments attracted into Singapore increased by nearly eight times, and the value added per worker of new manufacturing projects almost doubled between 1992 and 1997.

A key part of Singapore's excellence comes from its ability to perfectly blend traditional Confucian meritocracy with western civil service, making its government one of the most efficient and corruption-free in the world. In fact, every five years, the office of the Prime Minister selects more than twenty people from its Administrative Civil Service to enter its political arena. Mostly graduates from the National Singapore University, those chosen are immediately sent to overseas elite universities for further "fast track" education. These are future candidates for positions of chief executive, deputy minister, or minister. The Prime Minister's office has also budgeted S$10 million for encouraging new experiments to increase effectiveness and efficiency in government.

In addition, Singapore has saved and invested more than any other nation—even in the early stages of its economic development. By taking advantage of its supreme geographic location, investing heavily in infrastructure, focusing on efficient management, and responding rapidly to market changes, Singapore continues its drive for excellence.

Adapt to Constant Change

All of Singapore's successes really come from its deep commitment to economic development. For more than 40 years, Singapore's strategies for economic development have been tailored to meet her evolving needs as well as global changes. Singapore has always assumed that its future would be different from the present, so it is prepared for constant change. For example, the Public Service Division's website proclaims, "Change is the only non-changing thing. We've got to prepare for the uncertainties of the future for we do not want to be the slaves of the future world," demonstrating Singapore's continuous and urgent focus on anticipating and preparing for the future.

As part of the preparation for the future, Singapore is building "One-North," a multi-government agency effort to create a city-within-a-city where scientists, researchers, and entrepreneurs can live and work, exchanging ideas and collaborating on new research or product development. The government also initiated PS21 (Public Service for the 21st Century) in 1995. It advocates a code of conduct for people in public service that includes politeness, consideration, response, and efficiency as the core values for providing customer-oriented service. In Singapore, the boundaries between private enterprises and government agencies are becoming purposely blurred with the goal of assisting private enterprises. The government is keen to maintain its aggressive pace in terms of innovation and efficiency so that, as government employees are fond of saying, "Together, we make the difference."

As an example of the government's efficiency, everyone in government, from the Prime Minister to chief executives, uses email as the primary mode of communication. During interviews, many people spoke of receiving email from senior minister Lee as late as midnight. The most important aspect of email communication is that people get the immediate response they need, allowing them to make decisions and proceed without having to plow through interminable levels of hierarchy. This notion of non-hierarchical hierarchy,[13] initially used to describe the paradoxical relationships among the members and alumni of the EDB, is now widespread throughout Singapore's public service organizations. Every employee is expected to perform as if in a boundary-less organization, while at the same time following the traditional rules of an Asian organization in which hierarchy is dominant. As a consequence of this unusual cultural mix, each person is empowered to aggressively pursue their career but under the overall guidance of their "boss" as coach, patron and colleague.

Under the auspices of this "East meets West" government style, many top executives in the Singaporean government are simultaneously assigned multiple roles in different agencies. This practice helps leaders broaden their horizons; giving them many different perspectives and helping them make decisions that benefit all agencies. In addition, it helps every leader keep an open mind about the many different domains in government, allowing them to accept and work with a wide range of opinions.

Recognizing that central planning, the success formula for much of Singapore's economic development up to the 1980s, was a limiting strategy in the knowledge economy, Singapore began to shift to entrepreneurship in earnest in the 1990s. Entrepreneurship became a way to tap into the collective intelligence of Singaporeans to move in synchrony with the external environment. The creation of A*Star is a way to keep pace with the fast-paced knowledge economy, cultivating the necessary innovation from the entrepreneurial sector. Although the Singaporean government has done much in the past to drive the economy toward greater and greater success, it will be unable to do so in the face of the mind-boggling speed of change, the hallmark of the knowledge economy. The responsibility for innovation and change, then, falls squarely on the shoulders of the Singaporean people themselves, especially the entrepreneurs.

One of the potential obstacles to Singapore's continuing economic miracle is the shifting focus of its people. While the last two generations have developed a mindset of competitiveness as a result of the previously adverse environment, the current generation sees the world differently. The environment is no longer filled with adversity and the perceived threats in the environment are growing faint. This new generation is indeed the "me" generation and is often focused on instant gratification. How can Singapore maintain its competitive edge with the current generation's attitude? Yeo responded:

> *"The key thing is for Singaporeans to be mindful of how vulnerable Singapore is to adverse changes in the external environment. We have to work hard to get whatever we aim for. Nobody owes us a living. For this reason, we must have a 'can-do' attitude and a mindset of 'striving to be number one.'"*

Yeo doesn't see the nation's higher level of prosperity as a deterrent, so long as people maintain awareness of their past. In fact, greater prosperity provides Singaporeans with a sense of confidence, making it easier for them to upgrade themselves and develop Singapore as a global hub for knowledge driven industries. He continues, "From time to time, there is a danger of slipping into a sense of contentment and complacency. From this point of view, the Asian economic crisis is a blessing in disguise. It has brought home the realization that our past economic success and Singapore's competitiveness cannot be taken for granted. Only when we change faster than the outside world, will we continue to prosper."

The ability to adapt is clearly Singapore's key asset. The nation has cultivated top leadership capabilities in every major position in the government through its stringent process of selection, development, and empowerment, as well as a strong bond of trust between its people and the government. So long as Singapore can maintain its ability to adjust to changing world conditions at lightning speed, success will inevitably follow.

Towards A Gracious Society

Foreign travelers used to jokingly refer to Singapore as "Singa-Bored," indicating that despite its economic success, as displayed in its clean boulevards and glittering shops and low crime rate, the nation lacked soul. Fortunately, this situation is changing. For the past ten years, the government has been cultivating Singapore's presence in the world of the arts, just as it did in the worlds of economic growth and technology development. "Ballet Under the Stars" is one example. Not only does it receive 20% of its budget from the government, it also benefits from the "Home of the Arts" initiative, which allows the program to rent space in a beautiful historical site while paying only 10% of the actual rent. In fact, the National Arts Council provides subsidies of up to 90% for space in over 30 buildings for practice, studio, and administrative activities. Furthermore, the huge $600 million Esplanade Performing Arts Center, with multiple theatres on the bay, opened in October 2002 as part of a national effort to become a world capital of the arts as well as commerce.

Singapore is indeed reinventing itself once again, this time by augmenting its already stable culture with the flair and flavor of the arts. According to Yeo,

"One of the things which will propel young Singaporeans is the desire for a vibrant lifestyle. Young people want choice, variety, and fashion! They want to be hip, plugged in, on the leading edge. They want balance between work and play, excitement and new experiences. They want to be sophisticated and avant-garde. This will propel them to work and compete. We have established the clear principle that we reap what we sow. Singaporeans in ten years will still strive to be number one, because that's the way to get a more vibrant life."

It seems that Singapore, despite its small size and increasing competition from neighboring countries, will continue as a dominant presence in the world as it tirelessly pursues the goal of being number one. Relentlessly attracting top talent from around the world, cultivating a new spirit of entrepreneurship, maintaining life long learning, and using ecological thinking, Singapore is one blueprint for success that cannot be copied. Plus, with its attention newly focused on the arts, Singapore is developing the vibrant lifestyle so desired by its people. It seems that Singapore, as a society, is maturing graciously while maintaining its youthfulness. Striving to be the best is no longer just about economic development, but also includes artistic creation and the development of a "soul." Singapore, unlike so many of its competitors, is not just balanced on the edge, but walks the edge with grace and style.

Singapore's Path to Mastery

Singapore's evolutionary path to mastery, summarized in Figure 4.3, demonstrates that its infrastructure dimension is based primarily on its people, since it lacked the physical resources of other industrialized nations. In the 1960s, the founding period of the nation, it was blessed with a culture based on the traditional Confucian values of hard work and filial duty. This culture helped the Singaporean people to bond together with a determination to work towards a better future for their children.

The shaded area in Figure 4.3 delineates Singapore's initial condition, which included a strong culture but a weak physical infrastructure and a lack of knowledge, the mental aspect. Using its strong culture as a foundation, the nation set a goal of full employment by attracting labor-intensive industries. During the 1970s, western meritocracy began to take hold throughout the government, mixing with traditional values, and the government began to upgrade its labor forces to handle skilled work, attracting the manufacturing industry to Singapore. From late 1980s forward, Singapore, already a presence in the international community as a place for trade and commerce, set its sights on becoming a leader in the knowledge economy, aggressively upgrading its workforce and attracting top international talent to initiate innovative R&D activities. Today, the nation is aggressively cultivating the arts to fulfill the desire of its people to have a vibrant and hip lifestyle. Perhaps Singapore is also on its way to transcending the spiritual dimension, the ultimate mastery.

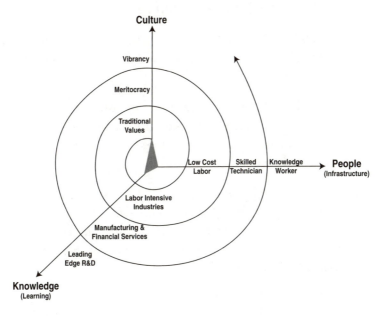

Figure 4.3 Singapore's evolutionary path to mastery.

The UCLA Bruins[14]
Be Quick but Don't Hurry

When I interviewed Coach Wooden, I was deeply impressed at how his "old-fashioned" values, common sense, and passion are so much needed in the 21ˢᵗ century.

When the UCLA Bruins played out of town games, students from the opposing school usually would bust into deafening boos to welcome the Bruins when they entered the court. Andrew Hill describes a typical scene:

> *"Then something really strange would happen: we would spend a few minutes running through the famous UCLA high-post offense. This could have looked pretty ridiculous (after all, no one was playing defense), were it not for the speed, timing, and crispness that were a trademark of Wooden's teams.*
>
> *Slowly, the booing and catcalls would die down, to be replaced by an awed silence as the capacity crowd watched this embodiment of 'Be quick—but don't hurry!' The sound of sneakers squeaking on hardwood and crisp passes slapping the palm of the outside hand of the receiver was the only sound in the arena. The crowd sat hushed as the Bruins gave a high-speed rendition of our most basic principle. What a remarkable sensation it is to experience a boisterous, obnoxious, rowdy group of fans turning their collective attention toward a carefully choreographed, high-speed dance of basketball poetry. They weren't sure why this was special, but they did know they were seeing something worth watching."[15]*

This scene, so typical of the UCLA Bruins, describes the very essence of John Wooden's formula for creating a masterful basketball team. Wooden led the UCLA Bruins to ten national college basketball championships in his last eleven years of coaching, seven of those championships occurring in a row. Unlike most of his peers, Wooden was more concerned about developing his players to their greatest life potential than winning championships. He taught the Bruins to run their own race and live in their Tao.

For Wooden, lifting the Bruins to mastery meant having them play at near peak performance as consistently as possible, regardless of the circumstances. He wanted his players to do as well in the opening game of the season as in the championship final. During his long tenure as the Bruins coach, he gradually developed a formula that empowered his players to perform at a consistently high level, a formula that included a new definition of success, practicing under pressure, a unique approach to learning, and, of course, balance, balance, balance.

Be the Best You Can Be

Unlike other college basketball coaches, Wooden never pressured his players to win. Nor did he resort to emotional appeals to motivate his players to go the extra mile during important games. Instead, Wooden coached his team with a business-like attitude, teaching them the fundamental skills necessary for high performance on a regular basis.

One of the key factors in the Bruins' success was Wooden's definition of the word success. Rather than using the traditional measure of success, the team's win/loss record, he created his own definition:

"Success is peace of mind as a result of knowing you have made the effort to do the best of which you are capable."

He notes that success, in his experience, is a byproduct of being happy or having peace of mind. While outer measures of success such as wealth or fame can be snatched away by unforeseen circumstances, the peace of mind that comes from doing one's best can never be taken away (see Chapter 5 for more details on his Pyramid of Success).

Doing one's best thus became the fundamental value of the Bruins team. By putting focus on his players' effort rather than on winning, Wooden took the pressure off, allowing the players to reach previously unheard of levels of performance. He often told his players, when they had put forth their best effort, that they had succeeded even when they lost a game. Other times, he considered winning games to be failures because his players had not demonstrated maximum effort.

Following this philosophy, Wooden has always taught his player to control those things that can be controlled, namely, their own effort, while staying detached from uncontrollable events. He often said to his players, "You can only deal with things that are under your control. Never try to be better than somebody else, but always be alert to learn from them."

Under his definition of success, each Bruins player only had to be accountable for his own effort, not for winning or losing games. Freed from the pressure to win yet motivated to do their best, the Bruins players created, as a byproduct of Wooden's unique definition of success, a long-term winning record. More importantly, each player learned a significant life lesson—the joy, peace, and success of always doing their best as a way to fulfill their own highest potential.

Practicing Under Pressure

New Bruins players often found themselves in the unique situation of feeling more pressured during practices than during actual games—and often about the oddest things. For instance, at the very first squad meeting each season, Wooden taught his players precisely how to put on their socks! Wooden knew that socks with wrinkles caused blisters that interfered with performance during practices and games. He also taught his players how to lace and tie their shoes, so they would stay tied during games and banned long hair, which interfered with a player's vision. Bruins players were constantly under pressure to learn and remember all of these seemingly ridiculous and minute details. Yet, the conscientious practice of these details produced, over time, a championship team. Says Wooden, "These seemingly trivial matters build into something very big: namely, your success."[16]

Wooden was famous for his scrutiny of every detail during practices. In his later years at UCLA, he would spend two hours each morning with his coaching staff planning the day's practice session. Every minute of practice was planned in minute detail, including how many basketballs to have on the court at once and how many minutes to spend on each drill. Every detail was recorded and Wooden would compare every practice session against sessions from years before, also recorded with stringent accuracy. From the beginning, Wooden taught his players by his own demonstration to be carefully prepared for every practice or game. He was fond of saying,

"Failing to prepare is preparing to fail."

During the practice session, players found themselves moving with precision from drill to drill. Efficiency and intensity were the keynotes of these sessions. Wooden deliberately kept practices short but fast-paced so that players could achieve conditioning as well as improve their skills. For instance, one shooting drill required each player to make ten shots in a row before moving on to the scrimmage. Wooden constantly told his players, "Practice does not make perfect; only perfect practice makes perfect." He deliberately put more pressure on his players during practice sessions than opponents ever put on the team during games. He reasons, "When an individual constantly works under pressure, he or she will respond automatically when faced with it during competition."

Wooden has always focused on consistency. For instance, Wooden forbade his players to make cross-court passes because they might be intercepted. On fast breaks, the guard with the ball was required to stop at the free throw line. Wooden banned wild drives and blind passes, both of which interfered with accuracy, and favored banked shots over fall-away shots for consistency. What the Bruins lacked in fancy plays and showy players, they more than made up for with incredible precision and accuracy.

It was a running joke among the Bruins staff that on any given game night, the team manager would have to run out to the stadium and get a copy of the program before he would know which team the Bruins were playing that night. That joke, while humorous, also demonstrates how Wooden created a precise focus for his team. He taught his players to put so much attention on their own performance during practice that the opposing team offered comparatively little pressure.

By learning to constantly perform under pressure during practices, Bruins players found it natural to perform well during games. Wooden taught his players to be at their best at all times and under any conditions. As such, the last foul shot at the end of the game, when the Bruins were behind by a point and there were only a few seconds remaining, should have the same consistency and accuracy as the first foul shot at the beginning of the game. Under Wooden's stringent coaching, the Bruins delivered stunning performances game after game.

Four Steps to Learning

In his long career coaching the Bruins, Wooden had many opportunities to study the process of learning. His fundamental belief about learning is that mistakes are part of learning and should not be penalized. Players who are afraid of making mistakes are afraid to do or try anything. Says Wooden, "I learn from mistakes. If you worry about making mistakes, you will never do anything. I used to say that the basketball team that makes the most mistakes probably wins because they are doing things. The doer makes mistakes so they are not full of themselves."

To reduce the number of mistakes, though, and to increase the speed of the learning process, Wooden developed a unique four-step approach to learning: demonstration, imitation, correction, and repetition. He determined that with this approach, his players were more likely to repeat only desired behaviors and make fewer mistakes. Many of his players blossomed under this approach, and Swen Nater, one of Wooden's former players, felt inspired to write this poem, *The Four Laws of Learning*,[17] to capture the essence of the approach:

> *"At the start of all your teaching,*
> *You would show me what to do.*
> *Always leading by example,*
> *DEMONSTRATION of 'how to.'*
>
> *Then you'd say, 'Why don't you try it.*
> *I have shown you how to be.'*
> *IMITATION—I attempted,*
> *As you watched me lovingly.*
>
> *'Do it this way, do it that way.*
> *Try it once again like this.'*

Your CORRECTION drilling habit,
As we watched my skills progress.

With occasional assistance,
You retreated humbly.
You were finished—I have learned it.
REPETITION was the key."

Balance, Balance, Balance

To help his team maintain precision and accuracy, Wooden always kept a sharp eye on the balance of the team. On the individual level, Wooden worked with each player to enhance their physical, mental, and emotional balance, the main ingredients for peak performance. He explains how athletes respond when they are balanced in these three areas:

"They react, and when they react, they don't have to think. They are able to do that because they have learned the fundamentals and the value of balance. They are under control. They have physical, mental, and emotional balances, but if they lose one of them, they are out of control."

Wooden's deliberate focus on the development of fundamental life skills such as accountability, precision, and attention to details, along with his carefully monitored practices, kept his players in top physical, mental, and emotional balance.

At the team level, Wooden carefully balanced the skills and needs of individual players against the greater good of the team. For Wooden, teamwork was never a preference but an absolute necessity. While he concedes that the team with the best players almost always wins, he welcomed good players who were willing to lose themselves for the greater good of the team. He comments,

"I would rather have the great players. No one really wins without them…[but] I can settle with good players, not sensational ones, who are closer to realizing their own potential and will be more successful than some with great potential and individual ability

who don't put their individual abilities to work for the welfare of the group."

With the balance of the team in mind, Wooden coached those players who often sat on the bench that being a supportive team player on the sidelines was one of the greatest contributions that a player could make. When asked how he would coach two great players, such as Shaquille O'Neil and Kobe Bryant of the Lakers, Wooden shed light on his approach:

"I would make sure that the rest of the players could help those two win. You [the rest of the players] need them, but they need you as well. While they form the engine of the team, they need the wheels. If the nuts come off, they will lose the wheels and the engine will be of no use. Everyone has a very important role. Kobe and Shaq will be all right. They want to be good and they are good, but they need the other players. I think Jackson did a great job in getting other players to accept the roles that are best for the team. Don't worry about Kobe and Shaq, they will come out all right."

At the personal level, Wooden always maintained balance between his personal and professional life, and helped his players to do the same. For instance, he insisted that one of his players, Eddie Sheldrake, be with his wife for the birth of their first child, even though it meant missing a crucial out of town game. Wooden considers basketball to be a part of life, not life itself. During his coaching career, he kept the balance between his family, his faith, and his work as a way to maintain peace of mind.

On the Edge

His long career with the Bruins and the team's later consistent success demonstrate that John Wooden takes the long view of life. Rather than pushing for quick victories early in his career, he patiently cultivated the UCLA basketball program until it became the balanced, precise, and consistently successful program he sought. Wooden is fond of saying: "Good things take time and you have to realize that good things should take time."

Patience, though, is not an excuse for sloth or simple laziness. Wooden has always coached his players with the phrase, "Be quick, but don't hurry." In other words, while patiently waiting for the desired outcome, he continually pushed his team for greater precision and balance. He required his players to be quick but never to cut corners. He pushed his team to play balanced on the edge.

In the long view, Wooden has always enjoyed the journey more than the destination. Winning ten national championships was never his aim. Instead, Wooden focused on using the basketball program to develop well-rounded individuals fully prepared to live happy lives. During our interviews he recalled many games that gave him equal or greater satisfaction than winning so many national championships, games that pleased him because his players prepared fully and performed at the height of their abilities. He explains, "I derived my greatest satisfaction out of the preparation, the journey, day after day, week after week, year after year." At the end of his career, Wooden summed up his mastery of basketball and his life this way:

> *"My development, the practice, is the journey, which is the only thing I missed after I retired. I don't miss the game. As someone once said, 'It's better to travel hopeful than to arrive.'"*

UCLA Bruin's Masterful Journey

Coach Wooden had already established good credentials when he assumed leadership of the UCLA basketball program. Not only had he been inducted into the college basketball Hall of Fame as a player, but he had, over the years, tried to create a basketball program that empowered players to blossom not just as basketball players but as people, too (see Chapter 5 on Wooden's leadership). In other words, he had already established the value of "being the best you can be," or the cultural aspect of his formula (as shown in Figure 4.4). However, he still needed to recruit great players for his team (the infrastructure aspect) and teach them the process (learning aspect). Wooden started with a strong culture and greatly enhanced the learning and infrastructure aspect as the Bruins basketball program matured and eventually reached mastery.

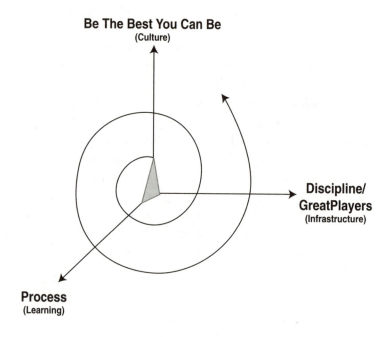

Figure 4.4 Bruin's evolutionary path to mastery.

Southwest Airlines[18]
Lean, Fit, and Ready

It's easy to see Southwest Airlines (SWA) as the happy-go-lucky, "party all the time" perpetual kid of the airline industry. In contrast to its stodgy competitors, the airline offers outrageous advertising, crew and staff members who know how to party, and airplanes dressed up as killer whales. In fact, SWA seems bound and determined to prove that it's never too late to have a happy childhood. Don't be deceived. Beneath all the flamboyant marketing is the unstoppable juggernaut of the airline industry.

In shoot-outs with other carriers for resources and markets, SWA has unbeatable speed. For instance, when SWA announced new service in Little Rock, AR, a competitor announced service in the same city, hoping to preempt SWA with an earlier start date. How did SWA react? By immediately sending a team to Little Rock and securing subleases from Continental Airlines on all available gates. SWA was ready for service within 10 days, long before its competitor even showed up. To introduce the new service, it offered passengers a $10 fare for 10 days and secured a 25% share of the Little Rock-Dallas route just five days after it began offering service. Says Kelleher: "If you don't go get those assets immediately someone else is going to scoop them up. All your alarming is not going to make a difference because the gates won't be available, nor will the airplanes. I really do believe in ready, fire, and aim. In our business, if you keep aiming all the time you never get to fire!"

To stay on top of its game, SWA has boiled mastery down into a stunningly simple approach by managing in good times in preparation for the bad, keeping everything simple, and operating based on old-fashioned values. The airline's discipline and outright simplicity make it a serious threat to other carriers in the industry while its trusting culture and spirit of fun attract deeply committed employees. While SWA is definitely dedicated to having fun, no one ever forgets that very, very hard work comes first.

Kelleher's philosophy has always been one of frugality. From reusable boarding passes to generic trash bags, frugality is in the airline's blood. He says:

"Manage in good times so that you'll do well in bad times. People get carried away; they get euphoric in good times. It's almost like people have no sense of history, no sense of futurality because you don't have to be real old to remember some bad times and to know you have to be prepared for them. Be a squirrel at all times."

Because every penny counts, the leaders at SWA want every employee to be absolutely obsessed with profitability and frugality. In the November 1995 issue of the company magazine, *Luv Lines*, the airline's executives included an article on profitability to stimulate awareness. The article pointed out the surprising fact that, on average, only five customers on each flight produced the total annual profit:

"Our Finance Department reports that our break-even Customers per flight in 1994 was 74.5, which means that, on average, only when Customer #75 came on board did a flight become profitable!...

When you divide our 1994 annual profit by total flights flown, you get profit per flight: $179,331,000(annual profit)/ 624,476(total flights flown) = $287 (profit per flight).

Then, divide profit per flight by Southwest's system-wide average one-way fare of $58:$287(profit per flight)/$58(average one-way fare) = 5 (one way fare customers!)

The bottom line, only five Customers per flight accounted for our total 1994 profit!"

The above message, in simple language, conveys the seriousness of keeping each and every SWA customer happy. To lose a single one of those five customers means a 20% loss in profit for the entire flight! Is it any wonder that besides being frugal, SWA provides outstanding customer service? Additionally, the result of such education and awareness helps employees at all levels to think independently and funnel great ideas to corporate headquarters. For instance, flight attendant Rhonda Holley wrote to SWA President Colleen Barrett suggesting that the company remove its logo from the plastic trash bags used onboard its planes. Barrett acted on the suggestion, which now saves the SWA $300,000 annually. This obsession with frugality and the relentless drive to shave even pennies from operating costs gives SWA a consistenly low cost structure.

If small ideas like generic trash bags save tens of thousands of dollars each year at SWA, big ideas save even more. One of the airline's chief financial strategies is to carry very little long term debt. Says Kelleher, "For at least 20 years, we've never had to borrow money on a long term basis to bring in airplanes. We've always had a short term line of credit so if we need money, we'll borrow it for six months instead of going out and encumbering ourselves for six to ten years. It preserves our flexibility." What's more, SWA does not use market share as a yardstick to measure success. Kelleher explains:

> "I was the first one in the airline industry to say, 'I don't care about market share. I just want to be profitable.' If we're profitable with 3% of the market, I'm happy. If we're unprofitable with 97% of the market, I'm unhappy. Unless you have the total industry context, you can't really appreciate how much the other carriers were totally preoccupied with market share. I describe it as the elephantiasis syndrome. They are always saying, 'Well, we're doing this now because five years down the line, if we gain five points in market share, we'll be fine.' But in our business, there's always someone there to take you on."

Frugality, thriftiness, and savings are the great American values of past generations, but they live on today at SWA. In a society that lives beyond its means and drowns in uncontrolled debt, the crew at SWA continues to thrive on lower and lower cost structures. The results are clear to see. After the September 11th tragedy of 2001, when other U. S. airlines grounded 240 aircrafts, laid off more than 70,000 workers and lost a total of $6 billion, SWA kept all of its 375 planes and 35,000 people flying. While other airlines struggled with their financial conditions and talked constantly about "sacrifices," SWA was able to offer raises and stock options to its employees.

By managing in good times to do well in bad, this free spirit of the airline industry continues to offer unheard-of job security to all its employees. More importantly, the obsession with frugality is only one example of the discipline the people at SWA demonstrate in carrying out airline's purpose.

Keep It Simple

When your business owns assets that travel at 540 miles per hour, managing your resources becomes a tricky business. Says Kelleher,

> "You have to get all these airplanes that are flying all over the United States every day to show up in the right place and to adjust for the ones that have problems. The airline business is an intensely executional business."

To achieve such flawless execution, SWA sticks to a simple formula. Simplicity is a key component of Kelleher's disciplined operating philosophy. He describes one striking application of this philosophy:

> "Our strategy has remained constant and our tactics have changed a thousand times. You've got to be able to change. We've told our people over and over again that there are three ways of being innovative. One is doing things differently. The other is being innovative in imitation. If a competitor has done something that we have to generally emulate, put in a new program but let's do it our way. For instance, our frequent flyer program is based on trips instead of miles, you get your award automatically and it's transferable. The third way to be innovative is by not doing anything, not changing at all. By that I mean that when the weight of the world and the pressure is on you, you don't change. After deregulation we could have bought 747s and flown transcontinental from New York to Los Angeles. We sat down and thought about it and said, 'We're different and we're not changing.'"

With simplicity in mind the founders took drastic measures. Kelleher recalls, "Some years ago we burned all manuals pertaining to general behavior within the corporation. We replaced about 750 pages of precise, detailed manuals with a 52-page *Guidelines for Leaders*, and told everyone they were free to break the guidelines as long as they were doing it with the intention of helping another employee or the customer." Along the same lines, the airline buys only Boeing 737 planes, which not only simplifies the training and maintenance, but allows the pilots, flight attendants, mechanics and provisioners to focus on learning the specifics of the aircraft in detail. SWA can also substitute aircraft, reschedule flight crews, or transfer mechanics without delay.

To further simplify, as mentioned earlier, SWA abdicated the hub-and-spoke system used by almost every other airline. While such a system is good for loading the maximum number of passengers onto a plane, it doesn't offer efficient aircraft utilization for SWA, whose primary customers are short haul travelers. By going point-to-point rather than sending airplanes back to the hub, the SWA fleet is used 11.5 hours a day compared to the 8.6 hours per day that most carriers use their planes.[20] Since airplanes generate revenue only when they are in the air, SWA higher utilization generates more revenue and results in lower unit costs per flight.

SWA's boarding process is also simple. Passengers move on board in three groups. Recently, SWA simplified the process still further by handing out boarding passes at the check-in desk and through airport kiosks. Once on the plane, passengers don't waste time searching for assigned seats but have the freedom to sit wherever they want. While the process sounds a little like something from kindergarten, the results are astounding efficiency and a sense of fun that is enjoyed by both crew and passengers.

A key part of the success of SWA, despite its party-happy image, is the simple philosophy of tempering opportunism with its fiscal conservatism. The old adage usually goes, "Easy does it," but at SWA the adage should read, "Simple does it."

Old Fashioned Values

We mentioned in Chapter One that one of the airline's most remarkable assets lies in its trusting culture. Such trust did not blossom overnight at SWA, but comes only with accountability on the part of every employee. For a covenant relationship of trust and accountability to exist between SWA and its family of employees, every employee has to become accountable for his or her own actions. In today's society, such a covenant is both rare and precious. Kelleher never stops looking for ways to spread this message:

> *"I gave the Message to the field one year by talking to our employee about The Greatest Generation, Tom Brokaw's book. What made the greatest generation? They were not peacock proud, they recognized duty, they knew that honor was important, they never bragged. I tell you, I've never heard a World War II veteran who won a Medal for valor ever say anything about even having been in World War II. They were not boasting. They just went out and did the job with a great deal of accountability and responsibility. That's what we need, accountability and responsibility at Southwest Airlines."*

In many companies words like "accountability" and "responsibility" are simply fixtures in the annual report. Not only are these words meaningless to employees, most have heard them so many times they simply turn a deaf ear. Not at SWA. The airline starts by hiring people who are eager to be accountable for their actions as a part of being on a winning team. SWA is extremely cautious about the people it hires, using a very stringent hirng process. Says Kelleher,

> *"From the first person you hire, make sure it's a good person. Make sure that it's a person who is a team player, who is willing to work with other people and who is willing to subjugate their individual ego to the well-being of the organization. Never hire any person other than that if you can possibly avoid it. One naysayer can destroy 40, 50, or 100 people in a given group in a very short period of time."*

In additionto hiring the crème de la crème, SWA is also careful not to dilute its culture by adding too many new employees at once. Plus, the hiring agents at SWA value a strong attitude and personal accountability. For example, Collen Barrett, President of SWA, started out as Kelleher's legal secretary. Certain ramp agents have risen to become pilots in the organization, one executive vice president joined the airline from the police force and one vice president never finished high school. Regardless of education, SWA hires based on talent. Kelleher describes this philosophy eloquently: "If the talent is there, go with it!"

Lean, Fit, and Ready

Like a first-rate athlete, SWA stays lean by being frugal, fit as a result of its focus on simplicity, and ready due to its trusting culture. This renegade airline has won not only government awards for excellence, but high loyalty from its customers, grudging respect from its competitors and lifetime dedication from its employees. Though its rebel strategies and offbeat advertising make it a maverick in the airline industry, its homespun family values make it stand out even more in the increasingly cut throat, competitive world of business. The spirit of the SWA people is proudly exhibited at the atrium of its corporate headquarters at the Love Field in Dallas:

> *"The people at Southwest Airlines are the creators*
> *Of what we have become—and of what we will be.*
> *Our people transform an idea into a legend.*
> *That legend will continue to grow only so long*
> *As it is nourished—by our people's*
> *Indomitable spirit, boundless energy, immense good will,*
> *And burning desire to excel.*
> *Our thanks—and our love, to the people*
> *Of Southwest Airlines for creating a*
> *Marvelous family and a wondrous airline!"*

The SWA Journey

From the very beginning, SWA has stood out from the rest of the field. Although it took four years to get its first flight off the ground, it has had a solid foundation in its culture, infrastructure and knowledge dimensions from the very beginning (see Figure 4.5). For instance, in terms of culture, SWA has always maintained its old-fashioned value of "making a difference," a value which mimics the founders' tremendous integrity and vision. By burning the 750-page manual, Kelleher has kept SWA's processes simple and streamlined. Finally, the airline has maintained its strong, low-cost infrastructure by hiring the right people and indoctrinating them in the value of frugality. In short, SWA started out by living in its Tao and has never stopped expanding the ways in which that Tao is expressed. Over the years, SWA has simply continued to push the boundaries outward, stay ahead of the curve, and operate on the edge, while always adhering to its founding principles.

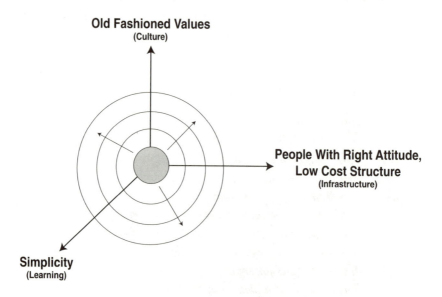

Figure 4.5 SWA's evolutionary path to mastery.

A Master's Journey

In the three stories of this chapter, we've explored varying degrees and methods of mastery. We've seen how mastery manifests itself in a variety of organizations, from corporate America to the Bruins basketball team to a tiny island-nation. What do these stories, and the ascending levels of mastery, tell us about this slippery, hard-to-define subject?

1. *Mastery is a Never-Ending Journey:* It would not be accurate to say that mastery is a journey without a destination, since every master in this chapter demonstrates that a clear and inspiring vision is a crucial ingredient to success. But it is true that mastery is a journey that never ends. With its continual reinvention of itself, Singapore demonstrates that the journey of mastery is one of continual growth, expansion, change, and transformation. As the forces of technology, culture, and commerce spin faster and faster, Singapore never stops pushing itself to harness those forces. Once focused only on raising its people out of the swamp, the Singaporean government now turns its attention toward creating a gracious society, befitting its standing and stature in the world. In the words of Philip Yeo, "Singaporeans in ten years will still strive to be number one because that's the way to get a more vibrant life."

2. *Mastery is About the Journey:* If you were to offer the true masters of the world a winning lottery ticket and a life of leisure, chances are that you would find no takers. For masters, the joy is in the journey and not in the achievement of some particular goal. For John Wooden, mastery of intimate details such as teaching his players how to put on their socks was a joy, whereas the goal of winning national championships was considered merely the consequence of doing your best (including putting on your socks the right way). The

joy of the journey, it seems, is truly the privilege of the masterful. As Wooden puts it, "I derived my greatest satisfaction out of the preparation, the journey, day after day, week after week, year after year."

3. *Tao Determines Level of Mastery:* Every leader in this chapter is striving to live in their Tao, working to make a difference in the world. Based on our interviews, it appears that the higher an organization's purpose, the easier it is for that organization to ascend the scale of mastery. Those leaders with very materialistic purposes seem to never achieve significant levels of mastery because their gazes are fixed on very low horizons. But leaders like Herb Kelleher, who seeks to free the skies so more people can live their dreams, seem to achieve mastery almost as a byproduct of their higher purpose and desire to improve the world.

4. *Masters Inspire with the Impossible:* Masters are aware of possibilities that ordinary people never see. Masters see and reach for the impossible. The people at SWA are constantly inspired because Kelleher applauds and vindicates the heroes of the impossible. When an agent on probation took the initiative and chartered five buses to transport passengers of a grounded flight to their destination, Kelleher raised her up as a hero. When the SWA Board was ready to close the airline after fighting for almost four years for the right to fly, Kelleher offered to fund a final round of the legal battle himself. When SWA got into a disagreement with another company, Kelleher settled the dispute with the chief executive of that company—by arm wrestling him! Masters use the impossible, the unheard-of and the unimaginable to align their people to the vision in every moment of the working day. It is the possibility of living the impossible dream that is the very essence of mastery.

Sun Tzu states that he who "wins without fighting" has mastered the highest form of strategy. In other words, the leaders who can inspire their organizations to focus on improving the world rather than winning the dogfight hold the keys to creating win-win situations. By empowering previously grounded passengers to fly with unbeatably low fares, SWA wins in the high-speed airline industry. By helping his players to excel in life as well as in basketball, Coach Wooden developed the most winning basketball teams in college sports history. In other words, masterful organizations always seek the inner win that, as a natural result, produces stupendous results in the outer world.

Striving for inner achievement, then, is a key to mastery. Because there is no judge or jury to declare a "winner" in the pursuit of inner excellence, the inward journey never ends. Passionate vigilance is the hallmark of such a journey, as the organization consistently seeks to test the very limits of possibility—all the while maintaining perfect balance, for balance is a necessity when walking the edge. With an eye toward maintaining this delicate and dynamic balance, SWA never hires more people than its culture can safely incorporate, while the Singaporean government actively reminds its people that the drive to be the best is the key to continued balanced growth and "a more vibrant life." Wooden, too, monitored the balance of the Bruins team with detailed precision, always measuring the team's needs against the development of individual players. Masterful leaders pursue aggressive growth and improvement tempered by unshakable balance.

At each stage of development, SWA, the UCLA Bruins and the Singaporean government have created or acquired the necessary ingredients for mastery. At the most basic level, organizations need discipline and talent. As Wooden says, "No one really wins without the great players." Talent is a must. At the next level, the entire organization must be inspired by an ultimate and pervasive passion that unites all the employees into a powerful and cohesve force. For instance, the Singaporean government leveraged its people's passion for a better life to literally pull the nation out of the swamps and into a position of world-renown and recognition. As each of these organization begins to quest for inner perfection, a collective wisdom begins to shape and guide it. For example, the UCLA Bruins understood that they control their own destiny by being the best they could be. Finally, at the ultimate level of mastery, companies must surrender to the higher purpose of making a difference. While SWA follows no ultimate master plan, it maintains a lean, simple, and agile organization, ever ready when the opportunity to manifest its Tao of "freedom in the skies" is presented. The leaders of SWA have surrendered control, relying instead on the accountability of its people and the "Spirit of SWA" as guiding forces. It is at this level that synchrony truly exists and the impossible becomes possible.

Perhaps the following statement from Jawaharlal Nehru expresses well the essence of a master's journey:

> *"There is no easy walk to freedom anywhere, and many of us will have to pass through the valley of the shadow of death again and again before we reach the mountaintops of our desires.*

V

The Art of Leadership

"The mark of a moderate man
Is freedom from his own ideas…
Nothing is impossible for him.
Because he has let go,
He can care for the people's welfare."
—Lao Tzu—

Two monks reach a river filled with waist-high water. The first monk observes as a woman tries several times to wade through the water, withdrawing each time from anxiety and fear. He walks over and offers to carry her over the river on his back. The lady accepts. The monk carries the woman across the river, sets her down on the far bank and, with the second monk, proceeds onward. After a few minutes, the second monk is unable to contain himself and bursts out to the first monk, "How can you break our vow so easily?" referring to the vow of having no contact with women. The first monk smiles at the second monk and replies: "I put her down at the river bank. Are you still carrying her?"

Kung Ming and Shih Ma Yi, two of the most famous generals in Chinese folklore, battled each other incessantly during the Three Kingdom period (220-265 A.D.). Kung Ming was considered the most talented general of the time and constantly outfoxed the less experienced Shih Ma—until, that is, their final battle.

Typically, Kung Ming was the more cunning of the two and held the upper hand during their mutual encounters. For instance, one famous story tells of how Kung Ming used Shih Ma's suspicious nature to win in a seemingly no-win situation. Shih Ma had been chasing Kung Ming for several days. When Kung Ming finally arrived at the town where he was to join up with reinforcements, he found that his expected troops had not yet arrived. Short of food, supplies and men, Kung Ming had no place to run, so he stayed. Knowing that Shih Ma was a very suspicious person, having been tricked many times before, Kung Ming ordered his soldiers to open the four gates into to city, and then hide within the city walls. Alone, Kung Ming sat on the city wall, drinking and playing his Chinese banjo. When Shih Ma arrived, he thought he smelled a trap and withdrew, exactly as Kung Ming knew he would. In refusing to step into another of his arch rival's traps, Shih Ma fell right in.

Years later, though, Shih Ma finally got his revenge. Kung Ming was on his sixth campaign to unify China, a promise he made to the late king, when he encountered Shih Ma's army blocking a strategic pass. For days, Kung Ming issued challenges to fight and for days, Shih Ma refused. As a last resort, Kung Ming sent Shih Ma a set of women's clothing, meant to shame him for being a coward and refusing to fight. But Shih Ma had learned his lesson well from his archrival. He merely circulated the women's clothes through camp to let his troops know of Kung Ming's tactics, but strictly forbade anyone from engaging enemy troops. Shih Ma simply waited, knowing that Kung Ming's long supply line through the mountains could not last forever. It turned out to be Kung Ming's last campaign, and he died unable to engage the enemy. Shih Ma had learned well from his teacher, Kung Ming, to release his ego and had thus risen to become Kung Ming's equal.

Releasing one's ego is one of the marks of a true leader. Perhaps no one demonstrates Lao Tzu's "mark of a moderate man" more than K. T. Li, the key architect of Taiwan's sustained economic boom from the 1960s to the 1990s, and the man most consider to be the father of Taiwan's science and technology revolution.

Although Li had been chosen to be the next Premier of Taiwan, he declined because of a heart condition. More importantly, he foresaw that Taiwan's booming economy, based on the land reform and value-added manufacturing he had spearheaded as the Minister of Economics, was reaching its peak and would soon slow down. He saw that he had much more important work to do—architecting the nation's next phase of economic development based on science and technology—and could not afford to be distracted by the trappings of power that came with the Premier's office. Instead, he chose to become a Minister without a portfolio. With only a small office in the basement of the Executive Building and one assistant, he went to work.

Li created an entire blueprint for Taiwan's second economic miracle, and pushed relentlessly for its actualization. He shared with me his metaphor of a river, which he divided into three sections—upper, middle and lower—as the basis for his blueprint. The upstream portion of the blueprint focused on basic research, with universities playing a key role. He proposed the development of various centers for advanced research in science and information technology, and actively recruited top talent from around the world. The river's midstream was dedicated to transferring the results of basic research to practical applications, as well as increasing the general public's awareness of the importance of science and technology. Toward this goal, he created the Institute for Information Industry (III) to promote and take the lead for automating the government. One of the events III manages is the annual "Information Month" to expand public awareness. Finally, the river's downstream area commercializes practical applications and spurs the creation of new companies. Li proposed programs such as the creation of a Science Park for commercial development and tax incentives for high-tech companies.

By dint of steady effort, Li finally fulfilled his blueprint for Taiwan's second economic transformation. Today, Taiwan is a major exporter of information technology. For example, it has dominated the world market for PC monitors, boasting such world-class companies such as Acer, a PC manufacturer, and Taiwan Semiconductor Corporation, a major chipmaker. His example demonstrates all the traits of a great leader: the surrendering of ego, the absolute commitment to succeed, and alignment with a higher purpose. While other people would have leapt at the chance to be the Premier of Taiwan, Li was driven only by the long-term good of his nation.

What is Leadership?

When a leader such as K. T. Li truly releases his ego and his attachment to outcomes, he gains the inner courage that empowers him to lead his organization without emotional attachment. In this state of detachment, he becomes willing to cannibalize his favorite business models, products or services in favor of innovation and positive changes.

Leadership, as embodied by people like Li, is not merely a concept. It's an action-oriented process that defines one's daily steps. Capturing the essence of leadership, we define it this way:

Leadership is the process of attracting the right people and influencing them to collaborate together towards a common vision, with unwavering resolve, while, at the same time, liberating their potential to achieve the best possible results.

In other words, the definition suggests that a leader needs to first envision a shared future to align the people in her organization and create a collective identity. She then needs to develop a roadmap to the future, understand the major hurdles she might encounter, and set up intermediate goals, such as R&D projects or acquisition targets, to overcome these potential obstacles. Finally, she would be persistent in hiring the right kind of people, training them, and allowing them to fulfill their own highest potential while they embark on the tasks to co-create the shared future. We visualize the leadership process as shown in Figure 5.1.

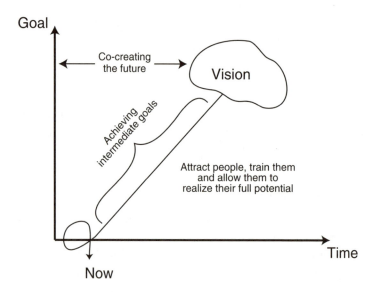

Figure 5.1 The leadership process.

Great leaders usually assume three different roles, either simultaneously or in sequence: visionary/architect, teacher/coach, and steward as shown in Table 5.1.

Roles	Functions
Visionary/Architect Create the context for accountability.	Envision the future and face reality.
Teacher/Coach Mentor without taking responsibility.	Recruit the right people, train them, and mentor them.
Steward Allow the people to fulfill the potential.	Create and maintain momentum.

Table 5.1 Primary roles of a leader.

The visionary/architect envisions the organization's destiny and designs a groundbreaking path. As such, the architect usually develops or institutionalizes the vision, purpose, and values (VPVs), which provide the context for people to walk the path and be accountable for their actions (see Chapter One). For example, Li envisioned that Taiwan's second economic miracle would be based on science and technology.

The teacher/coach, on the other hand, gathers the necessary people and resources to fulfill the organization's higher purpose. This involves recruiting top talent and mentoring them to greatness. The leader, in this case, acts as a wise mentor who provides guidance, being careful to mentor without taking responsibility. Teachers develop the people around them as leaders, allowing each person to fulfill their own potential while at the same time subtly expanding her or his own influence throughout the organization. Individual leaders developed under a steward's influence mimic and spread the leader's message effectively even though sometimes invisibly. Though Li had only one executive assistant, his influence in Taiwan from the 1960s to the 1990s was enormous, as clearly demonstrated by Taiwan's enormous rate of growth and productivity during those years.

The steward guards the longevity of the organization by creating lasting values for its stakeholders, hence maintaining the organization's momentum. Li not only recruited the necessary top academic talent to Taiwan, but he also helped, through the appropriate policies and incentives, numerous entrepreneurs to become highly successful leaders in global enterprises to sustain Taiwan's economy.

We see K.T. Li as a *compassionate leader* who mentored people by sharing a compelling vision and served his people by allowing them to fulfill their highest potential. While demonstrating a powerful way of life, he never took responsibility for the people he mentored, always allowing them to reach their own potential in their own unique style. This higher purpose liberated people from their ordinary concerns and unleashed their passion, so they could move forward without fear. Li co-created Taiwan's future together with those he mentored.

Walking With Leaders

K. T. Li is an exceptional leader by any measure. It is almost impossible to understand leadership merely from his life work because it leaves so many questions unanswered. For example, how does a leader define success and prepare for leadership? In the case of General Shih Ma, for instance, his leadership was defined not by the number of enemy soldiers killed but by his ability to release his own ego. There are also other questions. How can a person get started on a leader's journey? How do leaders make decisions? What is the process of leadership in action? These questions, like all the questions posed in this book, can best be answered by direct experience, experience that we convey to you through the stories of these once-in-a-lifetime leaders.

To gain that experience, dive into the stories of three exceptional modern leaders: John Wooden, legendary basketball coach of the UCLA Bruins; Earl Bakken, co-founder of Medtronic, the largest biomedical engineering company based in Minneapolis; and Herb Kelleher, co-founder and Chairman of Southwest Airlines, the most profitable and now the largest domestic U. S. airline. We will explore the multiple leadership roles they each perform in helping their organizations to be effective and efficient, although we don't always talk about these roles explicitly.

John Wooden[1]
Success is Peace of Mind

When I interviewed Coach Wooden on August 27, 2001 at his home, he was already 92 years of age. What impressed me most about him was his spirit, conviction, and his ability to totally be in the present. Throughout the interview, he didn't waste a single sentence on non-essentials.

John Wooden was head coach of the UCLA basketball team for 27 years. His team, the Bruins, won 10 National Championships, with a record of 88 consecutive victories during his tenure as coach. He is one of only two men to be inducted into the Basketball Hall of Fame twice, both as a player and as a coach. He was named College Basketball Coach of the year seven times and named Coach of the Century by ESPN in 1964.

Early Influence

Basketball has been a part of John Wooden's life since the beginning. Raised on a farm in Indiana, Wooden began playing this all-American game using a homemade ball his mother had created (by rolling up rags and stuffing them into a cotton hose) and a makeshift basket built by his father. Wooden's parents gave him the tools that he would eventually use in his long tenure in basketball, but they also gave him something more—true values to live by. They imprinted their son with strong, upstanding values that carried him through every phase of his life. From his mother, Wooden learned that hard work and patience are the grist of life. From his father, he learned that a person's true strength lies in his gentleness. When Wooden graduated from grade school, his father gave him a card that contained a few guidelines for life. These were his father's creed, called "Seven Things to Do":[2]

1. Be true to yourself.
2. Help others.
3. Make each day your masterpiece.
4. Drink deeply from good books, especially the Bible.

5. Make friendship a fine art.

6. Build a shelter against a rainy day.

7. Pray for guidance and count and give thanks for your blessings every day.

Wooden carries that same card even today, and considers them the guiding principles of his life. Later in life, Lawrence Shidler, Wooden's high school math teacher, became a pivotal influence. Wooden credits his success as a basketball coach to Shidler, who assigned his students to write essays defining success. In researching for this assignment, Wooden had to ask himself a number of questions about success:

- How do you achieve it?
- Who has it?
- What is it?

In answering these tough questions, he once again returned to his father's wise advise, which was, "Always try to be the very best that you can be. But don't worry much about trying to be better than someone else." In our interview, Wooden noted that Webster's defined success in terms of "positions of power or prestige, or the accumulation of material possessions." Never one to follow the beaten path, Wooden refused to accept such a definition of success. For him, happiness is the epitome of success. Why? He answers, "I consider happiness to be more important as it is something that cannot be taken away from you." Happiness, in other words, is a lasting and permanent form of success, much like the success that Wooden achieved with the Bruins.

Be True to Yourself—The Pyramid of Success

To the disbelief of many, winning was never Wooden's primary goal as a coach. When he related this to me during our interview, he smiled and added, "Most people don't believe me when I say this." All his life he has been focused on creating true success, both in life and in basketball. After many years of research on the topic of success, he created the definition of success described in Chapter Four:

"Success is peace of mind that is the direct result of self-satisfaction in knowing you did your best to become the best you are capable of becoming."

Wooden, rather than focusing on being the best, taught himself and his players to be the *best they could be*, each according to his own potential. He explains: "You attempt to achieve the level of your own competency, not someone else's. I don't believe there is such a thing as 110 percent. I don't believe in overachievers. We are all underachievers to different degrees. No one is perfect." In other words, striving to reach the moving target of "the best" may or may not be possible, but being "the best you can be" is within everyone's reach.

Wooden measures his own success according to his character and his reputation. At the end of the day, though, it is his character that defines his true success. Says Wooden, "My character is what I am and I am the only one who really knows that." The measuring stick of success, for Wooden, is internal. Disillusioned with the way parents measured the success of their children using the grade point system, Wooden has always relied only on his own definition of success to measure himself and his players.

To truly communicate all that he has learned about success and the attainment of it, Wooden created what he calls "the Pyramid of Success" (see Figure 5.2), a structure that he built over 14 years. He explains,

"I want to define success in a language that people can grasp. I remember some years ago that someone told me about the notion of a ladder with five steps, and I thought that would be a good start. The process allowed me to think of the pyramid notion, and I went to work on that for the next 14 years. I placed success at the apex of the pyramid. The first two blocks I chose are the solid foundations of the structure; they are industriousness and enthusiasm—hard work and enjoying what you are doing. I think those are the cornerstones of success and I never think of changing them. Between them I chose friendship, loyalty, and cooperation."

We further explain each of these foundational building blocks of Wooden's Pyramid of Success in the following sections.

Industriousness: Wooden was famous for holding the shortest practices in the NCAA, with sessions lasting only 90 minutes. To develop industriousness in his player, Wooden kept careful notes on every practice, noting the differences in strategy and results between each practice and using the insights to plan upcoming sessions. With his staff, Wooden emphasized short and productive meetings, soliciting input from every member but moving forward quickly. Whether with team or staff, Wooden created a work environment where every minute was considered precious, and every exercise was designed for high speed, intense concentration, and great focus. In Wooden's mind industriousness is not the same as workholism or quantity of time spent, but a function of focus. He taught every person on his team to be fully present and focused on all levels—physical, mental, and emotional. At that level of focus, problems become elementary and immediate action can be taken instinctively.

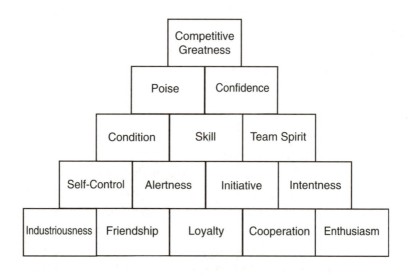

Figure 5.2 Building blocks of Wooden's Pyramid of Success.

Enthusiasm: Wooden believes that a great team is always enthusiastically willing to give its best while a lesser team is willing to work, but not highly energized. Enthusiasm is the result of a shared vision and purpose, in which every person takes full individual responsibility to achieve the aim. As a coach, Wooden was greatly enthusiastic about every aspect of his team, from the overall strategy to the smallest detail. His focus on details, such as the way his players put on socks or tied their shoes, in addition to their shooting or dribbling skills, demonstrates his philosophy that every person and every detail was equally worth attending to.

Friendship, Loyalty, and Cooperation: These three center blocks, the cement that creates the solid foundation for the pyramid, taught Bruins players how to work together harmoniously. True *friendship* requires people to develop mutual understanding, and requires the courage to eliminate the destructive finger-pointing and blaming that is so pervasive in many corporate cultures today.

Loyalty means being true to oneself—to one's own values and convictions. When we extend our loyalty to others, it drives and empowers us to reach far beyond our normal capabilities. Consider the Killer Bees, a high school basketball team from Bridgehampton, New York. The Killer Bees have an accumulated record of 163 wins and 32 losses.[3] The team qualified for the state championship playoffs six times, won twice, and finished in the final four two other times. While the team's record is certainly impressive, the true significance of the team is that it came from a small town with a declining population. The team consisted of only seven players, none of whom possessed extraordinary talent or ability. Killer Bees' former team coach, John Niles, describes the effect of the team's loyalty to its home town: "They are committed to bringing honor and recognition to their community, to protecting and enhancing their legacy, and to one another."[4]

Cooperation is the principle of accommodation, of solving problems by honoring and valuing the differences in any group. Without cooperation, there can be no synergy, and without synergy, high performance does not exist. The five building blocks of industriousness, enthusiasm, friendship, loyalty, and cooperation form the solid foundation upon which the other principles of success must stand.

The second and third tiers of the pyramid add richness and dimensions to the basic foundation. Wooden explains the process he underwent to create these next two tiers:

"I moved up to the second tier and had a lot of ideas. I ended up with self-control, alertness, initiative, and intentness. I could have said determination or perseverance rather than intentness. For the next tier, I chose condition, skill, and team spirit. You have to be in good physical condition whether you are a surgeon, deep-sea diver, or athlete. Whatever you are, you have to have the condition for it. However, you can't attain and maintain good physical condition unless you are morally and mentally conditioned. For skill, you need to have the knowledge and ability to properly and quickly execute. If it takes you too long, then you won't get to do it. For example, if you are on freeway and you can't react quickly or you just hurry a bit, you may not be around anymore. Team spirit is consideration for others with concern of others' welfare rather than just individual welfare."

Added to these two tiers are the building blocks near the top of the pyramid. Wooden describes them as follows:

"Poise is just being you. Don't act, don't pretend, and don't try to be someone else. On the other hand, don't aim too low. If you have poise, you will have the proper perspective, and then you will have to have confidence. You can't have confidence unless you are prepared. If you are not prepared, you prepare to fail. All these lead to competitive greatness—enjoying it when it is difficult. There is not always an easy road, but you can really enjoy it when it is difficult. And then, if you have patience and faith, you will reach success."

Although he recruited many great players later in his career at UCLA, due to the program's overwhelming success and record, Wooden knew that his players could accomplish only so much through sheer talent and effort. To create lasting success, Wooden taught his players to focus on success as "peace of mind," a formula which empowered them to soar far beyond their natural talent. He wanted his players to view the competition not as a threat, but rather as a catalyst that spurs each individual to rise up and meet the challenge. Instead of looking only to win, Wooden's players had far loftier goals, such as securing UCLA's place in history and becoming excellent human beings. On his website, Wooden advises people with the following words:

"The values, ideals, and principles of the Pyramid of Success are the qualities that I believe will allow you to stand tall, now and throughout your days. Furthermore, I believe that all of us have within us the building blocks of success. The potential is within each of us waiting to come forth. That's what you must always keep in mind. You have success within. It's up to you to bring it out."

Whether offering words of wisdom through his website or coaching his players, Wooden has never focused on winning or losing, but always on the development of each person to his or her greatest ability. Wooden taught his players courage in the face of difficulty, but it is Wooden himself who embodies perhaps the greatest courage of all— the courage to fly in the face of traditional wisdom and focus on building the long-term health and reputation of UCLA's basketball program. By consistently valuing effort and striving rather than winning, he relieved his players of the pressure to win, which conversely allowed them to do just that—win. By giving up on winning and focusing on his own definition of success, Wooden achieved both.

Be Quick But Don't Hurry

Business leaders and military strategists alike are fond of saying, "Timing is everything," referring to the wisdom of taking the right action at the right time. Wooden, in his usual manner, has a different way of describing this age-old wisdom. He says, "Be quick, but don't hurry" which is also the title of a book about his strategic thinking. This saying epitomizes Wooden's constant focus on balance. He wanted his players to operate as close to the edge of mental, physical, and emotional endurance as possible—without losing control. He would explain to his players, "If you hurry, you will be out of control. You have activities but not the achievement. I want achievement, but I want to do it quickly. If I can't do it quickly, I may not have the chance to do it. However, you don't want to be out of control either. For example, if you are hurrying to that corner, you may not make the curve (if you are not in control)."

At the same time as he drilled his players on balance, he also taught them to conserve and preserve their energy, acting only at the appropriate moment. Wooden was often heard uttering the phrase, "You don't want activity without achievement." He counseled his players on timing and patience, while he himself possessed the enormous patience and faith to develop his teams to their greatest possible achievement. Wooden explains his philosophy this way:

"You've got to have faith that things will work out, as they should. Much of the time we want the things to work out the way we want them to, not as they should. But we don't do things that are needed in order to make it into reality."

But Wooden never equated patience with lack of action. Vigilant and disciplined in all his affairs, he prepared religiously while waiting for the perfect moment of opportunity. From the proper way to throw a bank shot to the appropriate mental attitude, Wooden prepared every player to perform the right actions at the right time.

Focus on What You Can Control

While no one would ever accuse Wooden of being over-controlling, being one of the most relaxed a coaches during basketball games, he was nevertheless keen on focusing on those things he could control. As the famous coach of the basketball team of a major university, Wooden had to make hundreds of decisions regarding the Bruins' training. We give four examples to illustrate how he makes choices and why.

First, he put focus on "effort" rather than "winning." Winning was not within his ability to control, but effort was. While other teams sometimes had better players or situational advantages, the Bruins always had the advantage of freedom. Every Bruins player was freed from the stress and pressure of having to win, needing only to put forth their best effort to be a success. The Bruins' long-standing winning record is the by-product of this focus on effort.

Second, he placed a definite focus on teamwork: "Teamwork is not a preference, it is a necessity." While, like any other coach Wooden wanted great players, he was able to build great teams from good players who were willing to be team players. His focus on developing life skills (such as teamwork, balance and humility), not just basketball skills, in his players helped even benched players feel they were crucial members of a winning team.

Third, Wooden prepared his team for games with a counter-intuitive methodology. He put very little focus on the opponent, but focused mostly on his own team. Rather than pitting his players against the competing team, Wooden focused them inward on themselves, on being the absolute best they could be. In fact, the opposing teams were often seemingly irrelevant to the Bruins' games, acting only as the rebounding force that catalyzed each player to new heights.

Fourth, Wooden employed psychological warfare on his opposing team. For example, he never called the first timeout as he wanted to demonstrate to the opposing team that the UCLA Bruins had the physical stamina, mental focus, and emotional calm to outlast them.

These four examples resoundingly demonstrate that Wooden has always taken the long view of nurturing and cultivating fundamental values, and a long term vision rather than reacting to short term objectives such as win-loss records and statistics. Empowered choices rather than emotional reactions governed his coaching career, which produced not only winning records, but a legacy of players who became excellent human beings.

Learn

Since Wooden is famous for coaching the Bruins to stardom, many assume that he was a great teacher of basketball skills—and while he certainly taught these skills with great consistency and success, he focused on something far greater. As a teacher and coach, Wooden used his Pyramid of Success as a foundation to teach his players how to succeed, not just in athletics, but in life.

Wooden knew that to succeed in life, his players had to learn how to learn, and the fundamentals of learning that he taught were *listening* and *experimenting*. He says,

> *"One learns by listening. We listen when we read, with our ears, with our eyes, with our feelings—that's listening. Listen to the wind, the stars. Also learn from mistakes. If you worry about making mistakes, you will never do anything."*

He recalls an important lesson in personal relationships that he learned from basketball star Wilt Chamberlain. During a press conference, a reporter asked Chamberlain whether Coach Van Breda Kolff of the Lakers could "handle" him. Chamberlain's retort was, "You handle farm animals. You work with people. I am a person. I can work with anyone." Wooden believed that true leaders do not "handle" people, but seek to bring out the best in every person under their supervision. Wooden never referred to the UCLA Bruins as "my team" or the athletes as "my players." Everyone was on the same team, learning the basic lessons of life and striving toward the same goals.

Walk the Talk

Because leaders exercise such tremendous influence over those they lead, they have, in Wooden's opinion, a tremendous obligation to treat the role with grave concern. He says of leadership, "I consider it a sacred trust; helping to mold character, instill productive principles and values, and provide a positive example to those under my supervision." When asked how he guides young people to find their goals in life, he says: "I don't think they have the vision for their life (at this age). I think it's a gradual maturation. I hope by exemplar they will learn. As someone once wrote, 'No written words, no spoken plea can teach our youth what they should be. Nor all the books on all the shelves. It's what the teachers are themselves.' For instance, my relationships with my family and my co-workers will set the example. Young people need models more than critics."

"Walking the talk" by demonstration, then, is a leader's greatest daily act. Wooden goes on to add that one of the most important things that a leader can demonstrate is fairness. To bring the people in a team together in synchrony, leaders must be fair. As always, Wooden has his own definition of the word fair. He says, "Fairness is giving people all the treatment they earn and deserve." In other words, treatment can be fair but not equal. Each player received back in fair measure what he put forth. In fact, according to this definition, treating every person equally would actually be unfair, since not everyone earns the exact same treatment.

Let Go

John Wooden's most far-reaching influence as a coach is his principle of empowerment allowing those he coached to become the best they could. A coach's job, in his words, is "to allow his players to reach their full potential." Knowing this, he seldom paced the sidelines during a game. At game time, his job was done—his players had internalized all he could teach them, and he allowed them to fully deploy their own ingenuity, imagination, and effort to achieve success.

John Wooden's philosophy on leadership can be summarized as the ability to see differently, the courage to act on one's beliefs, and the discipline to create a masterpiece out of every action. The first creed from his father has served him well in his illustrious career. He summarizes in his own words:

"I am an ordinary man who is true to his beliefs."

Earl Bakken[5]
Ready, Fire, Aim

*When I walked into the North Hawaii Community Hospital
(NHCH), I was impressed with its pleasant interior, which was filled
with light and broad walkways that were twelve feet wide, much wider
than the normal eight foot walkways in traditional hospitals. Located in
the northwest town of Waimoa on the island of Hawaii and serving only
30,000 residents, the hospital nevertheless has developed an international
reputation. For example, one Japanese cancer patient who could hardly
speak English insisted on being treated at NHCH. Patrick Linton, former
CEO of the hospital, informed me that the hospital was situated in the
center of the energy vortex formed by five majestic volcanoes: Mauna
Kea, Mauna Loa, Hualalai, Kohala, and Haleakala. Native Hawaiians
have many sacred myths about this energy vortex, believing that it links
them to the cosmos.*

NHCH is yet another dream come true for Earl Bakken. Bakken,
co-founder of Medtronic (see Chapter One), has long dreamed of a
hospital that *blended* Eastern and Western healing approaches for the
benefit of patients. At NHCH, patient are usually under the care of
Western physicians, but are free to request the acupuncture and energy
healing treatments offered by the Eastern-trained professionals at the
hospital. While the local population and state officials doubted that
NHCH would ever open because of the difficulty in obtaining a
permit, the hospital defied all odds and opened in 1996. As with all
endeavors in his life, Bakken is never daunted. The word *impossible*
does not exist in his vocabulary. He recalls his quest to open NHCH:

> *"I think things happen by some divine guidance. Here at this
> hospital we have so many times reached points where if the right
> thing hadn't happened, we wouldn't be here. It's just like a bolt of
> lightning. Something happens out of the blue and we just go on.
> We don't look for failure. We know something's going to happen
> that will allow us to go through this."*

While Bakken is thrilled that the hospital is operational, he knows it's only the beginning. He has a bigger dream. Bakken, always fascinated with healing, seeks to bring a completely new concept of healthcare to the world, called a "Healing Island," a term he coined. Not satisfied with a healing hospital, Bakken strives to transform the entire island of Hawaii into a vortex for healing, envisioning it as the *21st century Kos of the Pacific*. Bakken's idea pays tribute to Hippocrates, the acknowledged father of Western medicine, who established a medical center and school more than 2,000 years ago on the island of Kos, located in the Aegean Sea.

Early Influence

It's not surprising that Bakken has always failed to see the factor of impossibility in his dreams, for he never encountered the concept as a child. His mother constantly encouraged his interests in science, allowing him to experiment freely at will. Almost at once, he developed a fascination for electronics and felt especially motivated by the horror movie *Frankenstein*, in which Dr. Frankenstein gives life to a collection of inanimate body parts through the magical power of electricity. As a youngster, Bakken spent his time experimenting with electricity in his home laboratory, building robots and even a simple telephone system that stretched across the street. He recalls his parents' willingness to support his interests:

> *"They didn't have much money but somehow squeezed out the money. My mother would go down to the basements of hardware stores to find old electronic equipment and bring it for me to work with."*

While his parents provided him with a nurturing environment in which he could explore his scientific interests to the fullest, it was his pastor, Dr. Christofer Hagen, who influenced Earl's later development. One day Hagen pulled Bakken aside to discuss the nature of science. Bakken recalls the essence of this conversation: "He said, 'Science is neither good nor bad in itself. What's important is how science is used.' He said it would be my responsibility, if I pursued a scientific career, to use it for the benefit of humankind and not for destructive purposes." Bakken has remained faithful to Hagen's creed, especially when he founded Medtronic. Says Bill George, former CEO of Medtronic, "What makes Earl unique, in my opinion, is his soul. Earl is a man with a mission to use science to benefit humankind. Bakken has always followed his heart."[6]

Dare to Dream

As Linton guided me through the hospital, we passed a huge mural hanging in the main corridor painted by native artist Wailehua Gray. The mural provides a visual representation of the hospital's philosophy, depicting the concept that healing works at all levels—physical, mental, and spiritual. Gray used an ancient *wa'a* (a Hawaiian canoe) with a modern-day health professional, the *ohana* (family) and a traditional healer aboard. The group in the mural exemplifies the hospital's commitment to the integration of high quality medicine and complementary care for the benefit of the whole patient—body, mind, and spirit—in the context of family, community, and culture. The following words, scripted in Hawaiian at the lower center of the mural, outline the fundamental philosophy of holistic healing:

Everyone paddles the canoe together,
Bail and paddle,
Paddle and bail,
Together we reach the shore.

The hospital's Mission, Vision, and Values are also written at the bottom of the mural:

Mission

Our mission is to improve the health status of the people of North Hawaii by improving access to care and providing high-quality services at a reasonable cost.

Vision

Our vision is to treat the whole individual—body, mind and spirit—through a team approach to patient-centered care, and ultimately to become the most healing hospital in the world.

Values

As ohana, we value an environment of aloha which nurtures trust, respect, self-expression, open minds, and hearts.

To Bakken, a company's mission is crucial because it provides guidance for making decision and inspires people to come to work:

"If you have a mission with a human purpose, profit will take care of itself if you operate wisely."

Equally important is the act of communicating the mission to everyone in the organization. At Medtronic, he formally inducts new employees who have been in the company for about six months with a "Mission and Medallion" ceremony. During the ceremony he reviews the history and founding of the company, its mission, and its values. This helps new employees connect with his fiery passion for healing. At the end of the ceremony, he invites each new employee to step forward and receive a bronze medallion, which is engraved with the Medtronic symbol of the "Rising Man" and the words "Toward Full Life" (see Chapter One). He also hands out wallet-sized mission statement cards that are meant to constantly remind each person of Medtronic's purpose for being. Bakken is fanatical about communicating the mission, saying, "You have to keep repeating it every time you talk. You have to talk about the mission."

Bakken believes that leaders distinguish themselves by *the length and breadth of their vision*. While managers tend to focus on the next quarter, true leaders are responsible for holding a much longer view, enabling them to navigate the marketplace for the next ten to twenty years. Plus, leaders must constantly learn. For example, Bakken subscribes to more than 170 journals, which help him keep pace with changes in technology, science, and business. While he does not read every journal cover to cover, he does scan them all, selecting certain ones to read in-depth. By reading so many journals on many different topics, Bakken expands both his horizons and his knowledge, believing that leaders should not restrict their vision to a particular domain of knowledge, which could cause them to miss the larger context. He says of leaders:

"They are aware of the growing impact on their environment of politics, economics, and the demographic changes the world over. They know that a trend toward more stringent regulation in a European country and the aging population of an Asian nation can have a great deal to do with business here at home."

Create a Roadmap for the Future

Bakken possesses the unique talents of both dreamer and engineer, a combination rarely found in our highly specialized society. When he is inspired by a new dream, his engineering talents spur him to define a roadmap for achieving that dream. With NHCH, he envisioned a patient-centered, high-tech, high-touch environment in which to practice "blended" or "complementary" medicine. Many of the practices in the hospital today stem from his patient-centered model for healing (see Figure 5.3).[7]

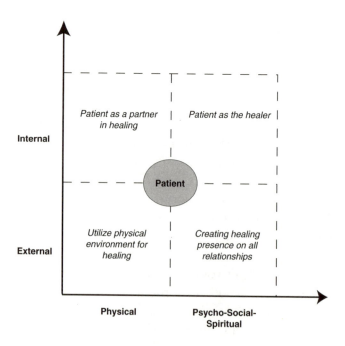

Figure 5.3 A patient-centered model for healing at NHCH.

The vertical axis depicts the patient's environment, both internal and external, while the horizontal axis depicts the nature of the environment in terms of physical or psycho-social-spiritual aspects. For example, the first quadrant encompasses physical elements of the external environment. At NHCH, windows are easy to open and every room has a sliding door that leads to an outside garden, which gives patients direct access to fresh air. Skylights are scattered throughout the hospital's rooms and hallways, and the décor features pleasing and lively colors. Patients are encouraged to choose specific works of art for their own rooms and closed-circuit "care channels" are programmed with music and video images developed specifically for healing. NHCH offers a wide assortment of fresh foods, as well as education on diet and nutrition.

The second quadrant of the model looks at the psycho-spiritual elements in the patient's environment. For Bakken, the relationship with others or the "healing presence" is the cornerstone for this quadrant. To facilitate maximum healing, the hospital offers a wide variety of Western and Eastern healing approaches, including acupuncture and energy healing. In addition to the traditional physician-patient relationship, the hospital uses the *primary nursing* concept, which assigns a single nurse to a group of patients rather than having different nurses perform separate functions. With primary nursing, each patient has a better chance of developing a trusting relationship with their nurse. In addition, NHCH uses the concept of a "care team," which brings the primary nurse aides and housekeepers together in groups of five to care for groups of eight patients. This facilitates closer relationships between the hospital staff and patients.

The third quadrant deals with the patient's internal environment. Contrary to the normal traditional Western physician-patient model, at NHCH the patient is considered a *partner in healing*. The whole spectrum of wellness, including dietary habits, exercise, smoking, drinking, and drug use fits in this quadrant.

Finally, the fourth quadrant addresses the psycho-spiritual aspects within a patient. In other words, what does the patient bring to the table for his or her own healing? Do they have a lot of self-love? Do they feel responsible for their life and their healing process, or do they feel like victims? This quadrant engages the healing potential within each patient, bringing it up to the conscious level to aid in the healing process.

Recruit Great People

In the process of transforming himself from an engineer to a corporate leader, Bakken learned that people are the most important asset in any organization. Knowing this, Bakken often uses his Board of Directors to cover his blind spots: "The Board of Directors meant so much to us...you need to set up a Board of Directors that rules, that directs you." Today, the Medtronic board is rated one of the Ten Best Boards in the nation.

Bakken also favors and nurtures the mavericks in his organizations. He discusses the value of mavericks:

> *"You want to have some people who are mavericks, who are out ahead five or six years. They are a terrible problem to manage. If you don't have them, you'd better grow them because that's what you need to keep the company out ahead. You've got to listen to mavericks. You don't let them rule, but you've got to have a system that at least allows them to be heard, and to have their opportunity to try and convince other engineers that they are on the right track. You've got to have products in the drawer that aren't authorized. You've somehow got to encourage people to try some other things. We have a system [at Medtronic] whereby if somebody has an idea that seems like it's within our province, we'll give him or her $50,000 to try it."*

Of course, the art of managing mavericks can be difficult. Bakken believes that one of the best ways to manage people, mavericks or not, is *to listen*, even when listening isn't easy. Great leaders neither suppress mavericks nor let them venture too far off the path. By offering a sympathetic ear to mavericks and using great imagination, effective leaders can turn their wild-card ideas to great benefit. At Medtronic, Bakken created the Bakken Society to honor the mavericks who made great scientific and technical contributions to the company. Medtronic is often able to stay far ahead of its competitors because of them. For instance, Bakken tells how a maverick idea of "beating heart surgery" is revolutionizing the entire industry:

> *"We build oxygenators for bypassing a heart when they stop the heart, and now we are promoting angioplasty and the beating heart surgery for bypassing the heart without stopping the heart, so we are putting ourselves out of business with the oxygenators. That's happening, but if we didn't somebody else would."*

By recruiting great people, Bakken has not only built a successful company, but also created a whole industry.

Customer First

Bakken always credits Medtronic's initial success to being at the right place at the right time. Ever since that initial success, however, he has followed the creed of "customer first" as the commandment of any organization he leads. He comments,

> *"A company's leadership, every bit as much as it's most distant field representative, must allow themselves to touch and be touched by their customers."*

Bakken is so dedicated to the "customer first" concept that he insists everyone in his organization have some sense of sales. He asserts that each person is in a position to help make a sale "by virtue of a pleasant, courteous, and sensible manner." Everyone must participate. Why? Because, as Bakken puts it, "If we don't make the sale, we lose our hard-earned place in the sun."

Ready, Fire, Aim!

Reflecting on his illustrious career, Bakken notes that leadership is an active process and that a person is leading only when they are doing. The act of doing provides leaders with experience, which Bakken considers to be the ultimate teacher. Effective leaders are well-traveled explorers who learn their lessons by doing, and who share their experiences by acting as coaches, communicating game plans and trusting their players to carry out their game plans.

Bakken summarizes his philosophy of leadership in three words: *Ready, fire, aim!* Medtronic created its first product when Dr. Lillehei and his colleagues at the University of Minnesota lost a patient during a massive power blackout, when the AC-powered pacemaker that was beating the patient's heart stopped. Bakken was on hand to witness the need for a battery-operated pacemaker. *Ready!*

A mere four weeks later, Medtronic had created the world's first wearable, battery-powered, transistor pacemaker. Dr. Lillehei and his team immediately began using the prototype to do heart surgery on children. *Fire!*

Because the pacemakers were not childproof, Medtronic had to alter the design. Once this initial flaw had been corrected, however, Bakken and company wasted no time in manufacturing the pacemakers on a commercial scale. Aim!

When Bakken mentors people on leadership, he uses "Ready, fire, aim." To get ready, he advises people to develop a personal mission, including vision, purpose and values (see Chapter One), which helps them create meaningful roles in their lives. He adds that people should believe in their own intuition, visualize the results and hold the vision until it manifests. Bakken also motivates people to think in unstructured ways and to chase the impossible dream.

The second step is to get fired up by acting on the vision and values. Bakken insists that just taking the first step is a positive move toward the vision because "failure is closer to success than inaction." To get and stay ahead of the curve, he encourages people to charge fearlessly into new experiences and activities.

Aim, the last step, is simply the result of persistence. The old adage, "Try, try again" is the very essence of aim. During the period of trial and error, one becomes broadly knowledgeable but remains focused on the goal. Bakken teaches, "A corrected aim eventually brings the envisioned success."

For his new dream of creating a "healing island" in Hawaii, Bakken is applying this philosophy once again. To clarify his direction and focus, he developed a table (see Table 5.2)[8] to illustrate the application of this philosophy. The first column describes the various needs for his dream (Ready), and the second column defines the resources, mostly newly created under his leadership to fulfill those needs. While the initial design or implementation of these resources may not fulfill all the needs, he can *aim* again to ensure that his purposes are satisfied, one step at a time.

Bakken proudly concludes about his leadership philosophy:

"Ready, fire, aim! It is indeed the lesson of a lifetime!"

Need (Ready)	Resources (Fire)	Purpose (Aim)
Resource Center	Friends of the Future/Tutu's House Health Maps™	Encouraging community members to learn about and take responsibility for their own health and well being.
Healthcare & Research	NHCH, Holistic Cancer Center, Holistic Diabetes Center	Providing quality integrated holistic healthcare and state-of-the-art technology and research.
Economic Vitality Jobs & Careers	Five Mountains Hawaii	Promoting, guiding, and supporting collaborative initiatives to realize the Healing Island vision for the Island of Hawaii.
Stimulation, Inspiriation, and Mentoring	Friends of the Future/Tutu's House Earl's Garage Makali'i Voyaging Program	Creating educational and cultural exploratory opportunities and incentives for children and youth.
Care Reimbursement	Medical Savings Accounts	Developing methods of healthcare financing that encourage prevention and enhance self-management of care.
Measurement	North Hawaii Outcomes Project	Gauging the effectiveness of community initiatives to assure that they improve the health-related quality of life.
Education & Research (K through Graduate)	The Kohala Center	Sustaining the natural environment, strengthening the social fabric, and developing the economy of Hawaii Island through innovations in research and education.

Table 5.2 A process for improving the health of the 30,000 people of North Hawaii.

Herb Kelleher[9]
Making a Difference While Having Fun

My first interview with Herb Kelleher actually lasted three and a half hours. During that time, Kelleher laughed, sometimes loudly. The most amazing thing to me was that he was totally focused on me during the whole time. When it was time for me to catch my flight back to Austin, he took me to the airport personally. On our way out, he waved to every person, calling them by first name and hugging many along the way. Then, at the main entrance of the Love Field Airport, we sat in the car for a few more minutes while Herb talked about his hobby in astrophysics. As I got to know him, I became mesmerized by his dynamic personality, exceptional intelligence, integrity, and compassion.

Kelleher is considered a legend in the worlds of aviation and business, and was voted by *Fortune* as one of the ten best CEOs in the U. S. His leadership skills, combined with his flamboyant and dynamic personality, have been envied by many but ably copied by few. Very few people are able to maintain his level of dedication to a higher purpose, his indomitable will to succeed, and his absolute lack of ego.

Early Influence

Kelleher's mother was the most significant and predominant influence during his formative years. As the youngest of the four children, Kelleher saw his family rapidly shrink from six members to two during World War II. He recalls his strong relationship with his mother, the only other member of his family to survive at home:

"She was both mother and father to me simultaneously. She had the strength to do both and she had very high principles. She was very ethical. She had a very democratic view of life and so really I was nurtured at her knees because there was no other knee. She had enormously wide interests in politics and business, so it was very educational in that respect, just talking with her. We'd sit up and talk to two, three and four o'clock in the morning when I was quite young, about how you should behave, the goals that you should have, the ethics that you should follow, how business worked,

how politics can join with business, and all those sorts of things. I was going to public school and it was like I was getting a combination of public schooling and home schooling."

Kelleher attributes his fundamental value of "doing good for others" to his mother, who taught him that a person's essential worth comes from the contribution that he or she makes. It's not surprising, then, that throughout his life Kelleher has never been concerned about position or title, and stands out as one of the few great American CEOs truly without ego. He remembers how he saw the pitfalls of outer success at an early age:

"I was about 12, I think, and there was a gentleman in our neighborhood. He was kind of a dandy, the way he dressed himself, and he preened himself like a peacock. I used to see him strutting around that way and lo and behold, within a relatively short time he was indicted for embezzling from this financial institution and sent to jail. And I said to myself, 'There is a first hand example of what my mother was talking about.'"

In fact, Kelleher was so determined not to become swept up in the chase for acknowledgement, position, or title that he almost got into trouble when he was 18:

"I was a basketball player at my high school, and the point record at that time was 29 points in a game, and this goes back to 1949. I had scored 29 points and everyone was asking me to shoot to break the record, and I refused to do it because that's not what it's all about. It's not about individual records, it's about teams winning, and it didn't make any difference to the team whether I broke the record or didn't break the record. I just refused to shoot until the coach called me over. He called a time out and said, 'Herb, everybody including me wants you to break this record. Now go ahead and shoot! That's an order!' But that's the way I felt about it."

Humility

When SWA built its corporate headquarters in Dallas, Texas, Kelleher appointed himself a windowless office away from a corner. Though flamboyant and often loud by nature, Kelleher is nevertheless humble at heart. Throughout his professional life, he has held true to the early values he gleaned from his mother, always treating each person as an equal. At SWA, Kelleher does not differentiate people by the positions they hold, choosing instead to honor the sacredness of each person as a human being. Says Kelleher, "It's very important to value people as individuals." Adds Barrett, who has worked with Kelleher for over 30 years,

> *"When he was practicing law, I was his secretary. He had two young lawyers and a law clerk that were assigned to him. Everything that he did, we did. At the time I didn't even realize that I was being given opportunities. I didn't know I was being mentored. I just thought that every legal secretary did that. If Herb went to court we went to court. If Herb went to Austin to lobby, we went to Austin to lobby. And he always treated us, really, as equals. He always asked our opinions about things. Remember, I wasn't even a lawyer."*

Jim Wimberly acknowledges Kelleher's humility as one of the trademarks of great leadership: "Some people have an open door policy. Well, he has an open door, which is different from an open door policy. There was none of the usual protocol. The hierarchy just never existed here. It's easy to get to him. He works seven days a week. Access was always there. And you felt comfortable going in."

At SWA, people can reach their executives, including Kelleher, almost anytime. Executives respond to emergencies immediately, usually within 15 minutes. One SWA pilot said about Kelleher, "If you've got a problem, he cares."

Kelleher recalls the early days of SWA, when he fought in court daily to get the fledgling airline off the ground against the more established airlines: "We had these just slashing battles in the courtroom, all day long, really bitter. And then, of course, I was very happy to go out and have a drink with the other lawyers after court. It wasn't personal." Wimberly observes, "Herb has made more friends out of enemies than any other person I've known. They all love him, whether they are friend or foe because he treats everyone the same."

When asked about the relationship between leadership and ego, Kelleher, as usual, focuses on doing good for others:

> *"You have to have the service mentality in the sense that you subjugate your own ego, and you subjugate a large part of your own life to really helping other people, being successful on their behalf."*

Unwavering Resolve to Succeed

When Kelleher was diagnosed with prostate cancer in 1999, he never stopped working. He would fly from Dallas to Houston everyday to receive his radiation treatment at the M. D. Anderson Cancer Center, and then return to work as usual. As with everything else in his life, he likes to win. Recalling his fight with cancer, he often jokingly says: "I just kind of kicked its ass."

During an interview, Barrett revealed that Kelleher never aspired to run an airline. In fact, his dream was to become a pilot. But after almost four years of battling in court against a slew of opposing lawyers for SWA's right to fly, he couldn't resist. In fact, the higher the odds, the greater his motivation to fight the good fight. He recalls his reaction to the early legal battles for SWA:

> *"It fired me up tremendously. As a matter of fact, in retrospect I think that was probably one of the greatest motivations, the most powerful motivation involved. The way I expressed it was, 'Look, we're offering to do something better for the people of Texas. I'm not going to let these guys frustrate the system and prevent that from happening.' It became sort of an idealistic issue. A societal issue with our legal system functioning the way it should."*

In fact, Kelleher became so inspired that he offered to personally finance the airlines' legal expenses when the SWA Board wanted to close the company.

Passion

Kelleher is a man of passion and he inspires others to work passionately in whatever they do. He used the football program at the University of Texas to illustrate the importance of passion at work. He said: "They brought in James Street as the quarterback to succeed Bill Bradley who was touted as a fabulous quarterback. Street didn't have nearly as many skills as Bradley. For example he couldn't throw as well. But when Daryl (Daryl Royal was the head coach then) replaced Bradley with Street, guess what? The University of Texas started winning because Street was the guy that could get everybody together to charge. And of course Bill Bradley was fabulous. He was a great defensive back for the Philadelphia Eagles thereafter. But if you had a punch list of who's bigger? Bill Bradley. Who's played quarterback longer? Bill Bradley. Who has the best arm? Bill Bradley. Who threw more accurately? Bill Bradley. And yet, there was Street and he took over and made them into a tremendous team, tremendous winner. Street's got passion!"

Kelleher continues: "When we talk to other people about Southwest Airlines, I always tell them that it's got to *come from the heart* not from the head. It has to be spontaneous, it has to be sincere, it has to be emotional. I said, 'Nobody will believe it if they think it's just another program that was conjured up for six months time and then you're going to drop it. The power of it in creating trust is that people have to see that you really radiate, that it's a passion with you, and you're not saying these things because you think they are clever or a way to produce more productivity or produce greater profits, but because you really want things to go well for them, individually.'"

Wimberly talks about Kelleher's love of people this way:

"He has the ability to remember not only names of people he's met but really significant details of their personal life or their business life, and he can go back and reinitiate a conversation with someone

that he met ten years before. He can recall those facts or those personal interest things of people that he met no telling how many years before. So he has just a unique ability to connect with people early, very early. And when he does it, it's not contrived. It's not like he's putting on this persona of trying to be a friendly guy. It's just the way God made him. I think with the instant connection he has with people, everyone is just mesmerized with him and they just fall in love with the guy, and for good reason because he does have that talent, he does have that God-given ability because he loves people."

One cornerstone of SWA's phenomenal success is its focus on loving people rather than following management trends—a clear statement of Kelleher's influence.

Walk the Talk

During several interviews with Kelleher, I discovered that he embodies tremendous consistency and integrity. Jim Wimberly comments:

"He's totally true to himself and totally consistent between his private life and his public life. He's totally consistent between his public speeches and his private speeches. You could look at a speech that Herb gave to the annual shareholders meeting of 2002 and compare it to his message to the field in 1992 and compare it to a letter to employees in 1982 and find tremendous consistency in terms of adherence to core values. So the absolute adherence to extraordinarily high professional principles of ethical conduct and fair dealing, is just remarkable over time. So he built up a reservoir of credibility not only among employees but other people."

Wimberly continues: "The other thing I would say about Herb is *what you see is what you get.* The public Herb is the private Herb. He doesn't have one persona for the TV cameras, the public Herb. It's not a Jekyll and Hyde situation where you have, when he's up in front of 1,000 employees he's one personality, but when he's in a small conference room he's another. No difference. Absolutely no difference."

Confidence

A person needs tremendous confidence to be a contrarian, which Kelleher has been all his life. For example, SWA was the first in the airline industry to bypass the hub-and-spoke system, long considered the most profitable way to run an airline. SWA counters this deficiency by focusing on short-haul, point-to-point customers, keeping a low-cost structure, and maintaining high efficiency. It was also the first airline that put its employees first by offering complete job security. SWA was the first airline to offer profit-sharing the moment it made a profit, and it is the first airline to focus on *profitability* rather than market share. Of course, it was also the first airline to offer permanently low fares on a widespread basis.

Kelleher possesses the confidence to respond quickly and decisively in almost any situation. For instance, as a result of a tax law change, a segment fee was imposed based on a percentage of the ticket price, putting SWA, which offered many short segments, at a competitive disadvantage. SWA responded immediately by offering longer flights with fewer segments. But people inside of the company then began to argue that the airline needed to start serving meals rather than peanuts, because customers would expect them on longer flights. Kelleher disagreed:

> *"Nope, we're not going to start serving meals, we're not going to start serving meals until our customers tell us that we need to start serving meals. But I don't think they will, and let me tell you why. Because we are going to fly them non-stop from Nashville to Los Angeles, for example, and we're going to charge them $1500 less than they are going to pay going through DFW and making a connection on American, or going through Chicago and making a connection on United. So they are going to save about 45 minutes or an hour on their trip, they're going to save $1500 in money, I don't think they're going to worry too much about whether they have a meal or not."*

When the financial community at large jumped in with similar suggestions, such as adding a first class, Kelleher responded the same way:

"Now, let's move to the coach portion of other airplanes. Have you flown coach recently? We give you more leg room. We give you as good as anybody else gets now, unless you just happen to hit the lunch hour, but when you're away from the lunch hour, what do you get? 'Oh, you get peanuts, you get pretzels.' What's the difference? That's 97% of the market. We'll be happy to appeal to 97% of the market. We just had to tell them, 'You're way off base. You don't understand. If people can save $1500 and 45 minutes to an hour, believe me; they'll be driving to Nashville from other cities to fly us to Los Angeles,' which of course they did."

Focus

One of the things that impressed me most during my interviews with Kelleher is that he always put his full attention to me. Wimberly elaborates on this point:

"When you're with Herb one-on-one, there's no one else in the world. You could be in the Grand Imperial Ballroom with 10,000 people, and he could be the keynote speaker, but when he's with you, when he's talking to you there's no one else in the world."

Adds Barrett, "He could have 18 fires burning and he could know they were burning, but when he is focused on a person or a project that is all he is focused on."

Informal Communication

SWA is known for its flamboyant marketing ploys, including events like "Malice in Dallas" in which Kelleher battled for the right to use the advertising slogan "plane smart" against the Chairman of Stevens Aviation in an arm wrestling match. To Kelleher, communication comes in all shapes and sizes. He said:

"Communication is seeing somebody that works in your department and saying, 'Emily, I sure am glad to see you back. I heard you had a little difficulty with the baby. How's the baby doing?'"

Demeanor is also a form of communication. Kelleher recalls a situation in which a manager's demeanor strongly affected his people: "I got a call from a department that has always had superb performance and they said, 'Herb, we don't know what we've done wrong. Our vice president walks through every morning and doesn't say hello to any of us, looks at the ground, got his shoulders slumped.' I said, 'Really? I need to talk to him.' So I talk to him and I say, 'What's the matter?' He says, 'Well, I'm in the middle of a divorce, and I'm really upset, really disheartened by this divorce and it's really gotten me down, I'm depressed.' I said, 'Well, do you realize that you're communicating that to all the people in your department? They think there's something wrong with them, that they're not doing their jobs right.' His very demeanor was a form of communication. He was a good guy and had just inadvertently made everyone think, 'Gee, I'm doing a lousy job.'"

Be Quick But Stay Balanced

Kelleher is a man of action who is known for making quick decisions. He says:

"If you make quick decisions and they're wrong, you also have to be ready to change direction instantaneously. Or fix things. Sometimes it's not going as well as you would like, but that's because there are little imperfections on it, so you smooth out the imperfections and keep going. I really do believe in ready, fire, aim. In our business, if you keep aiming all the time, you never get to fire."

Make a Difference While Having Fun

Throughout his life, Kelleher has adhered to the basic principle of "doing good for others." Over time, this principle has evolved into the golden rule in SWA, which is "Do unto others as you would have them do unto you." Even this rule has evolved into the more encompassing principle of "Making a difference." During his early years fighting for the airline's survival in the courtroom and on the field, Kelleher instilled in his people his vision of helping millions of people to fly, of making a difference.

Today, every employee at SWA still believes that they are on a crusade in the business of *freedom*. They believe that their company exists for a purpose, not merely to make a profit. As such, they almost always focus on serving the legitimate needs of the customers. They believe that their own needs will be met as a result of making a difference to the millions of people who fly SWA.

At SWA, people are encouraged to express their personalities in their work and savor the individuality of each person. While they work hard for a cause, they also don't take themselves seriously. In fact, making work fun is a trademark of SWA. Kelleher is well known for clowning and bringing fun into the workplace. Nothing is too small or strange to be celebrated at SWA. SWA celebrates milestones, people with big hearts, heroes, and oddities. Celebrations enliven SWA family, reminding them that they are on the winning team, a team that considers love, fun, play, and celebrations to be part of a typical day at work. Says Kelleher, "I want flying to be a helluva lot of fun!" Kelleher attributes his fun loving personality to his Irish origin. He says:

> *"The fun part really probably comes from being Irish, number one, and being around a lot of Irish people, because they do seem to know how to have fun, I must say. Also, the Irish are very ecumenical in their approach to people. But if you don't have fun with what you're doing, then why are you doing it? I mean, it's just such a drab alternative. I mean, do you want to die and be remembered as the person who had the least fun?"*

Adds Colleen Barrett:

> *"I read somewhere that laughter is really good for your body because it does something to your enzymes or something. I swear, that man, I bet he laughs three hours out of every 24. I'm talking belly laugh. If I go to an event that's got 2,000 people, I can always find him just because of the laugh. I can find him in the most crowded rooms. He enjoys everything he does."*

LUV, the ticker symbol of SWA, in my opinion, stands for what Kelleher is about, in his own words:

"I would characterize myself as a person who always wants to make a difference while having fun."

Essential Qualities of Leadership

Every excellent organization bears the stamp of its original leaders as shown in the stories throughout this book. This small group of leaders mentored a larger group of leaders that, in turn, creates a whole organization of leaders. Great leaders translate an inspiring original vision into synchronized daily executions that make a marked difference in the world.

Art Collins, Chairman and CEO of Medtronic, talked about what he would say if his grandchildren asked him, "Grandpa, what did you do in your life that was really important?" He would reply:

> *"I don't tell them I delivered an extra penny per share, not that that isn't important. But I tell them about all the good Medtronic did for millions of people around the world, and the small, but hopefully important, part I played in that effort."*

Collins has compassion because he shares the joy of the peoplerecovered to full life with the help of Medtronic products, and sympathizes with their pain during his frequent visits to doctors, continuously redoubling his efforts to ease their pain with innovative new products. In fact, all the leaders featured in this chapter are compassionate, a result of letting go of their egos in order to serve and to make a difference.

We capture the essential qualities of leadership, as embodied by K. T. Li and others featured in this chapter (see Figure 5.4), and explain these attributes with additional short stories to facilitate your understanding.

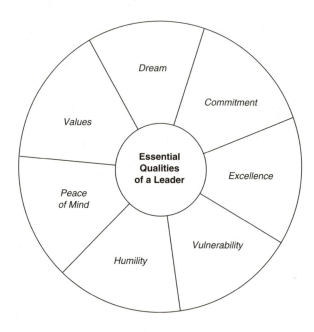

Figure 5.4 Essential qualities of leadership.

1. Values

All great leaders are defined by their characters in terms of how well they uphold their values, such as integrity. No organization can survive when led by people who fail to talk and act according to ethical values. The disastrous results of leaders failing to walk the talk have been abundantly demonstrated by corporate fiascos such as Enron, Arthur Andersen and WorldCom.

Consider the legendary story of Bill Hewlett, co-founder of HP. When he stopped by the company storeroom to pick up a microscope for the weekend, he found the equipment cage locked. He simply broke open the latch and left a note instructing that the room not be locked again. Keeping storerooms and parts bins open became a symbol of trust, a trust that is central to the way HP does business. This trust, of course, began with Bill Hewlett and David Packard, as demonstrated in the arrangement of their offices. In the first HP building on Page

Mill Road in Palo Alto, California, Hewlett and Packard worked in adjacent offices separated by a single door, and they arranged their desks so they could see each other through the connecting door. Leaders like Hewlett and Packard who maintain consistency in both word and action develop strong, lasting bonds with people both inside and outside their organizations. They walk the talk.

> *Ethical behavior is an expression of how a leader*
> *upholds his or her values.*

2. Dream

Great leaders create dreams that galvanize people into action. For example, Thomas Edison founded General Electric (GE) in 1879 to fulfill his vision of a company that would light up the nation by providing all the necessary components, from electrical power stations to electric lamps. The scope and depth of his vision impelled those who followed in his footsteps to build a world-class company that has succeeded for over 100 years.

Consider Sony. In the fall of 1945, in the midst of demoralizing conditions, one man, Masaru Ibuka, followed by a small group of loyal friends, refused to cower in the countryside and instead moved to Tokyo. He believed that the hub of new research and development in Japan would be in Tokyo: any engineer who hoped to work on the cutting edge of technology would have to do it there. While barely able to even feed himself at the beginning, Ibuka nevertheless held steadfast to his vision, later restated by his co-founder and lifetime friend, Akio Morita:

> *"Sony is a pioneer that never intends to follow others. Through progress, Sony wants to serve the whole world. It shall be always a seeker of the unknown."*[10]

All the leaders we mention in this chapter subjugate their personal desires to a compelling vision or higher purpose with the aim of making a difference. That urge to improve, enhance, revolutionize, and better the world is what separates the great leaders from the average. A higher purpose establishes a collective identity so that people's passions are unleashed and the organization achieves many multiples of performance when compared to the average organization.

Red McCombs, namesake of the business school at the University of Texas at Austin and owner of the Minnesota Vikings football team, talks about his philosophy this way:

> *"I am grateful everyday while I have it, and make best use of it to do something worthwhile to make a difference. I never have making money as a goal. I don't ever want to be broke ... I want to make whatever I do count."*

> *Passion is an expression of a leader's dream.*

3. Commitment

Leaders commit totally to their causes. Total commitment means they must persevere despite the sometimes overwhelming odds against them. Three necessary ingredients for preservation are *forbearance, self-discipline, and courage.*

Sir Winston Churchill once shared an essential life lesson in a commencement address at Eton (a well known private school in England). After the headmaster spent twenty minutes introducing the great leader, Churchill stood up and said,

> *"Never give up. Never give up. Never, never, never."*

Then he sat down, having given perhaps the shortest but most powerful commencement speech that effectively captured the essence of his leadership.[11]

Another well-known political leader, Abraham Lincoln, embodied that same *forbearance* as he struggled through failure after failure (see Table 5.3) during his long political career. His persistence eventually paid off and he went on to become one of the most famous American Presidents.

1831	Failure in Business
1832	Defeated in Legislature
1833	Failure in Business Again
1834	Elected to Legislature
1835	Sweetheart Died
1836	Nervous Breakdown
1838	Defeated for Speaker
1840	Defeated for Elector
1843	Defeated for Congressional Nomination
1846	Elected to Congress
1848	Defeated for Congress
1855	Defeated for Senate
1856	Defeated for VP
1859	Defeated for Senate
1860	Elected President

Table 5.3 A short chronology of Lincoln's political career.

Leaders are highly competitive. *Self-discipline,* therefore, is a necessary foundation for their eventual success. Without such discipline, Churchill would not be able to resist the enormous pressure from the German bombardments in the early phase of the WWII, nor would Lincoln be able to outlast all the disappointments of his public life. Self-discipline provides consistency in a leader's behavior.

Commitment is the forerunner of courage and it is infectious. Consider the legacy of Mahatma Gandhi. On a hot day in May of 1930, a group of 2,500 of his followers staged the first major non-violent protest 150 miles north of Bombay. After a morning prayer, the first column of protesters marched toward the great saltpans, where the government stored the salt it monopolized. The saltpans were surrounded by great ditches and hundreds of policeman. When the marchers refused to obey commands to halt, the policemen rushed at the protesters, clubbing them down with iron clubs and rifle butts. Not a single protester offered any form of resistance, neither using their arms to block the blows or striking back. As one column of marchers was beaten down, the next doggedly took its place. Each set of protesters marched silently and deliberately with heads held high until they were struck down. The same scene was repeated over the course of several days, resulting in many deaths and thousands of injuries.

As the Indians continued their protest, neither cringing nor breaking ranks, the British Empire became absolutely powerless. Despite the fact that nothing had changed legally, India nevertheless gained its freedom. The Indians, inspired by Gandhi's leadership, committed to free India through acts of non-violence. Their total commitment to a cause gave them the courage to face injuries and death, and hand their oppressors a complete moral defeat.

Lao Tzu succinctly describes this kind of leader:

> *"A man with outward courage dares to die;*
> *A man with inward courage dares to live!"*
>
> *Courage is the ultimate expression of commitment.*

4. Excellence

Great leaders strive for excellence in their quest for mastery. As they let go of the perception of fear, they achieve confidence. John Wooden is a shining example of unwavering confidence. His confidence is based on the concentration and effort he puts into preparation, not the outcome. Such leaders have a bias for action.

When Admiral Bob Inman set up the Microelectronic and Computer Company (MCC) in 1982, a consortium sponsored by twenty major corporations to compete with Japan's fifth generation technology, he invited me to Austin to consider the position of Vice President of Software. After a short forty-five minute meeting, he offered me the job. I was curious about the process behind his quick decision—since he hardly knew me—and asked him about it. He replied. "First of all, I've done due diligence on you. Secondly, if I sleep on it for a week, I'll still make the same percentage of mistakes." He later elaborated, "Fast decisions are usually the best decisions. Furthermore, if I made a mistake, I can always correct it fast."

Red McCombs shared a similar story with me. When he was considering buying the Minnesota Vikings, he discussed it with his wife Charlene, who reminded him that he was already past age 70. He responded by saying, "Well, this means that I need to do it fast!" and bought the team the next day. Inman and McCombs demonstrate the decision-making process typical of effective leaders. They have a bias for action and no fear of making mistakes—Ready, Fire, Aim!

Confidence and a bias for action are expressions of excellence.

5. Vulnerability

Leaders have a sense of vulnerability, knowing that they need other people to help in achieving their dream. Great people, however, do not always start out great. They need to be nurtured and guided. A reporter once asked Andrew Carnegie how he came to have 35 millionaires working for him. He answered, "They weren't millionaires before they got here. We treat people like you would mine gold; I look for the gold in people, not the dirt that surrounds it." Vulnerable leaders trust in others, embrace diversity, and see the unique gifts that each person brings to the organization. Such leaders empower people to develop and maximize their gifts—to realize their own highest potential. Max DePree, former Chairman and CEO of Herman Miller said:

> *"Leaders owe a covenant to the corporation or institution, which is, after all, a group of people. Leaders owe the organization a new reference point for what caring, purposeful, committed people can be in the institutional setting. Corporations, like the people who compose them, are always in a state of becoming. Covenants bind people together and enable them to meet their corporate needs by meeting the needs of one another."[12]*

To cultivate covenant relationships, leaders must communicate. Communication means listening as well as talking. Leaders use communication as a way to inform, heal, and solve problems. Throughout this book, we have seen how leaders emphasize the importance of communication of all forms—formal and informal. Neal Kocurek, co-founder of Radian and President of St. David's Healthcare System, suggests these guidelines for communication:

- Listen to all parties who hav an interest.
- Collect, analyze, and present data—again and again.
- See that all parties involved/affected are educated.
- Create "our" idea.

Perhaps Kahlil Gibran's poem[13] provides the most touching insight on the relationships between leaders and the people they lead:

"Your children are not your children.
They are the sons and daughters of life's longing for itself.
They come through you, not from you.
And though they are with you, they belong not to you.
You may give them your love but not your thoughts,
For they have their own thoughts.
You may house their bodies but not their souls,
For their souls dwell in the house of tomorrow, which you cannot visit, not even in your dreams.
You may strive to be like them, but strive not to make them like you. For   life goes not backward nor tarries with yesterday.
You are the bows from which your children as living arrows are sent forth.
The archer sees the mark upon the path of the infinite, and he bends you with his might that the arrows may go swift and far.
Let your bending in the archer's hand be for gladness;
For even as he loves the arrow that flies, so he loves the bow that is stable."

Empowerment is an expression of vulnerability.

6. Humility

Gordon Moore is a consummate leader with personal humility. When I asked him about all the great things that happened at Intel, he refused to take the credit. For example, he credited Robert Noyce as a great idea person and Andy Grove as a great manager. Leaders develop personal humility by letting go of their egos. Their ambition is not for themselves but for their organizations. They exist to serve, as K. T. Li did for Taiwan, John Wooden for UCLA, Earl Bakken for NHCH, and Herb Kelleher for SWA.

When leaders truly let go, *reflection* becomes a natural habit as they tend to look at the whole picture rather than just themselves. Tai Yu Kobayashi, former Chairman and CEO of Japanese computer giant Fujitsu Systems, once shared his secret of success with me. Without fail, he got up every morning at 5:00 AM and spent an hour in his Bonsai garden, immersing himself in nature and becoming totally tranquil. He strove to maintain this state throughout the day, which allowed him to make decisions without emotional attachment. Bill Gates, co-founder of Microsoft, regularly schedules "thinking days" throughout the year that allow him to reflect. Bill George, former Chairman and CEO of Medtronic, meditates daily. Reflection helps one to look at the whole picture and assess:

- What's happening?
- What's not happening?
- What can I do to influence the outcome?

This kind of reflection provides insight into the big picture, and provides the necessary clarity to juggle long-term priorities and short term emergencies. More importantly, such clarity allows leaders to maintain poise under pressure. As Gordon Moore likes to point out, Intel's R&D budget seldom wavers, even during very tough times.

Service and poise are expressions of humility.

7. Peace of Mind

The leaders I interviewed for this book have a deep sense of satisfaction about what they have done to make a difference to the world. They have gained the peace of mind that comes from knowing that when their best was called upon, they delivered. They are on an inner journey, and when they win, no one else has to lose. They flow into their destiny with certainty, and have the patience not to force their will on their environment. They have a heightened awareness of their own being.

A common trait among the leaders interviewed for this book is the ability to focus on the *present moment*. Gordon Moore never took his eyes off me during our ninety minute interview on the Big Island of Hawaii. He was totally present. Similarly, Red McCombs was totally present when I interviewed him, never once glancing at his watch. McCombs shared his principle of being present with this story:

> *"When I got married, my job was always six days. I refused to work seven days—at least I had that much sense. I got to have time with my wife long before I got chucked. I think the difference is that when I got home at 8:00 or 8:30 pm, I was 100% hers. There was no part of me that was still at the office. I never take calls at home; I never do business at home. One time an associate of mine called me at 2:30 in the morning and told me that our Mazda building was on fire. I asked him, 'Are you in the fire?' 'No,' he answered, 'I am outside of the building.' So I told him, 'Don't get hurt, I will see you 7:30 in the morning.' That got to be a big conversation all over the place. People asked, 'Does Red care?' What can I do coming to a fire 2:30 in the morning. None of employees are in the fire; none of our customers are there. If I could have helped them, I would have come."*

All these leaders express joy as a result of finding inner peace, though they each express it differently—from Herb Kelleher's belly laugh to Gordon Moore's sparkling eyes full of curiosity and John Wooden's Zen-like quiet smiles.

Presence and joy are expressions of having a peace of mind.

The qualities of a leader are exemplified by the people mentioned in this chapter. The stories of Li, Wooden, Bakken, Kelleher, Moore, and others suggest that such a leader is detached from outcomes, since her purpose is to serve while simultaneously caring for the people around her, both at home and at work. She joyfully shares in their successes and sympathizes with their sorrows.

These stories also highlight a path for becoming a leader. The path requires a person to have a clear understanding of what she stands for (values). Then, with a firm foundation, she must possess the imagination to dream, and the discipline by developing a roadmap. But merely having that roadmap is insufficient; a leader needs to commit to her cause. She recognizes the need to recruit other talented people to her cause, establish covenant relationships among them and align their personal goals to a shared dream, while empowering them to realize their full potential.

A leader has confidence as she strives for excellence by letting go of her ego and confidently makes fast decisions as she understands that mistakes are inevitable. She also has clarity of seeing the whole picture, allowing her to remain poised under pressure. Finally, a true leader has the peace of mind gained from a deep satisfaction of focusing on the present and enjoys every step of the journey. We summarize the key expressions of essential qualities of leaders in Figure 5.5.

Figure 5.5 Expressions of leadership qualities.

Leaders are dreamers first and foremost, who follow their hearts and bring their dreams into reality, many times facing tremendous obstacles. The path to leadership is truly the process of becoming yourself. Karl Wallenda once said, "Walking the tightwire is living; everything else is waiting." Perhaps this poem by T. E. Lawrence will help the leaders of the future begin walking the path:

"All people dream, but not equally,
Most dream by night, in the dusty recesses
Of the mind, and wake in the light of day
To find their dream was vanity.
But then there are the dreamers of the day—
Dangerous people,
Who act on their dream with open eyes
To make it possible."

VI

In the Footsteps of Giants

"No house should ever be on any hill
or on anything.
It should be of the hill,
belonging to it,
So hill and house could live together
each the happier for the other."
—Frank Lloyd Wright—

A rabbi set out to change the world. Since he wasn't making much progress, he tried to change his country. But this also turned out to be too much for him so he tried to change his neighborhood. When that failed, he tried to change only his family. Even that was easier said than done, so he finally focused on changing only himself. When he successfully changed himself, his family also changed. And when his family changed, his neighborhood changed. When his neighborhood changed, his country changed. And when his country changed, the world changed.[1]

One of the most famous houses designed by renowned architect Frank Lloyd Wright is the Kaufman House at Fallingwater, in Ohiopyle, Pennsylvania. Perched above the Bear Run River over a spectacular waterfall, this daringly cantilevered house is an architectural wonder, a quintessential example of organic architecture that facilitates harmony between man and nature. The sheer ingenuity of the architecture seamlessly blends the transition from indoors to outdoors. Floors made of polished sandstone give visitors the sensation of walking in an indoor stream, while rough stone walls and multiple roofless terraces bring the great outdoors inside. Such harmony between the inner and outer worlds provides a total sensory experience of quiet reflection. Wright's poem at the beginning of the chapter expresses his insight into the highest forms of human design: harmony, order, contrast, equilibrium, and unity. These are the key elements of the arts first defined by the ancient Greeks. Why, then, shouldn't we also design business enterprises with these characteristics?

In music, the eight basic musical notes (in diatonic scale) can produce an endless number of melodies, while the three primary colors can manifest an infinite number of hues. In the same fashion, Sun Tzu believes that all strategies are combinations of the five basic strategic arts discussed in this book. He understood that an ideal army must have the capability to deal with all kinds of changes, flowing like water to adapt. He asserts,

> *"For just as flowing water avoids the heights and hastens to the lowlands, so an army avoids strength and strikes weakness. And as water shapes its flow in accordance with the ground, so an army manages its victory in accordance with the situation of the enemy."*

When we view an organization, such as an army, as a living organism rather than a machine, we see new possibilities. By treating organizations as machines, we see only transactions, which are the snapshots of dynamic changes occurring within and outside of the organization. However, when we shift from a mechanistic perspective to a more quantum perspective based on relationships and wholeness, we see enterprises as consisting of *flows* of cash, knowledge, work, material, people and information. *Flows* provide the links between transactions and processes, bringing the business environment to dynamic, adaptable life.

Logistics companies such as UPS and FedEx, when viewed from a transaction perspective, can provide value to their customers only at the final transaction, that is, when the package is delivered to its ultimate destination. However, when viewed from a perspective of flow, new value can be created many times prior to the delivery of the package. For example, two minutes after the first transaction of picking up the package, customers receive value via the ability to track the package. Indeed, almost any form of information can provide value along the supply chain, such as financial or customer demand information for vendors. Flow, then, shifts the organizational consciousness from rote transactions to rich and dynamic relationships that constantly provide value as witnessed by virtually integrated organizations such as eBay, Wal-Mart, and Dell. Flow is the key to harmonious and mutually beneficial relationships with the ever-changing business environment.

When Sun Tzu asserts that "the best strategist wins without fighting," he transcends the normal consciousness of conflict resolution that is the modus operandi of war to see the whole picture. From that high level of consciousness, he is detached from notions of good and evil, high and low, difficulty and ease. These are merely two sides of the same coin. The effective use of the five strategic arts, as illustrated in this book, are the essential tools necessary to raise organizations above the usual chaos of conflict to the serenity of winning without fighting. These arts shape whether an organization is ruled by freedom or fear, order or disorder, strength or weakness, joy or boredom. The top organizations that we have profiled in this book have what all their competitors seek: profits, market share, high returns for shareholder, excellent branding and more. But what they seek to achieve is far greater; they seek to make a difference in the world. The difficulty or ease of their mission rarely enters the picture, only continuous striving via the five strategic arts.

The stories in this book illustrate the experiences of working in the best modern day organizations—in organizations with soul. Such an organization is like a river that constantly flows, collecting new ideas (diversity) while at the same time being anchored by the river bed (cohesion as a result of values and vision). Such an organization is inclusive and always in an open and interconnected state of being, waiting expectantly with acute awareness for each cubic centimeter of chance to present itself. It acts with lightning speed, almost instinctively, when such a chance appears, with the appropriate people in the organization leaping to take the initiative. In this way, a living company constantly and deliberately creates the future in which it thrives.

The stories of the modern day business "artists" in this book show us that the five strategic arts, the highest form of strategy, create the foundation for excellence. These masters suggest that the five arts form a high level strategic framework for any organization, as depicted in Figure 6.1. Such a framework begins with an organization finding its soul using the *Art of Possibility*. A roadmap to the future can then be developed so that the organization is constantly in alignment with its destiny by practicing the *Art of Timing*. Choosing the specific market to pursue at any given time belongs to the *Art of Leverage*, while establishing and maintaining operational excellence is guided by the *Art of Mastery*. All these arts are coordinated by extraordinary leadership at all levels of the organization. This strategic framework, which we call the *T-Strategy*,[2] provides a guideline of how the five arts, each a necessary ingredient, relate. The use of these five arts, however, overlaps constantly, much as waves in the ocean do, even though the framework is limited by its two dimensional geometry and seems to suggests a sequential order.

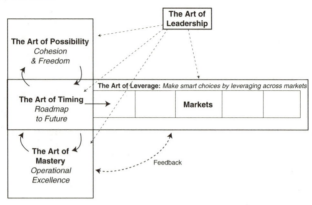

Figure 6.1 Interrelationships among the five strategic arts.

These stories also show us that the leaders who successfully practice these arts must first look inside to understand themselves and their purpose. Only when they discover themselves can they expect the people around them to change, as suggested in the story about the Rabbi. With this inner knowing, leaders can successfully use the five arts to:

1. Mobilize people around a shared future (the Art of Possibility).
2. Adapt rapidly to changing conditions (the Arts of Timing, Leverage, and Mastery).
3. Innovate constantly using the ingenuity of a company of leaders (the Art of Leadership).

These five arts create a long-term dedication to a vision along with an adaptable strategy and highly motivated workforce. The effective use of the five strategic arts, then, translates into constant exploration and renewal. The following poem captures the essential spirit of these strategically masterful organizations:

> *"We shall not cease from exploration*
> *And the end of all our exploring*
> *Will be to arrive where we started*
> *And know the place for the first time."*
>
> *—T. S. Eliot, Four Quartets—*

<u>Epilogue</u>

I hope you have enjoyed reading these stories about the fascinating giants of industry as much as I have enjoyed writing them. These stories suggest that leaders are always on a journey of inner satisfaction, a journey of doing their best to make a difference by surrendering to a higher purpose. While I have outlined their footsteps for you, perhaps you can best define your own path by asking yourself the questions below—questions that the leaders profiled in this book have answered for themselves:

1. Am I true to my beliefs?
2. How committed am I to my path?
3. Do I see and utilize the gifts each person brings?
4. Do I have time to think whole?
5. Do I put in my best effort into whatever I do?
6. Am I providing joy?
7. Am I making a difference?

As you embark on your way, perhaps this quote from Nelson Mandela's inaugural speech may act as a poignant reminder for you:

"And as we let our light shine,
We unconsciously give other people permission to do the same.
As we are liberated from our own fear,
Our presence automatically liberates others."

Thank you for reading this book and best wishes for your continuing journey!

Notes

Chapter 1

1   For more details on this concept, see *The Tao of Physics* by Fritjof Capra for scientific explanation of Tao.

2   All unreferenced quotes are taken directly from interviews with Earl Bakken and Art Collins by the author of this book.

3   Birger, Jon. "The 30 Best Stocks From 1972-2002." Money. Fall, 2002. Vol 31, Issue 11, p. 88.

4   George, Bill. 2000. Authentic Leadership: Rediscovering the Secrets to Creating Lasting Value. New York: John Wiley & Sons.

5   Yunus, Muhammad. 1999. Banker to the Poor. New York: Public Affairs.

6   Counts, Alex. "Stone Soup for the World," in Stone Soup for the Soul, ed. Marianne Larned, New York: MJF Books, 1998.

7   Yunus. Banker to the Poor.

8   All unreferenced quotes are taken directly from interviews with the following executives of Southwest Airlines: Herb Kelleher, Colleen Barrett, Jim Wimberly, and Ron Ricks. Interviews by the author of this book.

9   Donnelly, Sally. "One Airline's Magic." Time. October 28, 2002. Vol 160, Issue 18, p. 45.

10 Birger. "The 30 Best Stocks From 1972-2002."

11 Bennett, Randall, P. and James, M. Craun. "The Airline Deregulation Evolution Continues: The Southwest Effect." U.S. Department of Transportation, Office of Aviation Analysis, 1993.

12 Kelleher, Herb, Chairman of the Board, Southwest Airlines. Interview by the author of this book, January 14, 2003, Dallas, Texas.

[13] Freiberg, Kevin and Jackie. 1996. Nuts! Texas: Brad Press.

[14] Wimberly, Jim, Executive Vice President for Operations, Southwest Airlines. Interview by the author of this book, March 3, 2003, Dallas, Texas.

[15] Freiberg and Freiberg listed low cost, family, fun, love, hard work, individuality, ownership, legendary service, egalitarianism, common sense/good judgment, simplicity and altruism as the SWA values from their book Nuts!. We have abstracted this smaller list, which subsumed the list above based on interviews with Herb Kelleher and the Southwest Airlines staff.

[16] Birger. "The 30 Best Stocks From 1972-2002."

[17] Heskett, James L., Sasser, W. Earl, Jr., and Leonard A. Schlesinger. 2003. The Value Profit Chain. New York: Free Press.

[18] Rob Lebow and Randy Spitzer have written a good book titled *Accountability* in which they give detailed discussions about control-based and freedom-based cultures.

[19] Larned, Marianne, ed. Stone Soup for the World. New York: MJF Books. 1998.

Chapter 2

[1] Mizuno, Dr. Yukio, former Senior Executive Vice President of NEC. Interview by the author of this book.

[2] Schwartz, Peter. 1996. *The Art of the Long View.* New York: Doubleday/Currency. 1996.

[3] Davis, Ged. "Scenarios as a Tool for the 21st Century," *Probing the Future Conference.* Strathclyde University, July 12, 2002.

[4] De Geus, Arie. 1997. *The Living Company.* Cambridge, MA: Harvard Business School Press.

5 These scenarios are documented in greater detail in the book *Synchronicity* by Joseph Jaworski, edited by Betty Sue Flowers.

6 Knight, Margaret M. "2020 Visionary." <u>Rensselaer Magazine</u>, December 1999. Also located on the Internet at http://www.rpi.edu/dept/NewsComm/Magazine/dec99/visionary1.html.

7 Watts, Philip. Remarks at *Energy Needs, Choices and Possibilities—Scenarios to 2050*. New York City, October 3, 2001.

8 Kahane, Adam, Pieter le Roux, et al. "The Mont Fleur Scenarios." <u>Deeper News</u>, Volume 7, Number 1. Emeryville: Global Business Network, 1992. Also located on the Internet at http://www.gbn.org/scenarios/fleur/fleurIntro.html.

9 Kahane, Adam. "How to Change the World: Lessons for Entrepreneurs from Activists", working paper.

10 Ibid.

11 Ibid. ·

12 All unreferenced quotes by Gordon Moore are taken directly from interviews by the author of this book.

13 Moore, Gordon with Kevin Davis. "Learning the Silicon Valley Way." Working paper.

14 It turns out that the properties of silicon drive the dynamics behind Moore's Law. In silicon, the smaller the semiconductor transistor the faster it performs and the less power it needs. The result is that the chips keep getting smaller and more powerful, with more and more transistors being packed onto a single chip. This is the basic prediction of Moore's Law.

15 Yu, Albert. 1998. *Creating the Digital Future*. New York: Free Press.

16 Grove, Andy. 1996. *Only the Paranoid Survive*. New York: Currency/Doubleday.

17 Yu. *Creating the Digital Future.*

18 All unreferenced quotes are taken directly from interviews by the author of this book with Southwest executives: Herb Kelleher, Colleen Barrett, Jim Wimberly, and Ron Ricks.

Chapter 3

1 This poem was introduced to me by June T. Kunimoto of the Hawaii District Health Office in a workshop on *Healthy Community* on the Big Island on November, 2001.

2 Microsoft. 2000. *Inside Out.* New York: Warner Books.

3 Ramamoorthy, C.V. "A Study of Service Industry— Functions, Features and Control," <u>IEICE Transactions on Communications</u> vol. E83-B, No. 5, May 2000, pp. 885-902.

4 Hof, Robert D. "The Ebay Economy." <u>Business Week,</u> August 25, 2003, pp.124.

5 Ibid.

6 Walton, Sam with John Huey. 1993. *Sam Walton— Made in America.* New York: Bantam Books.

7 Birger, Jon. "The 30 Best Stocks From 1972-2002." <u>Money,</u> Fall, 2002. Vol 31, Issue 11, p. 88.

8 Walton. *Sam Walton—Made in America.*

9 Ibid.

10 Heskett, James L., Sasser, W. Earl, Jr., and Leonard A. Schlesinger. 2003. *The Value Profit Chain.* New York: Free Press.

11 All unreferenced quotes in this story are taken directly from interviews with Michael Dell and other executives of Dell by the author of this book.

12 Dell, Michael with Catherine Fredman. 1999. *Direct from Dell: Strategies That Revolutionized an Industry.* New York: Harper Business.

[13] Dell, Michael. 2001. *Direct from Dell*. New York: Harper Business.

[14] Park, Andrew and Peter Burrows. "Dell the Conqueror." Business Week. September 24, 2001, p. 92.

[15] Yeh, Raymond, Keri Pearlson and George Kozmetsky. 2000. *Zero Time*. New York: John Wiley & Sons.

[16] Park and Burrows. "Dell the Conqueror."

[17] Magretta, Joan. "The Power of Virtual Integration: An Interview with Dell Computer's Michael Dell." Harvard Business Review, March-April 1998, p. 72-84.

[18] All unreferenced quotes in this story are taken directly from interviews by the author of this book with Herb Kelleher, Colleen Barrett, Jim Wimberly, and Ron Ricks of the Southwest Airlines.

[19] Donnelly, Sally B. "One Airline's Magic." Time, October 28, 2002, Vol. 160, Issue 18. p. 45.

[20] Hawkins, Lori. "Southwest Flight Attendants Visit Airport in Effort To Seek Better Pay." Austin American Statesman, August 14, 2003. Also available on Internet at http://search.epnet.com/direct.asp?an=zw6419040983&db=nfh

[21] Donnelly, Sally B. "One Airline's Magic."

[22] Ibid.

[23] Heskett, Sasser, and Schlesinger. The Value Profit Chain.

[24] Bennett, Randall D. and James M. Craun. "The Airline Deregulation Evolution Continues: The Southwest Effect." U. S. Department of Transportation, Office of Aviation Analysis, 1993.

[25] Clausewitz, Carl Von, and Michael Howard and Peter Paret, editors and translators. 1984. On War. Princeton, N.J.: Princeton University Press.

Chapter 4

1 <u>Hero</u>. Director Yimou Zhang, DVD (in Chinese). 2003.

2 Musashi, Miyamoto. 1993. *The Book of Five Rings.* Translated by Thomas Cleary. New York: Barnes&Noble Books.

3 Sullivan, Gordon R. and Michael V. Harper. 1997. *Hope is Not a Method.* New York: Broadway Books.

4 Tichy, N. and S. Straford. 1999. *Control Your Destiny or Someone Else Will.* New York: Doubleday.

5 Heskett, J. L. "GE…We Bring Good Things to Life." Case Study 9-899-162, Boston, MA: Harvard Business School, March 16, 1999.

6 All unreferenced quotes in this story are taken directly from the notes of interviews by the author this book with Philip Yeo and many other people from Singapore.

7 Special Advertisement, <u>Washington Times</u>. October 3, 2002.

8 Ibid.

9 Schein, Edgar, H. 1996. *Strategic Pragmatism.* Cambridge, MA: MIT Press.

10 Ibid.

11 Educational Booklet, *Singapore Ministry of Education.*

12 <u>Washington Times</u>. October 3, 2002.

13 Schein, Edgar. *Strategic Pragmatism.*

14 All unreferenced quotes in this story are taken directly from an interview by the author of this book with John Wooden on August 27, 2001 at his home in Los Angeles.

15 Hill, Andrew with John Wooden. 2001. *Be Quick— But Don't Hurry!* New York: Simon & Schuster.

[16] Wooden, John with Steve Jamison. 1997. *Wooden: A Lifetime of Observations and Reflections On and Off the Court*. Chicago, Ill: Contemporary Books.

[17] Hill, Andrew. *Be Quick—But Don't Hurry!*

[18] All unreferenced quotes in this story are taken directly from interviews by the author of this book with Herb Kelleher, Colleen Barrett, Jim Wimberly, and Ron Ricks of the Southwest Airlines.

[19] Zellner, Wendy. "Holding Steady." <u>Business Week</u>. February 3, 2003, pp. 66-68.

[20] Gittell, Jody Hoffer. 2003. *The Southwest Airlines Way*. New York: McGraw Hill.

Chapter 5

[1] All unreferenced quotes in this story are taken directly from an interview by the author of this book with John Wooden on August 27, 2001 at his home in Los Angeles.

[2] Wooden, John R. with Steve Jamison and Coach John Wooden. 1997 *Wooden: A Lifetime of Observations and Reflections On and Off the Court*. Chicago, IL: Contemporary Books.

[3] Katzenback, J. R. and D.K. Smith. 1994. *The Wisdom of Teams*. Boston, MA: Harvard Business School Press.

[4] Ibid.

[5] All unreferenced quotes in this story are taken directly from interviews by the author of this book with Earl Bakken and other people from Medtronic.

[6] Bakken, Earl. 1999. *One Man's Full Life*. Minneapolis, MN: Medtronic Corporation.

[7] Bakken, Earl and Patrick E. Linton. "Acute Care Design: Healing Environment Case Study- North Hawaii Community Hospital." Journal <u>of HealthCare Design</u>, Vol VI.

8   "Hawaii Island—Healing Island—Health and Wellness Works." (a loose leaf booklet.) The table was revised April, 2002.

9   All unreferenced quotes in this story are taken directly from interviews by the author of this book with Herb Kelleher, Colleen Barrett, Jim Wimberly, and Ron Ricks of the Southwest Airlines.

10 A. Morita, with E. Reingold and M. Shimomura, 1986. *Made in Japan: Akio Morita and Sony.* New York: Dutton.

11 This story was related to me by Neal Kocurek, co-founder of Radian and President of St. David's Healthcare System in Austin, Texas.

12 DePree, Max. 1989. *Leadership is an Art.* New York: Dell Publishing.

13 Gibran, Kahlil. 1923. *The Prophet.* New York: Alfred A Knopf.

Chapter 6

1   Kahane, Adam. "How to Change the World: Lessons for Entrepreneurs from Activists." Centre for Generative Leadership, Hamilton, MA. This unpublished paper has inspired much of our thinking in Chapter Three.

2   Yeh, Raymond, Keri Pearlson and George Kozmetsky. 2000. *Zero Time.* New York: John Wiley & Sons.

Index

Quotes from Business Giants We Interviewed

"You work here not just to make money for yourself or the company, but to restore people to fuller lives."
—Earl Bakken, Co-founder, Medtronic

"If we have 99% {market} share of Ford Company, the question to us is, 'How do we improve the customer satisfaction in order to get that additional 1% share?'"
—Michael Dell, Chariman and CEO, Dell, Inc.

"Think small and act small, and we will get bigger. Think big and act big, and we will get smaller."
—Herb Kelleher, Chairman, Southwest Airlines

"Think backward while moving forward."
—George Kozmetsky, Co-founder, Teledyne

"Ask only what you can contribute, never what's the reward."
—K.T. Li, Former Minister of Finance and Economics, Taiwan

"One thing a leader does is to remove the stigma of mistakes."
—Gordon Moore, Co-founder, Intel

"Failing to prepare is preparing to fail."
—John Wooden, Former Coach, UCLA Bruins

Visit www.**TheArtofBusinessBook.com** for more information and additional stories.